THE CHINA CRISIS

HOW CHINA'S ECONOMIC COLLAPSE WILL LEAD TO A GLOBAL DEPRESSION

JAMES R. GORRIE

WILEY

Published by John Wiley & Sons, Inc., Hoboken, New Jersey.
Published simultaneously in Canada.

Library of Congress Cataloging-in-Publication Data:
Gorrie, James R.
   The China crisis : how China's economic collapse will lead to a global depression /
James R. Gorrie.
       pages   cm
   Includes bibliographical references and index.
   ISBN 978-1-118-47077-0 (cloth); ISBN 978-1-118-47080-0 (ePDF);
   ISBN 978-1-118-47079-4 (Mobi); ISBN 978-1-118-47078-7 (ePub)
       1. China—Economic conditions—2000- 2. China—Economic policy—2000-
3. Global Financial Crisis, 2008-2009.   I. Title.
HC427.95.G67   2013
330.951—dc23
                                                              2012049233
Printed in the United States of America.
10 9 8 7 6 5 4 3 2 1

I dedicate this book to my beautiful wife Lulu,
who supported and encouraged me throughout
the long writing process with a timely smile, loads of patience,
and the occasional yet indispensable glass of wine.
Her heartfelt faith in me is much appreciated.

I would also like to dedicate this book to my three boys,
Brandon, Oliver, and Alexander,
whose playful interruptions and numerous video game sessions
gave me much-needed breaks along the way.

Finally, I would like to dedicate this book to my parents,
Dr. Douglas and Marjorie Gorrie,
for their love and encouragement throughout my life.

James R. Gorrie
Austin, Texas
November 30, 2012

"Men in the game are blind to what men looking on see clearly."
                                                        —*Chinese proverb*

Contents

Acknowledgments

When I decided to write *The China Crisis*, it was sort of an intellectual homecoming for me. As an "economically challenged" doctoral student at the University of California at Santa Barbara more than a few years ago, I had just passed my comprehensive exams and gathered my dissertation committee together when I lost my funding amidst budget cutbacks. My choice was either to go into debt another hundred grand while I wrote my dissertation on the political economy of China (and probably live out of my 1969 VW camper van, which was all I had at the time) or forage for a job in the "real world" outside the protective walls of academia. I chose the latter. It has been quite a winding path, to say the least.

Fast-forward 20 years, and I have finally written the book that I had wanted to write. Though now far removed from graduate school, I have never lost interest in the world at large, nor of watching China as it grew and transformed itself, year after year, into a formidable, fascinating and greatly distorted economic power. Needless to say, completing this book is a dream come true for me and a very personal accomplishment. In getting my thoughts out of my head and into print, there are a few people who truly made it happen for me and they deserve my sincere thanks and acknowledgment.

My heartfelt thanks and gratitude belong to my wife Louise, who always found a way to make much of the long road a bit smoother than otherwise would have been, and remained with me through the very rough spots. I could not have a better companion with whom to travel life's winding, adventurous path.

I want to also thank MaryEllen Tribby, who not only is a fan of my writing, but was at one time also a colleague. Of course, I also want to thank the people at John Wiley & Sons: in particular, Deborah Englander, for her faith in me, for agreeing to go along with my idea for *The China Crisis*, and for giving me the opportunity to write for such an esteemed publisher. I could not have asked for a better home for my first nonfiction book. I would also like to express my personal appreciation to my editor, Judy Howarth, for all her help with the book, her flexibility, and her wise suggestions along the way.

Finally, I would like to thank my good friend, Al Hyam, for his insight and perspective, (though sometimes challenging my own, highly valued nonetheless) and for more than 20 years of great conversation and friendship through good times and some not-so-good times.

JRG

Introduction

When I discussed writing this book with my publishers , I mentioned that I wanted to make it as informative yet easy to read and digest as possible. I wanted the book to appeal to the business individual as well as academics and those with a causal interest in what's evolving in China. As a former academic, I am used to academic writing, but the vast majority of the public—including business people and those with a general interest in what's happening in the world—are not. That is not a dig against academia; it's just a fact. Most people get their information from Internet sites and so I have attempted to keep the writing as informative and engagingly conversational as possible. Also, I will use statistics as reasonably and effectively as possible without turning the book into a chore to get through.

My main purpose in writing this book is to inform the reader just what is going on with China's economy, and to provide a more balanced and accurate picture of some of the enormous challenges that China faces, which seem to get overlooked in popular news reports. As noted above, I use statistics where needed or helpful, but at the same time, I am mindful of avoiding presenting a dry, quantitative recitation.

Rather, my objective in writing *The China Crisis* is to view China from a macro perspective, to look at the broad forces that are at work within China's economy, its demographics, its environment, and the Chinese Communist Party. I want to connect the dots as I see them in a plausible fashion that is interpretive in style, scope, and intent. Like any predictive effort, there is the promise of being ahead of the curve in some areas, and the danger of misreading the meanings of events or facts, and, of course, of being just plain wrong. Whatever the case may be, I can bear the risk of being publicly wrong on certain points; after all, no one is right all of the time, and when someone thinks they are they tend to be a bit of a boor anyway. That said, I think the risk is worth the effort. The worst-case scenario for *The China Crisis* is that it will provide a context for many provocative conversations about the subject going forward.

Like so many other observers, when I first began thinking about China and its fantastic rise in the world, I was greatly impressed by how far that country has come in such a relatively brief period of time. It was not too long ago that China was the bicycle capital of the world. From the opening of China in the late 1970s up through the early 1990s, almost any newscast from Beijing—with the possible exception of the Tiananmen Square Massacre in 1989—would include the obligatory camera shot of thousands upon thousands of Chinese riding their bikes on Beijing roads. "The Bicycle Kingdom" was a kind of standing joke about the industrially backward and communist Chinese.

Suffice it so say, those days are long gone. Today, people speak of China's "economic miracle," which has lifted hundreds of millions of Chinese out of poverty and strengthened the prospect of China's growing role on the world stage. Such speculation is not altogether unfounded. In fact, on the face of it, there would seem to be nothing standing in the way of China in becoming the greatest power on Earth.

This is only a slight exaggeration, but there is always an awe factor when a nation of 1.3 billion people—one-fifth of the world's population—challenges the United States, the world's most powerful nation, in such a brazen and rapid fashion as China most certainly is doing. There is certainly no question that China already has surpassed the United States in several economic measures, and will continue to claim more firsts as their wealth and economy expand. Having said that, I explore reasons why China's economy is more likely to contract rather than expand, and what this means in the larger context of China's expected rise to global dominance.

But even as the Chinese economic machine begins to slow down, China's accomplishments in its development are far too great to ignore. In 2006, the size of China's economy grew to be second only to the United States in the world. By 2010, China had 85 million cars on the road and had become the manufacturing capital of the world, again surpassing the United States. By 2015, there are expected to be 150 million cars on China's roads; the country is already the largest automobile market in the world and is on its way to becoming the global leader in consumption of most, if not all, commodities. Since the mid-2000s, China has widely been viewed as the possible—if not eventual—replacement for the aging United States in leading the world through the twenty-first century.

In fact, Asia seems to be the newest place for rising wealth, with China leading the way. The BRIC nations—the emerging economies of Brazil, Russia, India, and China—are looked at collectively and in the case of China, individually—as viable substitutes for the U.S. economy as the world's engine of growth. China's economy, of course, is the largest out of all of the BRICs, and there is no doubt that enormous wealth has been created in China via its "Beijing Model" of state capitalism. So much so, in fact, that the Beijing Model has been touted as, again, the replacement model of development for the twenty-first century, superseding free market capitalism and the international trading system, both instituted and managed by the United States. *The China Crisis* looks at this from a more contrarian perspective, in light of the manner in which China, and the Chinese economy, has been managed by the Chinese Communist Party (CCP) over the past 60 years.

But regardless of how fast China has industrialized itself, it was the financial crisis of 2008, and the Euro Crisis in its wake, that truly drew my attention back to the Middle Kingdom. (I say "back" because, as a doctoral candidate in the early 1990s, my dissertation was to be on China, but I dropped out of the program for financial reasons before completing it.) Both the United States and Europe were hit hard by the crisis, but China was widely perceived to have been relatively unaffected by it. Therefore, by 2011, there was great speculation and hope that China would, in one way or another, come to the rescue of the Eurozone. And why shouldn't there have been? China possessed trillions of dollars in cash reserves (and still does) and the Eurozone was on the verge of collapsing (and still is). More to the point, the Eurozone was, and at this writing remains, China's biggest trading partner.

But as explained in this book, there are some fundamental aspects of China's internal arrangements that seem much less optimistic, even ominous, upon closer inspection. China's "economic miracle" more resembles an economic nightmare that is only now beginning to reveal itself in some very big ways. The aspect of China that makes it the most difficult for me to buy into the idea of China as the next global leader is the fact that it is, for all intents and purposes, still a communist nation with a command economy. I am certain that many Marxist scholars would challenge that assertion, just as others would challenge the assertion that China has embraced market capitalism, and both camps would technically be correct in doing so. After all, economically, China is not 100 percent communist anymore, although as conditions there continue to deteriorate, they are certainly re-embracing state-owned means of production with great zeal. No, China's political economy bears more resemblance to the fascism of the 1920s and 1930s with some new, "Chinese characteristic" angles thrown in. Though state capitalism is also an accurate label for China in many ways, it doesn't do the Chinese model justice when it comes to its impact and damage to Chinese society. I will elaborate more on that in the chapters ahead.

But politically, the CCP brutally retains its monopoly on political power and controls Chinese society to an amazing and depressing extent; in large measure the CCP *does* control the economy. Whatever economic policy or activity is undertaken must be approved by the CCP at some level. Thus, from my perspective, therein lies the fatal flaw in China's rise as a sustainable economy and as a global power. China's government, with all the wealth that has come to China, suffers from a legitimacy crisis amongst the vast majority of its citizens—even among many of the wealthy and middle classes.

Illegitimacy from the merchant and manufacturing classes is an enormous problem for the CCP. Unlike the low and vast labor classes, the middle class knows what freedoms their counterparts enjoy in the West, and they increasingly reject the political paternalism and intellectual straitjacket that the CCP demands they accept. Furthermore, as the Chinese economy continues its slowdown, and the state confiscates more factories and wealth from the middle class, the middle class is no longer satisfied with prosperity in exchange for political docility. This illegitimacy problem is not only showing itself at a critical juncture in China, but it will not be improved by the actions of the CCP; rather, it will only be made worse.

The overarching reason I say this is because the history of communist governments and economic growth is, with one very qualified exception, a dismal one. (The exception is primarily for China from 1979 through 1989, and, one could possibly argue, up through 2008.) The reality is that over the long term, every communist country has ultimately failed to bring about sustained economic growth, technological innovation, or rising standards of living for the majority of its people. This was eminently true for the late Soviet Union, whose ossified economy failed to feed its people, failed to innovate (with the exception of technology theft), and left itself and its client states 30 years behind the West by the time the Soviet Union finally collapsed.

A similar comparison can be made between the communist North Korea and the capitalist South Korea. With the exception of its nuclear weapons, North Korea exists in a time warp, with little development to show for its 60-year run of totalitarian socialism except darkness, fear, oppression, and hunger among its people. Other communist regimes such as Cuba are not really much better off than they were 50 years ago. Ironically, what remains of the Castro regime may actually possess a fortune in its now impressively antique fleet of 1950s-era automobiles; Havana may now be the classic car capital of the world for the simple fact that its communist government has been unable to move the country past 1959.

But all ironies aside, there are several traits that all communist governments have in common; among them are a few that are very crucial in their impact on how communist states run, or rather, how they run their economies into the ground. One crucial factor is the primacy of the one-party state. In every communist nation, the communist party is possessive of its power and has a history of doing whatever it takes to remain in power. That characteristic applies to China as much as—or even more than—it does to Cuba.

Another common trait is the Party's antagonism toward market forces. When there is only one party and no market to provide economic signals for pricing of goods or the allocation of resources, corruption in all its forms replaces market signals. And where there is corruption and a monopoly on power, there is secrecy. And when there is secrecy, and the means to maintain it, there is every reason (and need) to make things seem better than they are. This was true in the USSR—China's mentor state—as well as every other communist country. It is no less true in China today.

Thus, the natural question is simply: Why shouldn't these factors, which are all prevalent in communist countries, also apply to China? The answer is that they most certainly do. In fact, the horrible truth is that the CCP has an astonishingly consistent record of making huge mistakes. This particularly applies to the Great Leap Forward and the Cultural Revolution, which collectively ended up costing some 60 million people their lives. It is my contention in this book that with its record of repeatedly bringing one national disaster after another, the CCP is pushing China toward the next disaster, which will also be of historical proportions. The vehicle for China's next disaster is the Beijing Model, which again has been brought to the Chinese people by the CCP.

As I discuss in the chapters ahead, the Beijing Model is the aggregate of muddled economic policies that create market distortions both internally and globally. It is also a license for the CCP to ravage the Chinese economy, its resources, and the country as a whole. I will show why the Beijing Model is not a market-based model but rather, a model that abuses the market in many ways for short-term advantage and long-term catastrophe.

But some would surely say that China *does* in fact use the market—particularly the international market—and therefore is no longer in danger of the communist disease of economic stagnancy, oppression, and such. Certainly, there is no doubt that China is among the world's most dynamic economies today. Since China adopted capitalism some three decades ago, by all appearances it seems to have successfully avoided the fate of the Soviet Union. But has it really? I will argue that China has not successfully avoided their fate as a communist nation thus far, but is in fact on the very cusp of meeting it today.

We will explore why this is the case in great detail in the chapters that follow. Before getting started, however, a word about perspective and objectivity is in order. I have always found the tendency of academic detachment with regard to discussing the advantages, disadvantages, and aspects of political and economic systems that behave monstrously toward their people to be intellectually irresponsible and morally repugnant. The justification of maintaining one's "objectivity" by not providing unvarnished criticism of a tyrannical regime is a moral failing on the part of too many who wish to maintain their good relations with and access to the CCP.

Critics and skeptics of my approach in *The China Crisis* may level the charge that objectivity has been cast aside in this book. My answer to that potential protest is that Sinophiles, for the most part, see mainly what they want to see, perhaps wishing to keep their viability with China officials intact, and too easily dismiss the more dreadful and inhuman aspects of the Chinese society as akin to "the costs of industrialization," or some other such obtuse or marginalizing dismissal. Still, credit ought to be given where credit is due, and I readily acknowledge China's many accomplishments across a broad spectrum of disciplines. But the human costs also need to be accounted for, don't they?

Let's be honest: on the one hand, the lexicon of academic discussion of almost any comparative political analysis is dry and almost always dehumanizingly sterile. On the other hand, in the criticism of one system and the advocacy of another, there always lies the danger of it becoming an exercise in jingoistic propaganda. In navigating between these two poles, I find the surest path in arriving at the proper tone is to simply follow the path of human decency. I ask myself, "Would I like to live there?" or "How would someone like me be treated?"

Thus, my criticisms of China's current system are many and harsh because that system and the society it has engendered are both unimaginably brutal and indecently harsh to its citizens. As for the effects China's policies have had on its environment, the damage is on a scale that leaves no other intellectually honest or moral alternative than to see it as a highly disastrous and destructive force.

To assess China's current system by any other measure would indeed be a moral failing; I believe that the world has seen enough of tyrannical political systems to know that moral equivalency is no longer a defensible position among academics, journalists, or free men and women. After all, which of us is willing to admit that we are, or should be, academically detached from the suffering of our fellow human beings? Which of us would wish to be?

Having said that, I do not excuse the excesses and failings of market capitalist societies; they are there, as well, but to a much lesser degree and frequency than in the communist regimes. The fact is that no society, political system, or economic system is perfect; it is, after all, an imperfect world filled with imperfect human beings. But are we not yet wise enough to see that some political and economic systems are better than others? Or has moral relativism, and its political pack mule, multiculturalism, stripped us of our ability to think critically, blinded us to seeing what is actually there, and stopped our tongues from calling a brutal, unjust, and inhumanly destructive system exactly what it is? Perhaps that is the case in some quarters, but thankfully, it is not yet so in all of them.

In this, I am reminded of the utter surprise and shock in both the intelligence community and academia at the collapse of the Soviet Union in 1991. I was in college when the 1987 Reykjavik Summit between President Reagan and Mikhail Gorbachev took place. It seemed evident at the time that Gorbachev, for a variety of reasons, was quite hungry to cut a deal on mutual defense spending cuts. This was an especially daunting time for the USSR because it faced the prospect of Reagan's so-called Star Wars nuclear missile defense shield program when Gorbachev knew that not only was the USSR bankrupt, but that it also had no way of competing technologically with such a program should it become perfected. Reagan, as we know, rejected Gorbachev's offer.

At a symposium I attended in the days after the summit, I recall political science professors stating confidently and critically that the United States had blown a historic opportunity to significantly improve relations with the Soviet Union, which would remain a force in the world for the next 50 to 100 years. The students in attendance, myself included, were assured that the USSR would be around for at least that long into the future, and that it might even outlast the United States. Less than 15 years later, the Soviet Union was no more. Even with all its spies in the Kremlin, the CIA was taken by surprise at the Evil Empire's sudden collapse. Talk about not seeing the forest for the trees.

Therefore, in proceeding with this book, I seek to clearly identify those crucial, undeniable facts that foreshadow China's collapse, in the context of the typical trajectory of a communist government. The broad premise underlying the arguments in this book is that communist governments in general, and China's government in particular, possess the following characteristics:

- *Unbelievably inefficient in resource allocation*—such that waste of resources, natural, financial, and human, pose a direct threat to China's continued economic viability.
- *Corrupt in every way possible*—which is, of course, a function not only of the nature of communist governments, but also due to inefficiency, as referenced above.
- *Socially destructive*—not only is the entire political class corrupt, but Chinese society as a whole has become coarse and inhumane, and consequently suffers from what former Chinese Premier Wen Jiabao called a "degradation of morality and lack of integrity."[1] The corruption, through every stratus and quarter in China, has all but destroyed civil Chinese society. Decades of mass relocations, the One Child policy, forced abortions as a policy, and bribery and theft as the only way to survive have reduced much of China's society to the ravages of the more base elements of human nature.
- *Fostering the Tragedy of the Commons in all areas of life*—With the people enjoying "ownership" over all of China, and yet the people being represented solely by the CCP, no one (other than the CCP) really owns anything. This leads to abuse of all things that belong to no one in particular. This includes farmland, rivers, lakes, oceans, and, of course, the air. This command economy, communist-related phenomenon is on full display in the level of pollution and environmental deprivation seen in China today.

The effects and impacts of these facts have direct consequences for China on many fronts, but are mainly reflected in the country's growing instability. These impacts include:

- *Growing economic hardship*—As both the economic and social dynamism slow down in China, the gap between the rich and poor will grow, as well. This is already a hot-button issue in China and will only get worse.

- *Widening economic disparity*—a symptom of the above, but also a warning of things returning to pre-1979 conditions in terms of teeming Chinese masses dissatisfied with the leadership of the CCP.
- *Inability to produce enough food*—As uncontrolled industrial development continues headlong into oblivion, the *tragedy of the commons* and corrupt land policies are both playing a huge part in rapidly driving China into an era of want and hunger.
- *Political inability to adapt to changing world*—This is perhaps the greatest handicap of communist governments. The overriding need for political primacy results in a high level of repression and a restriction of ideas and the free exchange of information, leading to social stagnation and a depressed and dissatisfied society. This is why communist governments tend to be largely technology transfer economies rather than innovative knowledge-based ones.

Despite the successes of China's Beijing Model, it is also a model for disaster in the long run for several reasons. First of all, the Beijing Model's development path is not a sustainable one. Rather, it is the path to wreck and ruin in China. It combines the worst aspects of both communism and capitalism. The Beijing Model retains the oppressive aspects that are endemic to the communist system, such as the political exclusivity of the Party, institutionalized disrespect for humanity and the environment, and excessive corruption throughout society and the Party itself. But it is also marked by an unbridled greed that would put any nineteenth-century oligarchy to shame, including currency manipulation, Dickensian labor exploitation, and adversarial trade practices. And internally, market forces and the price mechanism for resource allocation are typically grossly distorted or abrogated by CCP policies and corruption.

As such, we will see how the Beijing Model has not changed the nature of communist government in China; it just bought the thugs in the CCP better clothes and allowed merchant and manufacturing classes to develop—for a while. We will also see why, even as you read this, these classes are rapidly being reabsorbed into state ownership. As I explain in the chapters ahead, the first step of the Beijing Model was actually the beginning of market capitalism in China, with the requisite freedoms and private property rights growing with it. But the CCP could see the direction in which the country was headed and crushed the flower of democracy and free expression in the spring of 1989. Tiananmen Square ended that phase of liberalism and market capitalism in China. The second phase is the cannibal capitalism of the Beijing Model, which is driving China to its destruction today.

In the concluding chapters, we will look at why China has reached critical mass and is ready to fall in upon itself through the perspectives of China as empire and the complexity theory. By *critical mass*, I mean that the collective impacts and effects of the Beijing Model, the rise of illegitimacy associated with the CCP, and the utter strain and desolation that have been put upon the waters and the lands of China, weigh down upon the country and its people; and China's leadership shows no ability or intention of adjusting to the destructive impact of it all.

Rather, the CCP leadership continues in its ways of overconsumption and abuse of its people as much as possible, at the expense of its aging population, its environment, its financial solvency, and its ability to feed itself. All of these problems will prove fatal to the current state of China. There is just too much damage done in terms of unsupported debt, currency manipulation, and widespread pollution, and too much privilege for too few people, as well as too much civil disorder and illegitimacy at the highest levels of society. China not only will fail to move up the development ladder from a manufacturing- to a knowledge-based economy, but its own manufacturing strength is also depleting and will continue to do so as labor costs rise, as other Asian competitors arise, and as poor-quality products and theft make China less and less desirable of a nation with which to do business. Ultimately, in the language of governments and bankers, China, with all its problems, is simply too big *not* to fail.

What will failure look like in China? With disparate development levels and regional favoritism, China's social and regional divisions will reach critical points and then result in regional fractures within the country. The new regime will not only feel pressure and threats from its competitors within the Party—which can be quite deadly— but also from regional Party authorities who will demand assistance to quell the growing resistance to Beijing's and the CCP's destructive totalitarian rule.

Those pressures may well cause a split within the CCP with divisions along hardliners versus reformers. If past is prologue, and the CCP's current policy of cracking down on dissent supports that presumption, then it will be the hardliners in the Party who will prevail. In that scenario, civil war, pitting one or more regions against the Party and Beijing rule is a distinct possibility. Compounding the impact of China's regional fractures may well be the lack of adequate food supplies, brought about by the extreme environmental degradation (which has the stamp of the Party all over it), drought, and overdevelopment and overgrazing. Rising food prices on the world market are already in play and may well become a major source of discontent for China's regional conflicts in the very near future.

Similarly, the Chinese need for energy, especially oil, will lead it to adopt a forward-leaning posture toward energy suppliers and an aggressive posture to capture oil-producing areas that are within China's military grasp. This is already underway with countries like Vietnam, the Philippines, and others where undersea oil fields are located under disputed territories. China's Communist Party newspaper *The Global Times* has already, in September of 2011, openly called for war against nations such as Vietnam and the Philippines who would seek to deprive China of those disputed resources and its proper place among great nations.[2] Foreign military actions would be expected to occur and rise in frequency and intensity as China's economic, financial, political, and environmental systems begin to fail in a cascading effect.

Finally, just as the first phase of Western-assisted capitalism rescued the CCP from an illegitimacy crisis in 1979, and the return of Hong Kong gave China a needed boost in 1997 by instantly becoming its sophisticated financial center, today, as conditions deteriorate, the CCP will also look toward Taiwan. Taiwan not only represents an ideological threat, as it underscores the freedoms and living standards that China still lacks, it is also a much healthier economy and source of abundant food. For all of these reasons, and more, China will be sorely tempted to bring the wayward province—as they regard it—under the control of the CCP at last.

And, according to Deng Xiaoping's message to his successors, the "Taiwan problem" needed be "solved" by no later 2012.[3] As of this writing in March 2013, that policy prescription remains unfilled, but as China struggles to stay afloat, the Taiwan problem will look like a needed opportunity to divert attention away from the epic mistakes and deep harm the CCP has put upon the nation. Such an invasion will also be an attempt to unify the fractured Chinese nation as much as it will be an effort to capture needed food and capital.

When reading *The China Crisis*, bear in mind that the statistics and facts I have presented may change over time—they may get better, and they may get worse. In fact, in all probability, they will not remain as they are at this writing for very long. Remember, like the world itself, China is a fluid place that is always evolving and is certainly unpredictable. With the recent transition of power, continuing challenges in the global economy, and heightened tensions in the region over oil, other resources, and ultimately, regional hegemony, China's obstacles to continue down the path it has chosen are formidable. The objective of this book is not to cast a pall of doom and gloom for its own sake over China, but to bring to the fore the very real problems and challenges that China's current leadership has largely created, and which it is truly unable and unwilling to successfully address, other than by tightening the screws of oppression. This is what the CCP is doing today in China and, if history is any guide, this is what it will continue to do in the future. Of course, as I intend to show, that is the path to failure.

The point of this book is not to attack China, but rather, to focus attention on the dangers that a Chinese collapse poses to itself, to its region, and to the global economy. It is true, however, that I hold the CCP responsible for the vast majority of China's problems and massive human tragedies that have befallen the nation since 1949. It is also true that the successful rise of a middle class in China is at least partly due to the policies of the CCP. However, the price of this rise has been inordinately high and, if my conclusions are correct, it may well be much higher in the very near future.

The upcoming period of trials that China is entering will, at the very least, cause China to look inward in terms of supporting, if not resuscitating, their own economy. This will not happen in a vacuum. A cessation of Chinese purchase of U.S. Treasury Bonds, for example, due to rapidly deteriorating circumstances at home on multiple fronts is a very real possibility; and not only is it an outcome that is reasonable to envisage, but it also would be dire and widespread in its impact.

Such an occurrence would be a precursor to a possible crash in the U.S. Treasury markets, and would likely cause a flight from the U.S. dollar, as well. Neither of these possibilities bode well for the United States' economy, nor for the Eurozone, or for that matter, for the entire global economy.

Furthermore, when nations are in distress, history shows us that striking out against their aggressors—perceived, imagined, or simply convenient—is how world wars begin. That is not a prediction in itself, but it is an acknowledgment of how serious and dangerous the situation can quickly become given the right—or wrong—set of circumstances. As I have mentioned in this introduction and will go into more detail in the chapters that follow, we are already seeing dangerous signs of this occurring today.

As global economic conditions grow worse, the temptation and need for foreign adventurism will grow for China's policy makers. It is no stretch of the imagination to say that the rhetorical foundations are being put in place on an almost daily basis. This includes not just China's neighbors in the Asian-Pacific region, but the West in general and, specifically, the United States. Even as China's greatest debtor—or perhaps on some level, because of its position as such—the United States is viewed as a main adversary in the political announcements of China's communist leaders. How this will play out remains to be seen.

Thus, a warning to the rest of the world regarding China's coming collapse is a wise precaution, and more than that, it is an absolute necessity. This is because the consequences and effects of communist China's descent into a twenty-first century catastrophe, rivaling or even surpassing those in its early history of the mid-twentieth century, will not be contained within China. The global recession in which the world finds itself will deepen considerably since the United States, and therefore, the world, now depends upon China's financial liquidity and markets. As China pays the price for its grave mistakes and willful abuse of its economy, its people, and its natural environs, the entire world will feel its pain.

James R. Gorrie
Austin, Texas
March 3, 2013

Notes

1. Wu Zhong, "Wen Won't Solve China's Crisis of Faith," *Asia Times Online*, April 21, 2011, www.atimes.com/atimes/China/MD21Ad02.html.

2. Miles Yu, "China Demands War," *The Washington Times*, September 28, 2011, www.washingtontimes.com/news/2011/sep/28/china-demands-war.

3. Mark O'Neill, "Taiwan's Forcible Reunification," *Asia Sentinel*, January 26, 2011, www.asiasentinel.com/index.php?option=com_content&task=view& id=2946&Itemid=386.

Chapter 1

A World on Edge

As the world passes through the second decade of the twenty-first century, we find ourselves in the midst of a global financial crisis that threatens the way of life of virtually the entire civilized world. From the United States to Europe, Russia, Eastern Europe, and Japan to South America, India, and the Middle East, and yes, even to China itself, most of the world's 7 billion people face a global economic crisis—perhaps even a global depression—that appears to have no rational ending in sight.

I say *rational* because the current course being pursued by the world's central banks shows no real potential for solving the crisis of debt and economic contraction that every major developed economy faces today. The policy of *quantitative easing* that every major economy, including China, is following—though temporarily helpful to some segments of the economy like the banks, stock markets, and corporate coffers—ultimately only adds more debt to an already debt-choked international financial system that sees productivity falling and is based upon a currency, the U.S. dollar, which itself is rapidly fading in value if not validity.

Consequently, the world finds itself at a crossroads. The current-but-broken international financial system, founded upon the vitality of the U.S. economy and a gold-backed U.S. dollar and held together by the imposition and enforcement of a set of rules by U.S. economic and military dominance, no longer works as it once did. The last pretensions of a gold-backed dollar disappeared in 1971 and the U.S. national debt and deficit spending have both been on a constant increase since then and are well beyond the point of anyone believing that such debts will ever be paid back. The global financial crisis at hand is perhaps the final symptom of this dysfunctional system before it crashes altogether. This now inadequate system, like an aging man, is full of frailties and weaknesses and is but a shadow of its former self, with a sclerotic capital system that is unsustainable and clogged with so much aggregation of debt that it can no longer be supported by falling productivity or the spent energies of 50 years of debt-fueled consumption.

One of the problems the world faces lies not just in where to go from here, but how to get there. At the same time, as the worst financial crisis the world has seen since the Great Depression continues to unfold (the 2008 credit crisis is neither solved nor cured, but is only being *managed* with massive amounts of new credit), military relationships and trade relations are being formed and re-imagined at this writing, which, to any careful student of history, ought to sound alarm bells loud, clear, and urgent.[1] The result of the last global financial crisis, the Great Depression, was the global conflict that became known as World War II. However, given our sophisticated and deadly technological age, large-scale and protracted warfare, particularly on the scale of a global conflict, is utterly irrational; and yet that is the direction in which much of the world seems to be headed in an unmistakable and disturbing hurry.

What Is the Proper Context in Which to Assess China Today?

Viewing China through the prism of the current global financial crisis is tempting and facile; with over a trillion dollars in reserves and deep trading relationships with both the United States and the Eurozone, as well as with Russia and Japan, China seems to be the nation least vulnerable to the negative effects of the financial crisis. But the dynamic of the global financial crisis is not the complete or only context in which to view China and its place and position in the world; as we'll see, it is truly not the most important either.

China's economic strength, whatever it is or may turn out to be, is a function of many factors, as are its military capabilities and diplomatic influence. Not least among those factors are the internal arrangements of China. By that, I mean the manner in which Chinese society is organized, the reliability and stability of its domestic economic and political structures, and how key economic and political decisions are made and carried out. Perhaps most crucial of all are the nature, history, and track record of just who makes the big decisions for China and why.

From that point of view, the global financial crisis is an external threat to China's economic viability, but so are the deep flaws and recurrent weaknesses in China's political economy that are being revealed in part by the financial crisis, and in part by China's exposure to the world as never before. The difference today is that China no longer exists in a state of autarky as it did for virtually the first three decades after the revolution. In fact, how China chose to engage in the global economy and arrange its economic footing—going forward from communism to a distorted form of state capitalism—is also a function of its Communist Party decision-making process and, as we shall see, is truly a fundamental and growing weakness in China's current economy.

Again, China certainly *seems* to be better positioned and more agile than either Europe or America in weathering the effects of the financial crisis. But is that really the case? How will China fare as the Eurozone slips into deeper levels of recession and Cyprus-style financial meltdown in 2013 and beyond?

There are essentially three schools of thought on how China will fare in the near future in the midst of the global economic crisis in which the world now finds itself. One view is that China will continue to weather the financial storm relatively well, given its level of economic development, the size of its internal market, its high level of liquid reserves, and other seemingly favorable facts and statistics on its economy. This may indeed prove to be the case, as those are certainly strong factors working in China's favor. Given that the Eurozone—the major economic trading bloc on the Eurasian continent—is on the edge of financial collapse, and that mass violence in the periphery nations of Greece, Portugal, Spain, and Italy threatens the legitimacy of governments and the stability of Europe itself, China, by comparison, looks to be in a much stronger position to weather the financial storm.

Is this true though? The crisis in the Eurozone has yet to reach its final stages, but China is looked to as the biggest source of market-rescuing capital for the Eurozone.[2] China, however, has yet to fulfill the role that some in the Eurozone fervently wish that it would. A very good question is, "Why haven't they?"

Another view on China's fortunes going forward (arguably less ideal, but perhaps more realistic than the first) is that China will continue to suffer some of the effects of the global financial downturn, but will prove to be flexible, agile, and smart enough to come through the next few years relatively well compared to Europe and the United States. This viewpoint toward China is still in the same orbit as the first view, but with a more or less bumpier ride built into the assumption. But still, it has China emerging from the crisis in a relatively more favorable position than it was in before the crisis.

Is this a realistic outcome for China? Is China, among the major economies of the world, truly best positioned to endure the financial crisis that threatens capital flows, investment, productivity, and consumption levels the world over? That is the implicit assumption underlying this viewpoint of China.

More precisely put are the facets of China's economy—its manufacturing base, domestic market, and technology sector—deeply embedded, nimble, diverse, and innovative enough to react to and overcome the challenges to which other highly developed economies such as the Eurozone, Japan, and the United States are struggling to adapt? This is an even more difficult question to answer in the affirmative when one considers the past history of decision making by China's leadership, its political culture, and its economic frailties that are now coming to the fore, and for which China has no immediate answer or cure.

This question, of course, leads us to a third view, one that is still shared by only a minority of observers. And yet, increasingly, it seems to be the most correct and likely view—that, in a nutshell, China is headed for another disastrous chapter in its history of disasters brought about by its communist leadership's decision-making process and inherent incompetence.

Although it may sound like political ax grinding between capitalism and communism, it is not. Rather, it is an acknowledgment that China's leadership has created an economic monster that is so distorted in its foundations and its execution as to render it incapable of reacting quickly enough or in the ways necessary to avoid a massive collapse of the system altogether in the face of rising internal crises which threaten China as much as, if not more than the global financial crisis threatens the Eurozone or the United States.

That more pessimistic view is also shared herein. It is not a wish or a hope, but simply an assessment of the conditions within the Chinese economy, population, and various policies that appear to conspire in their aggregate to cause a reckoning of sorts, which will not only be quite difficult for China to overcome, but poses real doubts about whether or not the China we see today will be recognizable in the next few years. More than its distorted economy, however, it is China's distorted political system that will be the country's undoing. China's Communist Party leadership and the political culture surrounding it are posed to catalyze the latest version of calamity that the Party leadership has brought to China since it took power over six decades ago.

China's Historical Context

A brief look into China's modern history provides useful insights into not only who drives China's policies, but also how and why they are driven as they are. It will also help illuminate the great flaws and resultant weaknesses and failures of modern China's financial and economic system and of its political culture, as well as the great and terrible implications and causations that it imposes not only on the Chinese people, but also on the very land and natural environs of the part of the planet that China inhabits.

Historical context is a wise place to begin to understand China, because nations, like people, are shaped by their pasts and their worldviews are influenced by what they have experienced. Understanding the past of a country can therefore help us in understanding, at least to some degree, its view of itself and of the outside world. That context, in turn, can help us to understand China's worldview, its perception of the current U.S.-dominated financial system, and how they view their role in the world going forward.

A full and in-depth history of China is beyond the scope of this book. However, a brief look at some salient points of China's experience in the twentieth century, leading up to and including the communist revolution and the main crises that followed the revolution, is helpful in understanding the major thrusts of China's experience as a nation in the twenty-first century. The discussion that follows, therefore, is useful in providing a context for viewing some of the more impactful of China's recent historical influences, but it is by no means intended as an exhaustive account.

China's Place in the World

Throughout antiquity, China's name for itself was the "Middle Kingdom" because it was located in what they considered to be the middle of the known world. There has been, however, no shortage of cultural perception throughout China's history that allowed it to regard itself as the most important country, and most advanced culture, in the world. This was true for centuries. Those nations and cultures outside the Middle Kingdom were, by definition, inferior and viewed as barbaric, lesser peoples from whom nothing useful could be learned. This was true for a time. But such a combination of conceit and insularity did not help China in developing itself beyond the agrarian stage, while Western European nations began to rapidly industrialize from the seventeenth century onward.

About 100 years ago, in 1912, the Republic of China was founded, ending over 2,000 years of imperial dynastic rule. The last of the dynasties, the Qing Dynasty, which was also known as the Manchu Dynasty, ruled China from 1644 to 1912. The republican government that was established in its place was far from stable or effective, but events within China and outside it hardly gave it a chance to succeed. By the early twentieth century, feuding warlords, divided interests, and meddling foreign powers repeatedly beset the Republic of China. Continuous sources of internal strife such as shifting allegiances and political missteps, as well as external influences such as the invasion of Manchuria by Japan all contributed to an ineffective leadership of China during this time.

In 1928, there was a loose unification in China under the Chinese Nationalist Party, also known as the *Kuomintang*, but this did not last, as rifts developed between it, the Chinese Communist Party, and competing warlords. This made industrialization and modernization progress, which China was striving to achieve, more difficult; it came to a halt altogether once the Japanese invaded China in 1936. From that time until 1945, China was involved in a war of resistance against Japanese aggression and occupation as the Japanese sought natural resources and territory for its imperial expansion plans.

At the end of the Second World War in 1945, with the Japanese driven out of China, the civil war between the Nationalist forces and the Chinese Communist Party forces resumed in full force for the next four years. Economic development plans were again delayed by that internal conflict, which involved more death and destruction. Thus, the Republic was only to last 37 years, when, in 1949, the Republic of China was defeated by the Communists in a drawn out and very bloody civil war. Sadly, the level of slaughter at the hands of the Communists under the leadership of Mao Zedong was unparalleled in all of human history, as 50 million or more Chinese were killed due to war and the resulting mass starvation.

Having lost the war to the Communists, the Nationalists fled the mainland for Taiwan, where they set up a one-party authoritarian regime with martial law, just as the Communists set up a one-party dictatorial regime on the mainland. The comparison between the two Chinas is an apt and useful one because both Chinas began as rigid political regimes with minimal liberties and effective marshal law in place. However, the Taiwan regime eventually liberalized its society beginning in the late 1970s, and actively adapted to the global economy and diversified its economy. It pursued more advanced economic activity and development as it adopted a market-based capitalist model for its economy. By 1986, Taiwan's Republic of China had reformed itself into a multi-party representative democracy with a rapidly rising standard of living.[3]

China's Self-Inflicted Crises

Meanwhile, from 1949 onward, Communist China, also known as the People's Republic of China (PRC), languished in underdevelopment hell. The country and its people experienced enormous tragedies borne of the unbelievably damaging and misguided economic and development policies made exclusively by the Chinese Communist Party leadership. The policies were the product of a combination of political paranoia, ideological zealotry, and utter stupidity and ignorance of the laws of supply and demand, coupled with an institutionalized culture of corruption and deceit that continues in China to this day.

Understanding how and why these self-inflicted crises came about in China is crucial because it reveals a recurrent pattern in decision making as well as those fatal political flaws that remain in their political and economic system today. They also explain why China will face similar crises of massive proportions in the near future. With their victory in 1949, Communist China's Mao Zedong began a vigorous purge of dissidents, the educated, and the landowners to eliminate enemies of the new Marxist state. After several years of consolidating power, Chairman Mao and the Communist Party put Leninist-based economic development plans in force. The first of these was called "The Great Leap Forward" and was put into action in 1957.

Great Leap Forward or Famine?

The Great Leap Forward was the first effort by the Communist leadership to reinvent China from a largely agrarian society to an industrialized one. The goal was to gain industrial parity with Great Britain in 15 years. Then, after only one year, that goal was, incredibly, changed to only a one-year timetable. That was just the beginning of the madness.

Immense social and agrarian dislocations occurred as forced communal farming was introduced by the Chinese leadership, and productive farmers were retargeted to produce steel in backyard furnaces, which proved to be a complete failure, producing low-grade metal virtually unusable in any industry. Meanwhile, more landowners and farmers who resisted the theft of their land or otherwise did not go along with Mao's vision were executed. Over 500,000 farmers, landowners, and dissidents were killed by 1958[4] and over 100 million people were forced into labor for massive industrial projects.

Facing such unrealistic industrialization goals, production numbers were inflated in all strata of the economy and the cadres, including food production objectives, in order to avoid punishment by the Party. Consequently, what was mistakenly thought to be surplus food was exported from China, leaving tens of millions of people to starve to death, while many others were beaten and killed by roaming bandits in search of food. Thus, by simple decree, without logic or informed reasoning, the very fabric of Chinese life was rent and put under enormous duress with tragic and catastrophic results. As Dali Yang points out in a *University of Chicago Chronicle* piece from March 14, 1996:

> No one is sure exactly how many people perished as a result of the spreading hunger. By comparing the number of deaths that could be expected under normal conditions with the number that occurred during the period of the Great Leap famine, scholars have estimated that somewhere between 16.5 million and 40 million people died before the experiment came to an end in 1961, making the Great Leap famine the largest in world history. People abandoned their homes in search of food. Families suffered immensely, and reports of that suffering reached the members of the army, whose homes were primarily in rural areas. As soldiers received letters describing the suffering and the deaths, it became harder for leaders to maintain ideological discipline. Chaos developed in the countryside as rural militias became predatory, seizing grain, beating people and raping women.[5]

The lessons to be learned here are not from the failures of the Great Leap Forward, although they are many and deserve to be remembered and condemned. No, the real lesson to understand is the absolutism of the Communist Party leadership and absolute failure of the Communist Party leadership to lead the country properly, as well as their failure to make wise and prudent decisions, and their complete willingness to let tens of millions of their fellow Chinese die horrible deaths in their quest to hold onto power.

Yang also notes in his book, *Calamity and Reform in China,* "Historical developments during more than four decades of Communist rule in China have again and again shown us how the unanticipated consequences of elite policies subverted their attempts at fundamental social engineering."[6]

He further warns of "the crucial importance of guarding against those who claim to know some magic route to the radiant future, be they politicians like Mao or party intellectuals who supported Mao or the new technocrats who claim to have found a scientific way to make China rich and powerful and who happily clamor for more power for themselves."[7] That idea of special knowledge has been and remains the vision that is sold to the people by the CCP to this very day; as we will see, that vision is much more of a recurring nightmare in China.

Cultural Revolution or Social Cannibalism?

As with the Great Leap Forward before it, a similar result was the out-come of China's *Cultural Revolution*, again, spawned by Chairman Mao and the Communist leadership in 1966 and continued up until 1976. In this 10-year reign of hell on Earth in China, no one is sure just how many people were killed, but the numbers are again horrific. China was once more torn apart as Mao sought such disruption as a means of main-taining power against various political challengers, including the Chinese Army itself.

For an entire decade, the educated, the able, the productive, and the wise were sought out, humiliated, excoriated, imprisoned, sent to re-education camps, and, of course, executed. Schools were also closed for the entire 10 years, leaving a whole generation uneducated.

The political reasons for the Cultural Revolution, its objectives as well as its manifestation in China, are almost unbelievable in their scope, destruction, cruelty, and stupidity. For instance, for what possible reason would the leaders of China stop all education for a *whole decade*? Were they mad?

A description of the Cultural Revolution, from the website *Ency-clopedia of Marxism*, is helpful in getting one's mind around such an epic, inhumane, and mind-numbing event:

> The "Cultural Revolution" was aimed at smashing the Chinese Communist Party, and rebulding an administration owing alle-giance to Mao alone. . . .
>
> In the first phase of the Cultural Revolution, the urban youth were mobilised against the intelligentsia and better-off or educated sections of the working class. To this end, Mao . . . taught the youth to regard all manifestations of culture as bourgeois and counter-revolutionary. Lessons were stopped, all entertainment and social life other than "politics" denounced, and "politics" reduced to mindless repetition of "Mao's Thoughts" and the witch-hunting of anyone unwilling or unable to reduce themselves to the same idiotic level.
>
> In the second phase, the atomised and terrorised population was mobilised against the Party. Mao declared that the "bourgeois headquarters" was in the top leadership of the Party itself, and

called on the population itself to overthrow the Party administration in their area. . . . Mao had no mechanism for controlling
or directing the "revolution." In all areas of the country, rival
groups claimed the mantle, and launched holy war, not only
against the "capitalist-roaders"—generally the best elements of
the Party—but against each other. China degenerated into the
chaos of factional fighting. . . .

Torture and murder were carried out quite publicly, by the
public, and were supplemented by very effective social control
through the eyes and ears of a thousand million neighbours,
friends and family members.

In the third phase, Mao had brought the country to the
brink of destruction. Some way had to be found to halt
the disintegration. To this end, the urban youth which were out
of control in the cities were broken up into small groups and
sent to the countryside to "learn from the peasants." Just at a
time when Soviet scientists were beginning to catch up for lost
decades. . . . Peasants lectured agricultural scientists instead of
the other way round.[8]

The Cultural Revolution ended only with the death of Mao in 1976.
But again, the people's "own" government, run by the Communist Party,
perpetrated a terrible reign of terror over and against them for purely
political purposes. The Chinese government estimated that around
30 million people died from political executions at the hands of roving
armed cultural Red Guards, who killed anyone who demonstrated
bourgeois tendencies (which meant virtually anyone who was productive), as well as by starvation or suicide.

Again, the lesson here is that mistakes are made on a grand scale in
China by a leadership structure and ideology that pits the Communist
Party and the state against the people, without having to answer to the
people. China's huge population not only makes human life expendable
on a mass scale, but it also requires, so it is apparently believed, a heavy
authoritarian state to rule them. (Note that China's neighbor, India, with
1.2 billion people, is the world's largest democracy.) This is particularly
the case when the policies that the leadership imposes upon its people
are not popular and cause millions upon millions of them to die.

Social engineering, as it were, and many of the political and economic policies deriving from it, became no more than a way to control the masses in China by setting them against themselves, rather than having them rise up against the leadership. It is repeatedly evident that the overriding goal is not just economic improvements to the nation, but for the Party to hold onto power at any and every cost.

The clear lesson here is that the "mistakes" of both the Great Leap Forward and the Cultural Revolution were part and parcel the result of not just the personality cult of Mao Zedong, but of the *personality* of the communist leadership structure of China. Long after Mao's death, the Communist leadership of China continued to make boneheaded economic moves and oppressive crackdowns on political dissidents, students, businessmen, artists, and writers—anyone who threatened the existing power structure by pointing out the obvious illegitimacy of their ruling position and their idiotic and destructive policies.

That is not to say that the Chinese Communist Party has cornered the market on mass executions, misguided economic policies that decimate the nation's food supply and leave millions to starve to death, persecution of political enemies, and an overriding drive to dominate all aspects of life for its citizens. No, that is the *personality* or intellectual framework of all communist regimes, a particularly toxic political ideology that bloomed in full flower ever so deadly in the twentieth century. Indeed, Lenin and Stalin in China's neighbor to the north, the Soviet Union, had shown the way 20 years before, and the regimes of Cuba and North Korea, both desperately poor and brutal societies, joined China as the remaining troika of their kind to survive into the twenty-first century.

The last public demonstration of the Chinese Communist Party's deliberate heavy-handedness was in Tiananmen Square in 1989, when thousands of students demonstrated against the leadership in China and for democracy, and were, after several weeks of global publicity, overwhelmed and killed by the Chinese army that included tanks and heavy caliber machine guns against unarmed youth. Think things have changed today? Many of the new leaders in power today were CCP underlings at the time, and, as we shall see later in this discussion, demonstrations and massacres in China are, to borrow a phrase, "like street cars. If you miss one, don't worry; another will be along shortly."

The abysmal fact is that China struggled for the first 30 years after the revolution to modernize with great and yet unsuccessful efforts at tremendous human costs. After several attempts to develop itself through various harebrained ideas culled from the pages of Marx and Lenin's proscriptions for development and Mao's own misguided musings (which all led to tragically inefficient collectivist farms and mass relocations of its populace to horrendous bouts of re-education, fruitless backyard iron ore furnaces, political purges, and tens of millions of deaths), the Chinese leadership concluded that they had to change tactics. This led directly to the opening of the Chinese labor market to American multinational corporations, which would soon become a deep trading relationship, swapping cheap Chinese labor for some of the highest levels of U.S. technological know-how.

The result? In a few short years, as the United States and other Western nations engaged in business with China, Chinese development took off at an astonishing rate. Private ownership of businesses was allowed and expanded by the post-Mao era Chinese leadership. It is key to understand that this cooperation with the United States and other Western nations was as much in order for China to develop as it was for the Chinese leadership to maintain its mantle of legitimacy.

To that end, Deng Xiaoping made the observation in 1978 that China must develop, or face being dominated by the West once again. To put a very fine point on it, the Chinese leadership knew that they would face extinction either at the hands of the developed Western powers, or at the hands of their own people if they were not successful in modernizing the country. It was obvious to Deng that communism was not going to do it for them. It was then that the leader of the Chinese Communist Party observed, "What difference does it make if the cat is red or white as long as it catches mice?"

Not long after, in the mid-1980s, the Soviet Union was already undertaking its own reform and restructuring efforts under Gorbachev's *Glasnost* and *Perestroika* policies. This was a last ditch effort by Gorbachev to save his communist empire from crumbling due to its ineptitude and stagnation. Undoubtedly, the Chinese leadership could read the writing on the Berlin Wall.

But on the national level, to learn from the past invariably means to be able to change the way of behavior from the past. Such changes, in the case of China, involved a restructuring of its society in some areas—those exposed to the West—and importantly, allowing itself to partially, and ever so carefully, integrate itself with the global economy.

How Has Economic Integration with the Global Economy Changed China?

Allowing itself to integrate with the global economy—and particularly with the United States—has, as noted, greatly affected the course of China's development. China has developed more rapidly and deeply in the past 25 years, albeit in a greatly imbalanced, unstable, and unjust fashion, than anyone could have foreseen. But at the same time, in addition to the blessings of development, there are also severe drawbacks that accompany the development path China has followed.

The greatest drawback is the threat that development in China, not only in fact but also in the means and methods of its development, poses huge risks for both the Chinese leadership and to the Chinese people.

What do I mean by that?

Simply that China's development path has led to a variety of social, economic, and political consequences, which pose direct challenges to the elite communist leadership and life-threatening conditions for the people that are only now coming to the fore. We will look into the ways of viewing China's challenges that will not only show the dangers of China's development path, but also the political and economic dangers of its one-party Communist leadership.

Today, far from being the exotic, strange land that it once was, China is now in the very center of the vortex in world politics, international finance, and negotiations for global stability. As you might expect, there are today more places in the world where China plays an active and leading role than ever before. Like the United States for the past 65 years or so, China's presence and influence is now felt and acknowledged worldwide, from the financing of bridges in Indonesia, infrastructure in Africa, automobile manufacturing for Volkswagen and

General Motors, to the manufacture of Apple Technology's most innovative products.[9]

Is China Becoming the Next Superpower?

Today, many leaders, strategists, academics, and political observers
throughout the world view China as the next superpower. Indeed, the
prevailing sentiment in that belief is that China is on the cusp of not
only supplanting the United States as the global hegemonic power of
the twenty-first century, but also, just as importantly, the United States is
in its last throes as a superpower.

Are either or both of these true?

The fact is that the ability of the United States to influence events
and outcomes throughout the world is declining both relatively and absolutely in the face of the increasingly powerful Asiatic colossus that China has
become. The rise of China into a global economic and manufacturing powerhouse certainly appears to be true, and in many ways it undeniably *is* true.
The nature and sources of China's ascension, however, need to be explored
and understood before assigning China the title of emerging superpower.

This is especially relevant when considering that the United States has
been to this day and remains the driving source of economic growth in
China. This may be a controversial position to take, but it is nonetheless true.
We will revisit this assertion in the pages to come, but it bears keeping in
mind as we review key aspects of China's power in the world and the prospects for its continued growth and, more to the point, its continued existence.

It is no stretch of the facts to point out that compared to other
nations like Russia or India, or even supranational entities like the Eurozone, China's power and influence in the world is not only growing the
most rapidly of all of them, but it is also the most far reaching. China's
rise is naturally, if mistakenly, compared to that of U.S. power, which, in
all its facets, is certainly not what it once was relative to the rest of the
world in general and to China in particular. That is a common and mis-
leading mistake in judgment, which leads to unfounded, and therefore
inaccurate, conclusions about China's present and future state. Taking a
brief look at where China is today is helpful in putting the depth and
scope of China's rise in the proper context.

Trading Partner to the World

China is the Eurozone's largest trading partner, and together they are two of the biggest traders in the world, with annual trade between the two exceeding $365 billion per year.[10] The rise in trading relations has been steep and deep, meaning that not only has the value of the relationship grown exponentially, but also the interdependent nature of the trade augurs for a long-term and economically symbiotic relationship between China and the Eurozone. Of course, the depth of trade relations between China and the United States should surprise no one. The United States is China's largest market, with an annual trade of $202 billion and its annual trade deficit with China has increased 18 percent since 2008 to $503 billion.

China is the second largest trading partner with the United States after Canada. United States trade with China in 2011 totaled about $400 billion, with the United States running a trade deficit of $295 billion.[11] To say that the economies of China and the United States are codependent upon one another is to state the obvious. The economies have been integrated with one another on a scale that is without precedent for both countries.

The codependency between the United States and China can hardly be overstated. China is the largest foreign holder of U.S. Treasury notes, with about $1.3 trillion, which makes it the biggest lender to the United States outside of the Federal Reserve, which only recently (2010) surpassed China as the United States' largest source of capital.

There is little doubt that China's purchase of U.S. debt is what supports the U.S. economy. And on the flip side of that, there is little doubt that the United States' vast consumer market sustains China's vast manufacturing base, which relies heavily upon exporting low-cost consumer products to the U.S. market for its very survival. Without access to U.S. markets, China's rise could never have occurred. And without access to China's capital, the U.S. economy would come to a halt almost immediately.

How deeply integrated has China become with the U.S. economy? In 2012, China was given unprecedented access to the U.S. financial system in several ways that were simply unthinkable just a few short years ago. For instance, China has been given direct access to the U.S. Treasury to buy—and presumably to *not* buy—U.S. Treasuries without the rest of the U.S. bond market having any idea of China's dealings with the U.S. Treasury. Also, for the first time ever, Chinese banks are being allowed to own and operate banks in the United States.

The World's Manufacturer

China has become the world's manufacturer, as thousands of firms from the United States and Europe have relocated their factories to China in the past three decades. Of course, China's rise in manufacturing was no accident; its extremely low labor cost coupled with the allure of over 1 billion people to sell to has proven to be irresistible to major and minor manufacturing firms from around the world. This has resulted in the oft-used phrase *hollowed out* to describe a nation's economy when its manufacturing base has been shut down and left the country for more favorable labor and materials costs overseas. Ironically—or perhaps not so much—the Chinese market has largely been kept at arm's length from most Western firms.[12]

Still, as firms built more and more of their products in China, the result has been that fewer and fewer products are made in the United States and Europe, two of the largest industrialized regions on earth. In the face of an aging population and social welfare states under immense financial stress, both Europe and the United States, and also Japan for that matter, found themselves unable to compete with China's lower labor costs. The lack of unions and plentiful workers at slave labor wage rates has given China a great advantage that they have made every effort to maximize.

The unparalleled expansion of China's rise as a global leader in manufacturing is significant because manufacturing is the base of a healthy economy, which, in turn, is the basis for a healthy currency. Furthermore, economic statistics are announced regularly that repeatedly make the case that China will replace the United States as the world's next superpower, such as news reports that China surpassed the United States as the world's number one trading nation in early 2013.

Does this validate the assessment of China as a rising superpower? It certainly is an outwardly positive statistic, but it does not tell the whole story, nor does it necessarily mean all is well with China's economy.

Is China really that productive? And what is the quality of that productivity? A look at the demand for commodities is a key indicator of China's—or any country's—level of productivity.

An Appetite for Commodities

As a manufacturing powerhouse, China has become the largest consumer of commodities in the world. This includes iron, nickel, copper, gold, silver, and numerous other manufacturing, energy, and food commodities. China's GDP growth rate has averaged 8 percent or more for the past 20 years,[13] thanks to the rapid transformation of China from a backward agrarian nation to a global manufacturing giant. Its economy has risen from the eleventh largest economy in the world 20 years ago to the second largest, behind only that of the United States.

Because China is one of the world's largest consumers of commodities, it is also one of world's greatest influences on the prices of commodities. This means that China is a market maker in commodities and therefore has terrific influence upon the economies of the world that are commodity based, like Australia, Chile, and others. Likewise, a drop in China's consumption of commodities is an indicator of a slowdown in demand in China. However, a decrease in China exporting a commodity may be a trade indicator of a different sort. Take rare earth elements, for example.

China's restriction and near monopoly of rare earth elements to the world market is a strong indicator of the CCP's adversarial view of trade. China was admitted to the World Trade Organization (WTO) in 2001. One of the criteria was for China to loosen their export restriction on rare earth minerals, which account for 90 percent of world exports. China's refusal to do so 10 years afterward, even after WTO ruling that it must do so, exhibits its adversarial trading habits that spill over into many areas of China's economic policies and activities. This attitude is in direct contrast to those of its U.S. and European trading partners. This is a policy decision made at the highest levels of Chinese leadership and indicates that the paranoid nature of the Party remains intact, as it always has.

Later in this discussion, we further explore the meaning and impact of China's great appetite for commodities. But for now, let us simply acknowledge that, whatever it may or may not do, China has become a major player in the global economy.

Why Does China Have "Gold Fever"?

China is not only the world's largest producer of gold, mining over 340 tons in 2010 (8.57 percent over the prior year's level), but it is also one of the world's largest consumers of it. In 2010, People's Bank of China (PBOC) bought over 209 metric tons gold, a 500 percent increase year-over-year. In 2011, PBOC's purchase of gold increased to 490 tons and Chinese mining output exceeded 360 tons, a 6 percent rise over 2010. In 2012, Bloomberg estimated that China purchased an additional 493 tons of gold. China will also seek to further increase its total gold production. There is much speculation as to why the PBOC is purchasing massive amounts of gold. Some view their growing gold reserves as a hedge against falling values of other assets, perhaps even against its own massive U.S. T-bill portfolio.

Tim Iacono wrote about China's gold fever, citing the *Financial Times* interview with Marcus Grubb of the World Gold Council (WGC):

China central bank gold buying is believed to have played a major role in the surge in China's (2011) fourth quarter imports:

China's imports from Hong Kong, which account for the majority of its overseas buying, soared to 227 tonnes in the last three months of 2011, according to data published by Hong Kong. Mine production in the country, the largest gold producer, stood at about 100 tonnes in the quarter, implying total supply of at least 330 tonnes.

That compares to demand of 191 tonnes for gold jewellery, bars and coins—which account for the vast majority of Chinese demand—reported by the WGC on Thursday.

Since China does not allow the export of gold, there was a domestic supply/demand gap of about 139 tonnes during the last three months of the year and central bank purchases likely accounted for some or all of that gap. This is consistent with the widely held belief that China's central bank will continue to quietly accumulate gold, buying on price dips such as the one in December and only revealing to the world the extent of their purchases long after the fact as they did back in 2009 when they said they had nearly doubled their gold reserves to 1,054 tonnes since it last reported its official holdings six years earlier.[14]

There is also the possibility of China eventually backing their currency, the yuan, with gold in order to make the yuan a competing currency against the dollar.[15] This would not only give the Chinese people greater spending power, but relative to the dollar, would also make U.S. goods more affordable to the Chinese. Whether commensurate amounts of U.S. goods ever get to the Chinese marketplace, however, is a dubious possibility, to say the least.

Today, the world's reserve currency, the U.S. dollar, is backed only by a promise to pay issued by a government that is financed on debt, runs huge trade deficits, and whose current economic growth rate makes it clear that for the foreseeable future, it will not possibly be able to repay its debts without inflating its currency at some point in the future. Is there any doubt that a currency issued by the world's second largest economy and backed by gold would challenge or even replace the dollar as the world's reserve currency?

That may be the case, as is posited in the October 1, 2012, edition of *Forbes*: "China is preparing for a world beyond the inconvertible paper dollar, a world in which the renminbi [yuan], buttressed by gold, becomes the dominant reserve currency."[16] Such an outcome jibes with China's desires to challenge the United States' global financial dominance in the world today.

But there may also be a different, less obvious reason. It may be that the current strength of the Chinese economy is not what the world thinks it is. If that is the reality, and I think that it is, then the gold spree may be just as much of a hedge against their own economy and currency as it may be against their U.S. Treasury bond holdings. Does that mean that the Chinese will not challenge the U.S. dollar-denominated financial system? It's unlikely, but doesn't automatically mean that the Chinese economy or currency will be able to replace that of the United States.

Getting accurate information about exactly who in China is buying what amount of gold is a difficult proposition in any case, as the PBOC doesn't release information or its plans. But the PBOC is not the only buyer of gold in China. As Gordon Chang notes in his January 29, 2012, article in *Forbes*, much of China's gold purchases may be from individual Chinese who are skeptical of China's economy and currency. Chang notes that the Chinese themselves may well have insights into the Chinese economic conditions that outsiders do not, and since the Chinese are not allowed to export gold, buying gold is their only hedge against an already overvalued yuan.[17]

What Does the Rise of Other Nations, but Especially of China, Mean for the Current Financial System?

The rise of competing nations will continue to bring competition and strife to the international dollar-denominated financial system. I say *continue* because the strife among the trading nations, amongst both allies and adversaries of the United States, has been ongoing and increasing as the global slowdown worsens. As the global economy continues its long, debt-laden decline, nations will use whatever leverage they possess to their full advantage, and that relates directly to the balance of power between the United States and China.

With the United States purposely devaluing the dollar by injecting trillions into the world economy through various stimulus programs and other funding mechanisms, the price of commodities has risen for other nations who must buy commodities in dollars on the world market. By doing so, the United States is, in effect, making U.S. goods and services more competitive by exporting inflation to the rest of the world, including China.

The very fact that major commodities in the world are priced in U.S. dollars has meant that the dollar has been guaranteed a certain level of strength and demand in the world simply because nations must have them to buy and trade in the world. Whatever country you may care to name, if it wants to trade on the world market, in the vast majority of cases, it will have to have dollars to complete the transaction.

Even with China's rise, today, roughly 80 percent of all trading transactions in the world are still priced and transacted in U.S. dollars. China is taking major steps to change that reality, and has overtly implemented some challenges to the United States' *dollar hegemony* that it still enjoys throughout the world. For example, it has entered into direct exchange and trade agreements with Japan, Russia, and South Korea to trade their respective currencies directly without using the dollar as an intermediary step. *Dollar exclusion zones* in Brazil, Chile, and other nations have also been established by China. It may seem that that is a direct challenge to the U.S. dollar, but the degree of the relationships is still comparatively small. There is the real possibility, of course, that it may change dramatically in the future.

Will the dollar's power diminish in the world as China's influence and power grows?

The dollar's role in the world may well diminish more in the very near future. But the possibility also exists that, as conditions in the Euro-zone continue to deteriorate, the dollar's role as important in the world may grow dramatically, or it may diminish entirely. This would especially be likely if China's current trajectory is altered, which, I argue within these pages, is quite likely to become a reality.

Marketing the China Brand

China's cultural footprint is also growing in the world. There are now over 60 Chinese cultural centers located on university campuses across the United States alone. And, as *World Affairs* reports, there are now

> two hundred and eighty-two Confucius Institutes scattered around the globe, all controlled from Beijing by the Office of Chinese Language Council International. China also has its own version of the Peace Corps, run by the China Young Volunteers Association, which sends young Chinese to do development work in countries with friendly governments, like Laos, Ethiopia, and Myanmar.[18]

Additionally, China is making a great effort to not only get its culture into the mainstream of ideas in the global culture, but it is also seeking to control its image, or brand if you will. This is especially true in the cinematic arts, which are the most efficient in reaching large, supranational audiences.

For example, the 2012 purchase of AMC Theaters, the largest theater chain in the United States, was a strategic purchase, just as financing and promoting films like *Crouching Tiger, Hidden Dragon*, which won Academy Awards and was seen and lauded around the world by hundreds of millions of people, was also a deliberate tactic to "sell" China—and most importantly, the "correct" China—to the world. Additionally, China's official "global media drive," a $7 billion project that began in 2009, is a deliberate policy designed to change the world's mind about China and culturally challenge the *American Idea* in the world.

China's shadow on the world stage grows larger every day, whether it is its unprecedented direct access to buy and sell Treasury Bonds from the U.S. Treasury itself, to its massive investments in farmland across Africa and North America, to its possible role in providing much needed financial liquidity to a Eurozone that stands on the edge of total economic and currency collapse at this writing. China understands that the various channels of power must include *soft power* like cultural affinity, good will, foreign aid, and the like, and has shaped its policies accordingly:

> According to Rumi Aoyama, Chinese public diplomacy has five components: "Publicizing China's assertions to the outside world, forming a desirable image of the state, issuing rebuttals to distorted overseas reports about China, improving the international environment surrounding China, and exerting influence on the policy decisions of foreign countries." This simple set of priorities has an admirable clarity that entirely eludes comparable efforts by the United States.[19]

Indeed, the Eurozone is already falling into a deep recession brought on by the debt crisis that originated in Greece. The crisis has since spread to Italy, Portugal, and Spain, and it threatens France. Eurozone officials continue to struggle with how to save the euro as a viable currency and the Eurozone as a relevant political and economic player on the world stage. Unfortunately, to date, the financial resources of the Eurozone have proven to be insufficient. In their hour of desperation, Eurozone leaders have called upon China to help out with its trillion-plus dollars of liquid reserves. Whether China does so or not is almost irrelevant; the point is that as the world's second largest economy and a perceived rising superpower, it is thought to be in a position to do so.

There are many other statistics and categories to illustrate the points already made herein—that China's rise to global prominence is real and has had great impact upon the rest of the world. However, when comparing one nation's historical path with another's—such as China assuming the mantle currently on the shoulders of the United States— clarity and objectivity are important, lest one see too much, or too little, in comparing the two.

That said, context, of course, is important when seeking to under- stand the meaning of events, to comprehend the dynamics of changing relationships, as well as to grasp the full and long-term impact of those changes. Context, in fact, is everything when seeking to understand such concepts as polymorphous and often ephemeral as the balance of power among nations and the sources of power within nations. Thus, context is also a necessity for the various definitions and advantages, real or imag- ined, of a country's national identity.

Be that as it may, the question, "Which context is the correct one?" begs an answer. In fact, at this time, it is virtually impossible to over- state China's *perceived* financial clout in the world. China's significance is undeniable, and its unavoidable influence around the world is in almost every field imaginable. But whether the decline in U.S. hegemony is fast or slow, and whether it will result in the fall of the international finan- cial order dominated by the U.S. dollar are both fascinating possibilities in their own right; in this book, though, we focus our attention on the prospect of China's rise in the world and determine if it is indeed poised to be the next great power on the face of the earth.

Does China Have a Bright and Powerful Future?

Given all of these impressive facts about the speed and breadth of China's rise to preeminence in the world, how can anyone conclude anything other than that a bright and powerful future awaits? How could all of the accomplishments and formidable signatures of a rising great power that are indeed a part of the picture of China be anything other than positive for the Middle Kingdom?

For one thing, as just noted, those things are a part of the picture, but not the whole picture of China. The description given is the picture that the Chinese leadership promotes and wants the world to see and to believe. And, in the vast majority of instances, we dutifully do so. Just as there is no denying that China's story the past two decades is truly nothing short of stunning, there is also no denying that desperate people in need of financial rescue and new markets tend to not look closely enough at the gift horse that China represents in the minds of so many.

But once we admit that this is the case, it becomes clear that we need to look deeper into the phenomenon that is China to get a more detailed and accurate picture. When we do, what we will find is a portrait of a deeply flawed and riven nation whose many weaknesses are not yet acknowledged by the rest of the world and that are certainly not advertised by the Chinese themselves. Like the Great Wall of China itself (which, ironically, is both the most apt metaphor as well as the most powerful symbol of modern China, as it was of medieval China), much that is not so evident on the perimeter of our understanding of China becomes more visible when we look behind that Wall.

And what is there to see behind that wall that much of the world does not yet see or perhaps just chooses to ignore? As we take a close and careful look, we will see that things are not completely as they seem to be. China's many weaknesses—some of which are of such enormity that they are scarcely believable—become more apparent as we cast our view ever deeper behind the Wall and see what has happened on the inside of modern—that is, Communist—China in the past 60 years and in the past six months. There is much to see that has not been recognized for what it is, and even more to understand. We will identify the key elemental weakness therein and put their meanings in the proper context.

What's Really behind the Great Wall?

What some see in China is not the next great superpower, but rather the next great collapse of a massively complex and brittle regime that is among the most brutal and oppressive the world has ever known. There is no crystal ball that tells us what will happen in the future, but there is known history in China, and China's modern history is one of great crises and spasms of social and political violence on a scale unknown anywhere else, with the possible exception of the old Soviet Union.

There is, of course, the history and historical collapse of their former communist neighbor, the former Soviet Union; that in itself is not a definitive indicator, but it can certainly suggest possible outcomes. After all, command economies, wherever they are tried, all suffer from similar fundamental flaws that have all resulted in cataclysmic disasters.

But it won't be just one crisis that China will have to handle; it will be many, and all at the same time or in quick succession. There will definitely be a domino effect in play as the crises overlap and magnify the impacts of the others. Before too long, hundreds of billions, if not trillions, of dollars will be lost in China—and in Chinese companies around the world.

We will assess China under the following criteria that apply to any nation. The contexts in which we examine the questions will include:

1. Stability. Does China have a history of stability or instability?
   a. Does modern/Communist China have a stable history?
   b. Is China's current development path a stable one?
   c. Does China's political system address instability, or does it cause instability?
2. Sustainability. Is the political structure and economic system sustainable?
   a. Is political corruption and deception in Chinese society the exception or the rule?
   b. Is the *Beijing Model* a sustainable model? Or is it an exhaustible model based upon external markets and false demand driven by unsustainable debt?
   c. Is the development model sustainable? Is the majority of Chinese society improved? Or is most of Chinese society—or too much of it—abused by the development model?
   d. Are resources used wisely? Are they extracted in the least environmentally damaging way possible?
3. Dynamism. Is there a healthy dynamic between society, the means of production, and the political system? Or is state capitalism absorbing and confiscating private capitalism, and physical and intellectual capital for political and financial advantage?

4. Justice. Is the political system based upon privilege? Is there legal redress for crimes committed by the government and state-owned enterprises against individuals and domestic and foreign business corporations? Or are massive land seizures, a caste system, and forced relocations of millions of people working for slave wages undermining legitimacy in the regime?

5. Political Adaptation. Is the political culture adaptive to challenges in society? Is the political culture an advantage to the business class in helping it adapt and overcome financial challenges? Or is the Chinese political culture one that increases oppression as wealth increases, and increases oppression as economic conditions deteriorate? Will State oppression, fraud, and illegal confiscation increase as economic hardship increases and State legitimacy diminishes?

6. Creativity. Does both the current economic system and political culture reward and encourage innovation? Is China a technologically innovative nation, or does it rely on theft and other forms of technology transfers? Do creative people stay in China, or leave? Is fraud-related creativity in terms of financial gain the highest form of creativity?

7. Renewability. Do the Chinese political and economic models allow for the Chinese economy to renew itself through innovation, creativity, and the free flowing and sharing of ideas and capital as economic conditions change? Is China's Beijing Model one that fosters renewability within China? Or are the massive levels of horrific pollution so great that renewability—including China's ability to feed itself—is symptomatic of China's Beijing Model, which is an exhaustive model sacrificing long-term stability and resource protection for short-term gains?

It will be from this framework that we will assess China's strength and possibilities going forward. And it will be through these lenses that we will take a closer look at China and its frail and brittle structure and identify just why—and perhaps even how and when—China will fall from within. We will also look at the potential ripple effects of China's coming collapse that will impact the rest of the world, but especially the United States, Europe, and the rest of Asia.

Notes

1. Charlie Devereux, "Ahmadinejad Meets with Chavez as Nuclear Talks in Moscow Falter," *Bloomberg*, June 22, 2012; David Nakamura, "U.S. Troops Headed to Australia, Irking China," *The Washington Post Online, Asia & Pacific*, November 16, 2011; Pavel Felgenhauer, "The Russian Military Has an Action Plan Involving Georgia if Iran Is Attacked," *The Jamestown Foundation*, April 5, 2012.

2. Li Wei, "How China Can Save the Eurozone," *The Guardian*, October 30, 2011.

3. Gary S. Fields, "Living Standards, Labor Markets and Human Resources in Taiwan," Cornell University ILR School, January 1, 1992.

4. William Harms, "China's Great Leap Forward," *The University of Chicago Chronicle* 15, no. 13 (March 14, 1996), http://chronicle.uchicago.edu/960314/china.shtml.

5. Ibid.

6. Dali L. Yang, *Calamity and Reform in China: State, Rural Society, and Institutional Change Since the Great Leap Famine* (Stanford, CA: Stanford University Press, 1996).

7. Harms, "China's Great Leap Forward."

8. "Cultural Revolution," *Encyclopedia of Marxism*, www.marxists.org/glossary/events/c/u.htm.

9. Deborah Brautigam, "China's Foreign Aid: The Economist Still Doesn't Get It," *China in Africa: The Real Story*, January 22, 2012, www.chinaafricarealstory.com/2012/01/chinas-foreign-aid-economist-still.html.

10. "China," European Commission, Trade, updated December 3, 2012, http://ec.europa.eu/trade/creating-opportunities/bilateral-relations/countries/china.

11. "Trade in Goods with China," U.S. Census Bureau, Foreign Trade, www.census.gov/foreign-trade/balance/c5700.html.

12. Derek Scissors, "The Most Important Chinese Trade Barriers," Testimony before the United States House of Representatives Committee on Foreign Relations, July 19, 2012, www.heritage.org/research/testimony/2012/07/the-most-important-chinese-trade-barriers.

13. Annual Data, National Bureau of Statistics of China, www.stats.gov.cn/english/statisticaldata/yearlydata.

14. Tim Iacono is the founder of the investment website *Iacono Research*, a subscription service providing market commentary and investment advisory services specializing in natural resources. He also writes a financial blog, formerly known as "The Mess That Greenspan Made," a sometimes irreverent look at the many and varied aftereffects of the Greenspan term at the Federal Reserve.

15. Ralph Benko, "Signs of the Gold Standard Emerging in China?" *Forbes*, October 1, 2012, www.forbes.com/sites/ralphbenko/2012/10/01/signs-of-the-gold-standard-emerging-in-china/.

16. Ibid.

17. Gordon G. Chang, "Why Are the Chinese Buying Record Quantities of Gold?" *Forbes*, January 29, 2012, www.forbes.com/sites/gordonchang/2012/01/29/why-are-the-chinese-buying-record-quantities-of-gold.

18. Helle C. Dale, "All Out: China Turns on the Charm," *World Affairs Journal*, July/August 2010, www.worldaffairsjournal.org/article/all-out-china-turns-charm.

19. Ibid.

Chapter 2

Stability and Legitimacy: A Chinese Crisis from Within

All nations go through periods of instability and crisis. Some of the causes are outside the control of the leadership, such as invasion from another country or famine caused by drought, crop failure, and other acts of nature. The communist leadership itself, however, has been *the main cause* for the crises and instability in China. As we will see in this chapter, the prospects for continued instability and even greater crises in China are growing and reaching the tipping point and once again will have been brought about entirely by the communist leadership.

When investors talk about the prospects for a country as a possible place for profitable investment, the question of stability is right at the top. "Is the country stable?" is always a very crucial question, because no matter how much opportunity may exist, if the country is not stable, then every investment is at risk. Unstable countries typically don't abide by the rule of law or comply with the standards of conduct normally associated with international trade agreements. Foreign capital investments in unstable countries are subject to all kinds of risks that are not found in stable countries with a legitimate government and a functioning and more or less accessible and transparent legal system. In some ways, *stability* is almost a synonym for *sufficiently Westernized* —not quite, but certainly very similar in its actual meaning.

What Kinds of Risks and Problems Are Typical of Unstable Nations?

There are certainly many risks and problems that come with trading with unstable nations, and there are many variations on that theme that are far too numerous and beyond the scope of this discussion. But a general and very usable framework can certainly be defined. Instability applies not only to how foreign investment is treated, but also to how that nation's citizens are treated.

Those risks and symptoms typically include:

- Unlawful seizure of capital or property
- A lack of legal recourse for foreign investors
- Routine intellectual and physical property theft
- A murky legal system that favors the ruling elite
- Steep capital restrictions
- Limits on foreign ownership in the country
- Lack of an independent and transparent banking system

These and other nasty habits basically work against the foreign investor getting their money back or against the citizen holding onto his or her capital. Unstable countries also have serious internal problems that are associated with poorly structured societies such as shortsighted economic and political policies, inconsistent laws, intrusive domestic police powers, censorship, and other invasions and restrictions on individual liberties, as well as financial and legal safeguards. No nation is perfect in any of these categories, of course, but it is largely a matter of degree. The more these risks are "the way things are done," the greater the level of instability tends to be in the country.

Stability and Instability: What Are They?

Stability has different meanings and sources. Ideally, from a Western perspective, stability in a country means that the people's needs for liberty, self-determination, and opportunity are being met by the political, economic, civic, and social policies of the government, with abundant individual rights recognized and honored by the ruling elite and defended by a transparent and independent legal system. There is also an accepted, embraced, and somewhat assumed order in society, with civic assumptions on the part of the people, such as voting, taking responsibility on a community level, and engagement in the direction of the country.

For all that to occur and function, there must be a relatively high level of calm and order in the country, and belief in the political system. Another phrase used to describe belief in the political system and how the government is viewed in the eyes of the people is "political legitimacy." Needless to say, social chaos is anathema to the above criteria.

But the ideas of stability and legitimacy as just described are the Western ideal; the reality in most parts of the world is usually a much more flawed system based upon political and economic exclusion for the majority of the population and excessive favoritism for the ruling class, with an authoritarian political system. The latter is certainly the case in China; and the ruling class is the Chinese Communist Party, or the CCP, and it spends an enormous amount of time and resources maintaining order and its grip on power in China.

That said, stability in the West is certainly much more than simply the absence of chaos in a nation. Although an absence of chaos is a great place to begin and is preferable in any case, stability as we understand it is based upon democratic Western values. That includes, of course, an actively engaged citizenry in the political dialogue of the country. Thus, stability means one thing in Western Democracies, and in the case of China, it means something quite different.

The basic truth is that "stability" in a nation can be obtained from either below or above. When stability is achieved from below by a democratic plurality, power tends to be diffuse among different political parties and organizations (unless the people vote themselves into dictatorship, which has happened before), people tend to be freer, ideas flow freely, the courts and legislature are, to a large degree, independent, and the electorate vote for their political preferences. This is the typical experience in most Western democratic nations.

On the other hand, when stability is achieved from above, the power tends to be concentrated in the hands of the few, and civil rights, economic liberty, and other traits of a free society are largely absent. The ruling party achieves stability by oppression and coercion. Often, crisis and instability are used and/or created by nondemocratic forces to seize or maintain power. But whether its source is from the people or the iron fist, stability might optimistically be defined as that condition existing in a country where there is some predictability and some level of civility that allows for at least the potential of minimal economic growth, a smidgen of opportunity for some, a modicum of scientific knowledge and social development here and there, as well as an arguably rising standard of living.

In communist-led China, just as it is in most nations of the world, stability has been achieved by coercion from above. But China is finding out, just as the late Soviet Union did, that a stability that relies on stifling the creative forces and commercial energies of its people has a huge downside: It is realizing that *its adaptability to a changing world will be severely limited, and eventually, will prove to be inadequate, leading to ultimate failure.* Thus, all things being equal, over time, oppressive regimes will tend to be inherently less stable and less successful than those nations whose governments derive from political pluralism. That is because in those more open and democratic societies, political expression, ideas, and creative energies are not only encouraged but are rewarded, and social pressures are acknowledged and accommodated through the democratic political process.

Perhaps a more enduring and practical definition of true political stability is the condition that allows a nation to successfully adapt to changes both internally and externally. Without the ability to adapt, it is nigh impossible for a nation to continue to develop as much as it needs to; even with stability, successful, self-sustaining societies with healthy economies can be a challenge for most nations. Thus, in less developed countries, political and social stability are tenuous conditions.

For a developed nation, however, political stability is one of the pillars upon which its successful society and economy have been built. There's no doubt that stability is needed before widespread economic development can take place, but the opposite is not necessarily true. Just because a nation is "stable" does not mean it will enjoy fantastic, double-digit economic growth year after year for a decade or two.

India, for example, is China's neighbor and the world's largest democracy, and its government generally enjoys widespread legitimacy[1] and stability. Although it has struggled to grow economically as fast as it would like, India's stability derives from below, based upon democratic pluralism, and so has been able to adapt to challenges over the years. Its economic development has been somewhat more evenly distributed, thus its society is less stratified than China's.[2] In the absence of a properly functioning economy such as China's, stability imposed from above becomes difficult to maintain as legitimacy is eroded when things deteriorate from bad to worse to unbearable.

The Source of China's "Stability"

When a state holds monopolies on information, communication, and technology, trades little with societies, and of course, retains a monopoly on force and is not shy about using it on a continuously grand scale, long-term oppression on a mass scale is easier to pull off. This was the case in all previous crises in China from 1950 onward, ending, in some sense, with Tiananmen Square in 1989, but in another sense not all. China's oppressive state continues to dominate Chinese life and make life miserable for most of the Chinese people. It does so, however, in a less public manner, if and when it can.

Since the Tiananmen Square massacre, some observers think that China's elevated position in the global economy makes it less possible or likely for China to do to its people today what it has done to them in the past. That viewpoint supposes that when a state is opened up sufficiently to allow, in whatever ways, competing (and quite frankly, better) ideas of freedom and openness, as well as cultural values that are based upon individual rights, human rights, and Western materialism, that their society will evolve and adopt those influences. He Zhi Hua, a man who recently protested the forced relocation of his Changsha village in Hunan Province by local Party authorities and who was summarily crushed beneath a steam roller for his trouble, might disagree with that suppostion.[3]

As a result of this "absorption of Western values," the theory is that China will become more like the West and less like itself. In some ways, this has happened. At the top levels of the party, there is some minority disagreement on whether China's economy is wholly China's or part of the global economy. The question has great implications for China's behavior in the world at large, but given the challenges it faces and the threat that openness brings, the CCP's choice is obvious. Its domestic policies and its behavior in the economic and foreign policy realms all belie a rejection of the minority viewpoint. On the whole, it is a foolish notion to think that the political elite of China would willfully allow such a transformation to take place at the expense of CCP leadership. On the contrary, China's communist leadership is doing all it can to resist it.

In terms of development, China falls somewhere in the middle realm of developed nations; it is highly developed in some regions—particularly the eastern regions such as Hong Kong, Guangzhou province, and in Beijing and the areas around it—but also resembles a dirt poor, backward agrarian nation in many of its other provinces. Such uneven development in itself is a source of growing instability and weakening CCP legitimacy.

For CCP-ruled China, stability has meant continuous oppression of all kinds of the vast majority of the people to keep public chaos and revolt to a minimum. Maintaining its grip on power in China may well be the defining political achievement of the ruling regime, but it is far from a permanent legacy. Another way of defining stability is to look at its absence in a country, which, of course, is instability.

What Are the Characteristics and Effects of Instability?

Usually, instability within a nation is marked by a significant level of civil violence—up to and including civil war—as political, economic, cultural, and/or religious adversaries compete with one another. A deep sense of alienation from the government among a significant portion of the population is also a part of the instability equation.

When such events occur, there is heightened competition and/or adversarial relations between the alienated group(s) and those who still support the government. One main reason for this is that even on the road to ruin, a government will have its institutional allies within the society, within certain industries, economic sectors, and social institutions like the ruling political party, and certain parts of the government. (This is important to remember in the context of China today; most of its party cadre will be with the CCP to the very bitter end, at which point, they will attempt to politically abandon the sinking ship *en masse*.)

By this definition, China's stability is indeed in question, isn't it? In the West, stability means, among many other things, the following:

- Regular elections where the people can make adjustments to the direction their governments have taken the country
- Referendums on the economy through representation
- Civil liberties like freedom of association, freedom of dissent, self-determination, and a host of other individual rights we take for granted
- An ability to effect change through political expression and activism
- An established and thriving middle class, through which most of the economic activity and social values derive
- An independent judiciary
- A representative legislative body
- A functioning legal system and due process

In China, pretty much none of these apply, with the exception of an emerging and simultaneously disappearing middle class, which is a key factor for both stability in China and the legitimacy of the CCP going forward and also its biggest threat.

The "risk" that foreign capital and foreign investment take by investing in China is loss of both, but often in a gradual and perhaps more calculated way than say, Argentina's sudden takeover of Spanish oil producer YPF's operations in Argentina in 2012. Rather, China will joint venture with foreign firms and often steal the technology and intellectual property of their Western business partner as a matter of course.

As Jeremy Hurewitz, China expert and former head of Business Intelligence at Nardello & Co., observed, Western firms have come to accept technology theft as the price of doing business in China. Volkswagen's experience, for example, of seeing its proprietary technology suddenly show up in China's First Auto Works (FAW) cars is not unusual. "What is Volkswagen to do?" Hurewitz asked. "China represents 35 percent of its business."[4]

Thus, the long-term risk in China is for both capital and technology theft, and, as China acquires more technology and perceives that it no longer needs the foreign partner, market access will more than likely diminish over time. This scenario is not unusual. It is, quite frankly, standard operating procedure in China. There are literally thousands of examples of this kind of behavior and they occur regularly and on every level of business, in every stratum of politics, and, needless to say, are very damaging to the foreign investor as well as to the sociopolitical culture of China.[5]

Does Stability also Mean "Legitimacy" in China?

As Deng Xiaoping understood in the post-Mao era, legitimacy is a crucial part of the stability equation; or at the very least, it makes it much easier to rule the nation.

Today, an interesting question to ask would be, "Do the Chinese people view their government as legitimate?" The answer would depend upon whom you ask. From the leadership's point of view, by virtue of the fact that they defeated Chiang Kai-shek and the nationalists in the civil war in 1949, and have delivered unprecedented economic growth and development to the country via the Beijing Model, they believe and would insist that they are the legitimate rulers of the country. Of course, the CCP is also viewed as legitimate by the upper-class communist authorities.

As noted above, in the West, stability grows out of political inclusion or pluralism. In China, stability has come from the iron fist of the CCP. But the question remains: "Is the Chinese government actually legitimate in the eyes of the people?"

Another way to answer that question is to look at the arrangement and size of the internal security forces. Those regimes with the largest and most powerful domestic security agencies have such forces because they are necessary to keep those whom they rule in line and under their bootheels. Legitimate governments, by and large, need no such protections from those whom they govern. In reality, the telltale signs of illegitimacy are the existence of large-scale censorship, tight restrictions on assembly, a corrupt or nonexistent legal system, unlimited detention without trial, and an advanced internal security service that is not just investigative, but paramilitary and widely present in its exercise in society. All of the above symptoms reflect a deep paranoia within the leadership of a country, and all of those and more are part and parcel of life in China. They are crucial for the Chinese leadership's hold on power.

But it can also be argued that legitimacy's definition depends on the beholder. To Mao and his followers, the existing Kuomintang government was not the legitimate government of China. And, as it turned out, by killing tens of millions of his fellow Chinese, Mao was able to convince the rest of his fellows that the Chinese Communist Party, based upon the quasi-religious, eschatological utterings scribed by Karl Marx—an atheistic German Jew who lived and died in nineteenth-century London—was, in fact, the legitimate form of government for twentieth-century China. How's that for establishing stability and legitimacy? Might makes right is the formula that works for tyrants and their regimes.

Is Legitimacy of the Government Necessary for Stability?

What is a "legitimate" government, anyway? Is it one that the people accept freely? Or is a legitimacy conferred upon a government—whether benevolent or malevolent—simply because it has been successfully imposed upon the citizenry by violence and the continuation of the same going forward?

It is no exaggeration to say that the people of China were better off—and certainly better fed—before the Revolution than during the 30 bitter years that followed. For as we know, the Communist government didn't bring stability or better times for the people of China. In that light, one could conclude that the most organized, ruthlessly violent, and best equipped force in a country will be able to control it and form a "legitimate" and "stable" government, which can last for decades, regardless of how monstrous its behavior may be—or perhaps, because of it.

The United States did not, in fact, view Communist China as a legitimate government until 1970, when it finally recognized the CCP and Mainland China in the United Nations and effectively demoted Taiwan's status. But even then, China was enduring continuous and great hardship under Mao and the ongoing Cultural Revolution. Was the CCP legitimate or illegitimate? As stated previously, it depends entirely on whom you ask.

It is true, however, that as the tough times dragged on through the close of the 1970s, Deng Xiaoping feared that the CCP was becoming illegitimate in the eyes of the Chinese people. More to the point, he feared that the CCP would not be able to restrain an uprising from the Chinese people if things carried on the way they were going. Losing legitimacy was Deng's way of saying that he feared losing power, legitimate or not, and more to the point, of being dragged by his heels from the seat of power by the people in the heat and rage of a righteous revolution. Legitimacy, we can conclude, is more or less in the eyes of the beholder; it is certainly helpful if the beholder has superior firepower and organization and is bereft of a conscience and any sense of human decency.

Certainly, the stability of the rule of the Communist Party and the continued existence of the *status quo* in China fits that description. The power and position of the CCP leadership lies in the existence and vigorous exercise of a ruthless internal security force that is routinely set upon the tens of millions of Chinese who have protested and fought against the ruling elite in the country for decades, and continue to do so even today. When necessary, the internal security apparatus has been backed up by a massive and well-armed military force with orders to kill rebellious civilians.

It is true that some level of acceptance of the ruling regime—that is, some level of legitimacy—is necessary for stability within a country. But legitimacy, like stability, can be a tenuous prospect. The manner in which that acceptance (legitimacy) is obtained, either from consent of the governed or in China's case, oppression from above, matters greatly.

Does Communist China Have a History of Stability?

For many China experts, the answer to that question is yes. China is and has been widely perceived as a stable and vibrant nation for the past 25 years, and in many quarters, it is thought to be getting stronger all the time, especially relative to the United States and Europe. China has become the manufacturing center of the world and boasts an economy whose size is second only to the United States. And, even with a so-called *soft landing* expected for China in the midst of the ongoing global financial crisis, China holds about $1.2 trillion in cash reserves while the rest of the world is choking on their own debt.

Furthermore, the same one-party system, the CCP, has ruled China for over 60 years through famine and virtual civil war; those two facts alone should be proof enough of China's stability and legitimacy of its leadership. Of course, the last quarter century of astounding economic growth and global political clout China has gained would seem to make China's future brighter than bright. Given all of these facts, what China watcher would argue that the largest nation in the world, with all the advantages it has, is not stable?

Besides, throughout history powerful and authoritarian governments have been the rule, not the exception. There are plenty of examples of stable societies and nations that have been so only because of their oppressive political systems with limited social and political freedoms. They remain in power via strict control of political, economic, and social activities, with the rules of society dictated from the elite, which are then enforced by efficient internal security agencies and outright military power against the people to maintain the status quo. By that standard and practice, China ought to qualify as a stable nation in good stead with the historical experience of stability.

But neither the nineteenth nor the twentieth centuries were kind to China. As noted in Chapter 1, foreign domination and both internal and external conflict plagued China through its last dynasty, through its troubled era of republican government, through Japanese occupation in World War II, and through civil war that lasted until 1949. And yet, the Communists' victory over the Chinese Nationalists in 1949 did not usher in a period of stability in the country; in fact, it was just the opposite. In the decades since the Revolution, China has lurched from one crisis to the next, all self-generated in one way or another. Throughout each and every one, from the Great Leap Forward and The Cultural Revolution to the Tiananmen Square massacre and even to the internal crises that China struggles with today, the costs have been huge, and as we shall see in later chapters, they will continue to be enormous going forward.

The reality is that under the care and guidance of the CCP, the Chinese people have endured tremendous and truly unimaginable human suffering, as well as colossal amounts of property destruction and the ruination of hundreds of millions of lives. It is also true that hundreds of millions of Chinese have been lifted out of poverty in the past 25 years. No one can deny that fact. But the new wealth of a portion of Chinese society doesn't erase the murder, theft, and injustices that have been visited upon the Chinese people on a continuous and grand scale since the revolution.

And for the most part, the world has done very little because, realistically, there was very little that the outside world could do to change things for the better in China. Furthermore, very little information escaped China for the first 40 years of Communist rule, which benefited the ruling elite and allowed them to "get away" with their horrific crimes against their own people for so long.

To bring the big picture of the Chinese regime's instability and legitimacy into focus, let's look at the sources of instability in China today. They are all a result of leadership decisions and unfortunately their impacts overlap and reinforce one another. They also tell us why and how the next great crisis in China is rushing toward it like a freight train under full throttle with a madman at the helm.

Does China's Beijing Model Lead to Stability and Legitimacy?

Although we will more deeply examine the Beijing Model of development in Chapter 3, suffice it here to say that China's opening of its vast manufacturing labor force to Western investment and involvement in manufacturing also brought about and/or unleashed several powerful forces operating at the same time in China. These forces, as noted above, have both lifted China out of its morass of poverty in some regions, and created more devastating poverty in others.

For example, there is no question that Western firms brought in technological know-how and the capital to develop China more quickly than could have happened without it. Again, an apt comparison is India, when in 1990, both countries, the two most populous nations on earth as well as Asiatic rivals and neighbors, had about the same GDP.[6] Within 10 years, however, with the West's capital and technology transfers, China's GDP had more than doubled, while India's grew only by about 40 percent. Today, China's GDP is four times that of India. The difference? Although there are many influences in both countries' development, the key factor has been the West's tremendous and sustained level of direct foreign investment in China year after year.

The downside to China's strategy is that its cheap labor-fueled development has led it down the path toward a less technical and less educated, manufacturing-based economy and not a knowledge-based one like India has strived to develop. This has been a big factor in inhibiting China from moving up the value chain in terms of economic development.[7] Likewise, India's focus on education has resulted in its rising up the development ladder into a knowledge-based, technological force.

For example, China's strategy of inviting joint venturing with Western firms has China importing or otherwise acquiring Western technology, but not adopting the value-added Western management styles or practices or disseminating knowledge throughout its people. This tactic of separating technology from human capital has left a tremendous gap in China's economic development curve. This division of knowledge from the development process is a function of the paranoia and corruption of the ruling party; the CCP knows that knowledge and ideas are a threat to their legitimacy, and it also knows it must reward party members with valuable technology enterprises and hire "business leaders" based upon party loyalty, not on business acumen.

The need for the CCP to maintain a monopoly on power compels it to adopt a distorted economic model of imbalanced development and promotion through political connection. Both of these practices rely on corruption as a means of perpetuating themselves. At some point, as the Chinese leadership is now finding out, the imbalances become too great and the corruption too widespread, which ultimately brings about economic instability and institutional illegitimacy of crisis proportions.

Notes

1. The exception may be India's Muslim population. See T. Riyas Babu, "Muslims Feel Alienated in the Country: Teetsa," *The Milli Gazette,* March 1–15, 2010, available at www.milligazette.com/news/4759-muslims-feel-alienated-in-the-country-teesta.

2. "India's Wealth Triples to $3.5 Trillion," *The Economic Times,* October 9, 2010, http://articles.economictimes.indiatimes.com/2010-10-09/news/27598451_1_wealth-osama-abbasi-trillion.

3. Brandon Jones, "Chinese Protester Crushed Under Steamroller, Okayed By Government Official," *The Global Dispatch*, September 26, 2012, www.theglobaldispatch.com/chinese-protester-crushed-under-steamroller-okayed-by-government-official-graphic-photos-78022/.

4. Jeremy Hurewitz, interview with the author, June 2012.

5. Michael Riley and Ashlee Vance, "Inside the Chinese Boom in Corporate Espionage," *Bloomberg Businessweek*, March 15, 2012, www.businessweek.com/articles/2012-03-14/inside-the-chinese-boom-in-corporate-espionage.

6. Stephen S. Roach, "A Tale of Two Asias," Morgan Stanley Research, June 2006, www.scribd.com/doc/6674213/Comparison-Between-India-and-China.

7. Richard Florida, "Why China Lags on Innovation and Creativity," *The Atlantic Cities*, April 2, 2012, www.theatlanticcities.com/jobs-and-economy/2012/04/why-china-lags-innovation-creativity/1604.

Chapter 3

The Rising Tide
of Instability

A s discussed previously, instability in China has been the one consistency of the Communist Party of China (CCP) since 1949. Not only has the Chinese leadership made enormous mistakes throughout its past; it continues to make them today. That is not to say that China's leaders have not made smart decisions as well, because they have. The highest growth period in China was achieved from 1979 to 1989, when liberalization in China—including property rights and greater freedom of speech—resulted in millions of new businesses being formed and an explosion of wealth and political expression. But over the long term, China's leadership has made huge, earth-shaking mistakes more often than not when it comes to running the nation, and they are making them again today.

As pointed out earlier, one of the smartest decisions the CCP made was to get the West to help them do what they most obviously could not do, which was to develop their country. It is no stretch of the facts to say that the West's involvement in China's economic development remains a major reason that the regime is in power today. China grew more stable, not less, since it allowed the Western capitalists to provide the capital to develop itself as a nation and an economic power. Just as the West did in its economic support of the Soviet Union through decades of wheat sales, Western capitalism saved the CCP leadership from facing yet another existential crisis from within. As noted earlier, 30 years of communist rule had left the country an economic basket case with nothing to show for it except decades of state-sponsored instability, poverty, famine, and widespread terror.

Only since the 1980s onward, with Western involvement and guidance in finance and technology, did some level of social and economic stability become present in China. As Edward Friedman observed, China's development was not derived from "Chinese ideas," much less policies originating from Marxist-Leninist ideology, but rather from the abandonment of them.

> Post-Mao China rose by abandoning its disregard for the market and both copying and plugging into other "varieties" of Asian capitalism. . . . In addition to the extraordinary advantage of being located in the most economically dynamic region of the world since the end of World War II, China (and also India, Turkey, Indonesia, Brazil, and other rapidly rising emerging economies) eventually benefited from the structural forces of post-Bretton Woods globalization. The fact is that broad international political economy factors, not culture, explain China's rise.[1]

Friedman's observation does not go far enough, however, in identifying the sources of China's development. He notes China's benefitting from "broad international political economy factors," China's favorable location "in the most economically dynamic region of the world," and "the structural forces of post-Bretton Woods globalization." But the unavoidable historical facts are that neither China's location in Asia nor any such "structural forces" caused China's development. If that were so, it would have done so much earlier. The key fact remains that it was not until China opened itself up for Western and, particularly, American economic activity—a policy choice made by Deng Xiaoping, not a structural fact—that China developed.

Ironically, the CCP is rapidly becoming a victim of its own success as well as of its excesses. The rise of a prosperous middle class not only rescued its legitimacy after 30 years of Marxist development failure, but today, the economic power, expectations, and dissatisfaction of the middle class with the regime's corruption and its wholesale theft of property and businesses threatens the CCP's authority and legitimacy once again.

This is because the rising discontent of the middle class reflects not only the growing usurpation by the state of wealth created by the efforts of the middle class, but also because of the failure of the CCP to maintain its promise of upward economic mobility. In addition, well-educated middle class Chinese have less trust in the ability of the CCP—that is, the political class—to deliver on policy promises, whether it's regarding pollution reduction or even in the accountability of the CCP in its economic policies. Rank corruption throughout the CCP and its political lip service to pressing economic and sociological problems have left China's middle class cynical, alienated, and angry.

Suisheng Zhao wrote about this rising dissatisfaction in middle-class China in his article, "Political Reform," in *The Diplomat*:

> The grievances of China's middle class over government policy have become more evident in recent years. The rising unemployment rate among recent college graduates (who usually come from middle-class families and are presumed to be members of China's future middle class) should send an alarming signal to the PRC government, as well as those who analyze Chinese elite politics. In a recent forum on China's response to the global financial crisis held by the Academy of Chinese Reform and Development in Beijing, Chinese scholars argued that the government should pay much greater attention to the needs and concerns of the middle class—otherwise the "sensitive" Chinese middle class will become the "angry" middle class.[2]

This "angry middle class" is not only a reasonable assumption but a rapidly evolving reality as well.

This is due to the fact that with regard to China's middle class, several things are happening at the same time. As noted above, the CCP has been rapidly transferring privately owned enterprises into state hands via takeover by state-owned enterprises as a way of transferring wealth out of the middle class up to the party elite. This is also done to keep the middle class in check by reducing its economic power. To add insult to injury, income and other taxes are also heavily focused on the middle and lower classes, where at least 60 percent of the tax burden falls. Contrast that with the top 20 percent in the United States paying 80 percent of the tax burden. China's tax policy is another way to keep the middle class in check and is an unhealthy dose of salt in a festering and widening economic and political wound.

The fraudulent land seizures by corrupt party officials and authorities are also a form of wealth usurpation and domination, which again sends wealth and power up the food chain to the political elite. Each of these ways of sucking wealth out of the middle and lower classes has not only served to erode middle class support for the regime and enrich party membership, but also to cripple China's domestic consumer economy. China's consumer market is not what it needs to be to sustain the domestic economy. In fact, as a percentage of its total economy, domestic consumption decreased 20 percent from 2006 to 2011. This is also one of the main reasons China has not ascended the value chain from manufacturing economy to service economy.

But there are other reasons, too. With the global financial crisis, the CCP is also caught in the vice of a slowing of foreign investment into the country on one side of the equation and continued economic contraction at home, as well as with its trading partners on the other.[3] Furthermore, as the slowdown and the corruption diminish the wealth of the Chinese middle class, they are now chafing at their political bit since their high expectations for a continually rising living standard are not being met. It is for all of these reasons and more that the ruling legitimacy and stability of the CCP is coming into greater doubt as economic conditions deteriorate.

Has China Been Influenced by Western Ideas?

The answer to that question is "yes", but it's not a simple yes, or even an affirmation of the positives of Western influence on China. The picture is much more complex than that. There's no question that China has been influenced by the West; but it's the manifestation of the West's influence on China that matters most.

China's decision to open itself to Western capitalists has been a double-edged sword for the nation and the CCP leadership. Beginning in 1978 with its Open Door policy, China cautiously and in its limited way transformed its economic structure, going from the command economy production matrices of communism to an authoritarian State Capitalism model, which later came to be known as the Beijing Model. This abandonment of Marxist economic ideas and embrace of at least part of capitalism allowed China to achieve fantastic growth and development in a historically unprecedented short amount of time. But the let some people get rich first attitude adopted by Deng Xiaoping has taken on a life of its own over the past quarter century in China, likely far beyond Deng's wildest expectations.

The effects that Western culture and newfound wealth have had on China are deep and multifaceted. For example, the student drive for democracy that resulted in the Tiananmen Square massacre in 1989 came out of the adoption of liberalization period that was necessary for capitalism to take hold in China. Indeed, the adoption of capitalism has had the greatest of all impacts upon China with the exception of the communist victory in 1949. It has both changed and challenged the relationship between the state and the people in radical ways over the past 20 years.

For one thing, as noted above, the adoption of capitalism in China has lifted hundreds of millions of Chinese out of poverty. The CCP deserves some credit for that achievement. The Open Door policy embracing capitalism created a middle class in China where none existed before. But the same forces of capitalism that brought about prosperity also created a hunger in the minds of Chinese for greater wealth and opportunity as well as for self-determination and a desire for more freedom of expression in all of its forms. This created a new generation of Chinese with a desire for greater political freedoms and a demand, in many instances, for greater control over decision making in their businesses and in their own lives.

This has led to greater demands being placed on the CCP by the middle class even as the CCP has levied greater demands upon it. The CCP's response to middle class demands has been mostly harsh. Beginning with Tiananmen Square, it cracked down on political expression and has kept a close eye on political activities ever since. It has also sought to minimize the impact of a reabsorbed Hong Kong by maintaining its hardline political repression, and today, into the second decade of the new millennia, the CCP's response to political expression and complaints from the middle class has been increasingly negative and oppressive.

The great wealth and transformative power China has gained in the past 25 years or so has not, however, led to the CCP becoming less intrusive, less dominating, or less guarded of its power. If anything, it has become more of all of those things. Even though this great wealth has been generated by direct foreign investment yoked to the energies of an emergent, entrepreneurial middle class, the privileges that the middle class expects and demands are contrary to the assumptions of the ruling party elites. Thus, the CCP is doing all it can to stifle the political and economic demands of the middle class while enriching itself at the same time. Of course, these two forces are mutually exclusive and, therefore, cannot co-exist for too long before they begin to rip China apart.

Sources of Rising Instability in China

To explore every single incident and indication of why and how China's economy and political systems are running off the rails would be a crisis buffet impossible to take in at one sitting. But it's not necessary to do so in order to grasp the magnitude of the situation and the urgency of its many manifestations. Nonetheless, it is important to identify enough of the impacts of forces at work in order to appreciate the scope and depth of the crises. To that end, following are the major political and economic trends in China brought about by policy choices of the Chinese leadership that are returning China toward the chaos and instability that has been its legacy since the revolution.

Rise of a Chinese Middle Class

As noted earlier, the emergence of a middle class in China has been the result of the Open Door policy of allowing capitalism to operate within China. Within a short period of time, the manufacturing base that was developed by the West created a commercial class within China that was allowed to exist and grow based upon an agreement between it and the CCP. The compact was simple: The Party would allow them to become rich, and the commercial class would agree not to challenge the political establishment.

As acknowledged, this arrangement lifted hundreds of millions of Chinese out of poverty over the past 25 years and led to the rapid development of many parts of China. China's subsequent rise in the global economy to become the second largest economy in the world—in one generation—is, however, proving to be both blessing and a curse.

On the one hand, some Chinese have a sense of optimism for the future like never before. Many in the Party and the upper echelons of business feel a sense of destiny today—that China is now ready to take its rightful place on the world stage. This is certainly a long ways away from the China of 1979, when the Open Door Policy began. A confident, economically powerful China with a vibrant middle class and a formerly agrarian society that has become the manufacturer to the world is an enormous achievement to the Chinese, and rightly so.

However, on the other hand, the wealth and comfortable living standard of the commercial/manufacturing class has become the baseline expectation for the new generation of Chinese. Needless to say, that has its political disadvantages in an economic downturn. But the expectations of continued growth and development within the middle class are not the only problem facing the CCP.

The new generation, with its wealth and lifestyle that is a lifetime away from the origins of the CCP and light years away technologically, is not satisfied with the restrictions on political expression of their parents' generation. Technology, such as cell phones, laptops, tablets, and the rise of the Internet—which the CCP controls as much as it possibly can—has given rise to an explosion of information and communication that has undermined the party's monopoly on information and political discourse.

In capitalist democracies, a greater flow of information has meant more efficient markets and therefore greater wealth. The irony is that this hasn't been allowed to occur in "capitalist" China. The CCP makes every effort to suppress information and communication within the country as it usurps wealth from the productive sectors of the economy. As a result, millions of micro bloggers in China, expressing political views and demands that if found out would lead directly to arrest, long prison sentences, and even death in some cases, nonetheless exist and thrive among the Chinese people.

The irony of the information age for China's middle class is hard to miss. What should lead to greater wealth in China has instead led to greater oppression. The secretive nature of the CCP is now threatened, if not entirely laid bare by these developments, and again, adds to the growing mountain of doubts within China's middle class of the CCP's legitimacy.

Decline of China's Middle Class

Another irony is that for Western democracies, the middle class has been a broad, stabilizing force for many decades, where the traditional values of the nations were not only observed, but also validated and supported. As noted earlier, the rise of a middle class in China has led to the optimism and sense of destiny for China's greatness. But it has also led to a rising undercurrent of discontent within the middle class against China's oppressive and corrupt political culture, resulting in a rising willingness to question the authority of the CCP and growing sense of dissatisfaction as the corruption of the party reaches in to take more and more of the wealth of the middle class for itself. The CCP's big problem regarding the middle class is therefore controlling—that is, minimizing—its political and economic influence, as well as its vast discontent as its income falls and wealth transfers continue upward to the Party. Thus, both the rise of the middle class and its concurrent diminishment are proving to be sources of instability in China today.

The decline in middle class wealth is no longer something that can be rationalized away as temporary or as being of minimal impact. But still, how serious is it? Job indicators are dire. Recent statistics show that college graduates in China—often the first family member in generations, if ever, to graduate from university—today have few jobs waiting for them upon graduation. In 2012, 38 percent of university graduates did not have jobs. And of those who were able to find work, the majority have taken jobs that are far below their level of academic accomplishment. Growing resentment and frustrations are the result of this and are aimed directly at the CCP leadership.

The truth is, every nation has times of transition and difficulty brought about by changing technology and changing ideas. What is becoming clearer every day, however, is that the *idea* of China as promulgated by the CCP, the home of an obedient worker class taken care of by the Party, no longer fits the reality of China today. Furthermore, much of the China that is a product of the CCP is rapidly becoming unfit to live in under modern and Western standards. In the greater context of this discussion, it is particularly crucial to bear in mind that the diminishment of the middle class is not simply a function of the global economic slowdown in the Eurozone and in the United States, but is much more a result of the rising levels of corruption in the CCP, which has led to greater levels of theft from the middle class to both keep it in check and to keep itself in power.

Decline in Traditional Chinese Cultural Values

Related to the success of the Open Door Policy and the rise of China's middle class is the change in cultural expectations and values that material wealth has brought to the commercial/middle class of China. Following the *old ways* of tradition has been replaced in China's major urban areas by the hustle and hunger for accumulating wealth and outward signs of status and power. This has brought a distinct level of coldness to Chinese society that is being mourned as much as it is being practiced. The One Child policy, the culturally widespread practice of killing of baby girls, the forced abortions, the abuse of the poor rural populations at the hands of urban ones, and of course, the callous disregard for the welfare of its people by the CCP have all inculcated a hardening within Chinese society.[4]

Men and women in China's larger cities no longer want to automatically adhere to the traditions of an assumed marriage and subservience to a paternal social order. Like their Western counterparts, the assumed roles of the past are being rejected in favor of an individualism that recognizes the primacy of the individual material wants and needs over those of society at large. This is partially supported by the Confucianist value of focus on a tight circle of family and friends and much less so for others. But it is also a reaction to decade upon decade of deprivation and hardship. The consequence of this is a new generation of materially hungry Chinese not satisfied with any limitations put on their lifestyle or their determination for accumulation.

This social detachment from the reverence of tradition is not only a rejection of the old ways, but of the outdated and unrealistic political compromise and the agreement that was put in place by their parents' generation and the CCP. Today's generation has been pulled toward a self-oriented concept of life that includes more freedom and riches, and less idealism or enthusiasm for the political message of the CCP. This is a major source of the CCP's rising illegitimacy and social instability in the eyes of this generation of Chinese. To lose the allegiance of the lower classes is one thing, but losing the support of the middle class is an unsustainable condition.

In China today, many in the new generation know that the CCP is a naked power. In a twist on the old fable where the emperor is discovered to have no clothes, the CCP has revealed to the middle class, and especially to the younger generation, that it has no political or economic clothes. Its politics stifle the people of expression, and its economic policy of growth at all costs has shown a great portion of the people that the CCP does not care for them or for China, but only for itself.[5]

Downward Corruption Cycle

As the economy continues to deteriorate at the hands of corrupt and inept state-owned enterprise directors, more of the wealth will have to be siphoned off from productive sectors to keep people in line with larger bribes, to maintain the patina of legitimacy, to keep up appearances of bogus economic figures, and to hold onto power. It's a vicious downward spiral of fraud, deceit, corruption, theft, and oppression on one side and economic contraction and political alienation on the other. Each side reinforces the other.

This phenomenon is seen in the rising levels of corruption amongst party officials from all strata of the Party throughout the country. The need to curb corruption is given lip service by the new leaders, as it was by the old, but the ways do not change because, short of a major bloodletting purge from top to bottom, they cannot change the system of corruption and remain in power. The system is built on corruption, relies on it for any and all actions and activities, and is the necessary means by which the Party, and the economy itself, operates.

The cycle or process of getting things done, implementing a policy, or ensuring that a law is followed, or at least is *reported* to have been followed, requires bribery and threats all along the food chain. Hence, as conditions deteriorate, the pressure to perform increases and the need and requirement for greater forms of bribery and punishment avoidance require ever-larger amounts of corruption and theft to keep the *status quo*. When one thinks back to the famine caused by the Great Leap Forward in the 1950s, it boggles the mind the level of corruption, theft, and fraud that had to occur in order to cause the starvation deaths of tens of millions of people. And yet, it happened. Today, the corruption is supported by a much greater level of wealth—both domestic and foreign—in China, allowing for a much higher threshold to exist; but in the end, the downward cycle will continue until it can do so no longer. At that point, the CCP will no longer be able to deliver economic viability and will shed its aura of superiority and claim to special knowledge in guiding China to power and riches.

Uneven Development

Uneven economic development is another source of instability in China today. The developed areas around China's coastal regions generate the majority of wealth and receive the lion's share of investment assets, social benefits, and focus from the Chinese government. Thus, distortions in wealth creation and distribution, which is a function of uneven economic development, is highly skewed in favor of the eastern urban centers, with a wide income discrepancy of the top 1 percent of households holding 40 percent of the wealth. This has led to high levels of discontent, violence, and street riots that have lasted days or weeks and have only been quelled by the involvement of thousands of police. Furthermore, with up to nearly a half-billion rural Chinese living in poverty or near poverty levels, that wealth and income discrepancy is only growing worse. Accordingly, such resentments and violent reactions to this widening wealth and income gap will only rise as well.[6]

Accompanying and indeed a part of China's uneven development model is the rampant exploitation and government seizure of rural lands for quick profit by local CCP authorities that not only lead to violence in the hinterlands and despoliation of them, but also contribute to the continued distortions in economic development. The urban–rural development distortions are enormous in their implications for rising instability within China, but they are not the only source of instability within China's development model and policies. There are others, from destructive forces at work that are inherent to capitalism itself to the heavy-handed statism that threatens to destabilize China and delegitimize the CCP.

And even where economic development has flourished in China, it presents its own dynamic destabilizing effects that are exerting growing pressures upon the existing regime. In fact, that is part of China's challenge. Its development path has enriched millions and created a wealthy commercial class and an ultra-wealthy political class, both of which are unwilling to alter the current path and unable to offer policies that would reconcile the deep divisions within the country. Rather, the opposite is true. The political class has *become* the commercial class (most CCP members are deeply entrenched and have become fantastically wealthy in their ownership of commercial/state-owned enterprises) and so enjoy continuous bribes and enrichment as being an integral part of the current power structure. This distorted process exists and is performed at the expense of the middle class and rural populations.

But as a result of China's uneven development policies, social stratification in China has never been greater and is manifested by the great wealth in the country's eastern and southern regions, as well as by the displacement, defilement, and looting of rural wealth throughout vast regions of China. Since China's population has become more urban than rural, the inequalities and tensions of uneven development will only worsen, as will the protests in both rural and urban areas, against the CCP.

Corruption and China's "Morality Crisis"

The pervasive level of corruption that plagues every strata of China is hardly a state secret. Hu Jintao, China's former president, said that China needs to create a harmonious society and that the country is in the grip of a morality crisis. President Hu mentioned the morality crisis because rapid economic growth has been accompanied by rabid corruption in every part of Chinese society, and China's newest leaders have launched a very public anti-corruption campaign. Whether the campaign is only for public relations or is a serious effort remains to be seen, but China's problems with corruption require no exaggeration to effectively stagger one's mind.

That is why the chances of real improvements or reform of corruption are slim. Other than carrying out token prosecutions meant for public consumption and painting the new leadership in a positive light, corruption cannot easily be excised from the society because it defines what Chinese society has become: corrupt. The entire country is in a frenzy of capitalism run amok, where everyone is trying to get rich in a socio-economic arena where there is no strong regulation or a transparent legal system, but rather a government that decides who will win and who will lose. This has led to an epidemic of very bad behavior throughout all levels of society, creating great ethical challenges and a moral vacuum within Chinese society where the key to success lies not in talent or hard work, but in *guanxi*, access to government officials.[7]

Thus, corruption at the top is more than just a moral failing; it is a threat to the entire social structure and yet paradoxically, it is also the structure itself. But in either case, growing animosities between the producers of the country and the takers (i.e., those connected with the Communist Party) are (as noted earlier) understandable, since massive seizures of factories and property from business owners to Party members have become the norm. This not only means replacing skilled leadership with inept but Party-connected leadership; it also means deep and widening rifts between the business classes of privately owned businesses and state-owned enterprises.

From the Great Leap Forward to today, fraud and corruption have been the constants of Chinese society. This was the case in the Soviet Union, and it is the case with China today. The levels of graft and deceit in economic statistics is so high as to make growth rates unreliable at best, and at worst, untrue to the degree that renders economic activity and decisions baseless and ineffective, while corruption leads the way to success:

Ever since President Hu Jintao took office in 2003, he has made fairness a central theme of his agenda. Hu, along with his power base in the Communist Youth League, view China's widening gap between rich and poor as a significant threat to social and political stability. The country's latest Five Year Plan, which was unveiled last November, aims to redistribute income more evenly in order to foster "inclusive development," reflecting a widespread belief among Party leaders that Deng Xiaoping's maxim—"let some people get rich first"—has gone too far.

By and large, your average Chinese worker admires people who have gotten rich through cleverness or hard work, because that's what they aspire to do themselves. What bothers them, though, is the growing sense that there's a special class of people who get to live by a different set of rules than everyone else.[8]

Corruption is also tearing the social fabric apart as land seizures increase to pay debt service on development loans taken out by local authorities for quick riches, which also happened to disenfranchise the farmers. As a result, civil protests are skyrocketing in China.

Another consideration is how such embedded fraud in the system has the effect of *hollowing out* the Chinese economy. That is, financial and economic calculations and projections based upon false assumptions have a devastating and magnified ripple effect throughout the economy over a period of time. The perceived—and claimed—strength of the Chinese economy is based on numbers and statistics that too often have no basis in reality. This is just now beginning to catch up and affect the overall economy, but will grow worse over time as the waters of recession and burst financial bubbles expose the ugly truth beneath the surface of Chinese economic vitality. Just as food production was grossly overstated in the Great Leap Forward, leading to a horrific famine and the starvation of tens of millions of Chinese, that same dynamic is at work in the Chinese economy today.

The financial sector is also built upon corruption, from false valuations of property and fraudulent profit margins of state-owned companies to fraudulent lending involving non-existent customers, baseless public investment projects undertaken, and inefficient, unnecessary, and poorly constructed infrastructure projects that fulfill no need. The degree of rot in the system is at levels that challenge the imagination. We will explore this further in Chapter 5.

Civil Unrest

As a result of all of these trends, civil unrest has reached near-crisis proportions in China. Between the failing middle class, the rot of corruption from top to bottom, and rampant seizure of property, the frequency and intensity of anti-government protests are rising rapidly. In 2002, the official number of "mass incidents" involving 10,000 or more people in China was 50,000. These incidents were for a variety of grievances and injustices. However, the year 2012 saw over 100,000 of these incidents with higher levels of violence. This helps explain why Beijing has allowed the emergence of urban militias to exercise more power than would normally be acceptable to the power-jealous CCP. It's a tacit acknowledgement of a rising problem that the leadership is not quite sure how to address. Uncontrolled and contagious mass civil violence against the state is the CCP's greatest fear. As the Chinese economy continues to deteriorate as a result of challenging global and domestic conditions, civil unrest may well become the leadership's greatest challenge.[9]

The civil unrest is becoming so widespread and frequent that urban militias have not been enough to subdue it. Municipalities are even hiring unlicensed security firms to maintain order and keep citizen protesters and those petitioning the government at bay. This cottage industry has led to kidnappings and illegal security activities against *regular* people:

> The Beijing Municipal Public Security Bureau launched a campaign Wednesday to crack down on rogue security contractors, which have been found to be committing crimes such as illegally intercepting and detaining petitioners.
>
> Zhang Bing, a deputy director of the bureau, told reporters that more than 130 companies and 300,000 security guards make up the capital's security market. Yet, nearly half of these contractors operate without a license, and many of the guards do not have a job certificate.
>
> "The city's security market is in complete chaos. Some companies have been operating outside the law and against regulations, and a few have even allowed their security guards to impede the flow of government work and to participate in illegal activities such as detaining people and setting up black jails, all of which will be covered in the campaign," Zhang said.

In one of the cases, a former security guard and 15 collaborators were arrested in August for running an illegal detention center in Changping district.

They were paid by five provincial and city governments to hold people who came to Beijing to submit petitions to higher authorities, in the name of "maintaining social stability," Zhang revealed.[10]

That is just in Beijing. The civil unrest and anti-government protests are occurring more frequently throughout China every year. Although the level of civil unrest in China seems to be a phenomenon that is minimized in the global press, this will not last for long nor alter the conditions on the ground. As conditions deteriorate in China, the protests will continue to increase both in severity and frequency, and the CCP will be forced to respond harshly, in ways that are not easily hidden or explained away. Such a response is, of course, nothing new, and is a measure that in the past the CCP has shown itself to be more than willing to apply if necessary. But will urban militias and state violence be enough to keep the CCP in power the next time a major revolt or demonstration takes place?

Loss of Economic Control and the Rise of a "Gray Economy"

Given the rising level of civil violence, the CCP is making efforts to address—at least superficially—some of the grievances of the people, such as missing pensions or insufficient remuneration for seized land. But it can do so only marginally. This is not only because of the size of the country in every aspect, but also because of the corruption levels, which again leave real policy enactment spotty at best. Policies are enforced on an inconsistent basis; local authorities have much greater control over local economies. What does this mean concerning the CCP's ability to effectively pull the levers on the economy?

Or, put another way, does the CCP really have strict control over the economic activities within China? It certainly can compel government banks to lend to state-owned businesses regardless of their profit levels, and can embark on massive infrastructure projects. But it cannot control the influx of hot money into and out of the country, even if it exercises capital controls with regard to its currency. But with a "gray economy" of over $1.4 trillion, where business and savings exist outside of the official economic state controls, there is no question that exclusivity in microeconomic affairs no longer exists in China, if it ever did.

The expansion of the gray economy is also closely linked to the widespread corruption in China and people's financial needs not being met by state institutions. Citizens of a nation understand the condition of the economy much better than outsiders do, and in order to avoid excessive taxation, confiscation of property, and other nefarious activities of state and local authorities, an underground economy of enormous proportions has emerged, both as a symptom of and a counter weight to the level of state corruption.

In fact, hidden income in China may be up to RMB 9.3 trillion ($1.4 trillion), which would be about 30 percent of GDP according to a recent study commissioned by Credit Suisse and conducted by Professor Wang Xiaolu of the China Reform Foundation. What's more, almost two-thirds of that hidden income goes to the top 10 percent of households and 80 percent belongs to the top 20 percent. This means that the per capita income gap between the top 10 percent and bottom 10 percent of urban households is much wider (26 times) than official statistics suggest (9 times).[10] It also tells us that the political and economic elite are cheating as much or more than the rest of the citizenry.

China's lack of control of its economy is further evidenced by its recent call for an increase in private investment. Why would this be needed? China holds $3.3 trillion in foreign currency reserves and, per an Associated Press article of July 30, 2012, "Major industries are state-owned enterprises that dominate major industries despite three decades of market-oriented reforms, and private investors remain unprotected from state-owned rivals."[11]

The fact is, the CCP does not control as much of its economy as one would think, and its control is largely restrictive or confiscatory. *It has difficulty controlling private reactions to public policies throughout the land.* State-owned enterprises, for example, are run or influenced by party authorities and cronies, but the party still does not have any real control over the performance of them, with the exception of looting their wealth. Profitability is rarely in that equation, although profit is officially reported to be on par or greater than privately owned enterprises.

The gray economy also perilously extends to the underground lending industry, which has a long history in China. Like the official state-run bank lending, the private lenders are now under great strain as non-performing loans and bankruptcies rise amongst their clientele. We will look at this more closely in Chapter 5.

Inability to Adapt to Cyclical Market Forces

The Communist regime is finding out that economic stability is not so easy to maintain with so many complex and inconvenient market forces at work, such as the effects of rising demand on prices, obtaining profit margins, high savings rates, low domestic consumption, and hot money flowing into the country, among others. On the other hand, rising economic and political expectations of its beleaguered middle class are not easily managed, either.

In the past, the great temptation of the CCP has always been to resort to overwhelming force to maintain power and re-establish stability in the country. But it is becoming much more evident that doing so will not be the solution that it has been in the past. As it faces these challenges and more, the CCP is finding it very difficult to put the genie of capitalism and economic expectations back in the communist party bottle.

Today, the realities of cyclical market forces both in the domestic and the global economy are not lost on the ruling elite in China; but they are hard pressed to address them in a manner that will be successful over the long term. The leadership's overreliance on real estate development and infrastructure investments, for example, to make up for falling domestic consumption are short-term fixes that have led to enormous distortions in the economy. The massive stimulus spending that The People's Bank of China (PBOC) has engaged in to support those investments has undermined their entire financial structure. Both events have served to undercut their legitimacy today, and quite possibly, as conditions worsen, their monopoly on power tomorrow. It may also expose them to greater scrutiny and thereby cost them whatever level of legitimacy that may remain. But either way, a loss of both may well be the inevitable outcome.

The hard truth that the rulers of China face is that the country's economic stability and the CCP's political legitimacy are both in jeopardy in the face of massive market distortions that are the direct result of CCP policies. Addressing such structural problems in favorable economic conditions is difficult enough to implement. But in response to economic downturns and the challenging conditions in China and the world today, it is politically impossible to do, as it would crash the economy even more quickly than it is crashing today, leaving political instability and chaos in its wake:

> Unfortunately, the structural reforms required to rebalance the Chinese economy and address the underlying causes of inflation will be politically impossible in 2011. They will hurt interest groups that have influence during leadership transition. Many top executives of state-owned enterprises and provincial leaders are members of the Central Committee of the Communist Party and senior leaders in Beijing need their support in gaining coveted seats on the Politburo for themselves or their protégés. Such reforms were deemed too difficult when the Chinese economy was in much better shape and the leadership transition was a dormant issue. Today, they are simply out of the question.[12]

To add to this dilemma, structural factors—rising labor costs, for example—have risen with the rise of the middle class in China, causing it to lose manufacturing business to Vietnam, Cambodia, the Philippines, and the like. Even some U.S. firms now find that the labor cost advantage in China has gone away, and consequently they are closing their factories in China and returning their manufacturing plants to the United States, to be manned by American workers. The political reality in China is that the necessary reforms simply cannot be carried out today; and yet, if they are not, the economy will crash all the same. The Chinese are discovering the great power of market forces and the inevitable creative destruction of capitalism, all in real time. It could be argued that China's power relative to the rest of the world has already peaked and is now on the downside as it loses control of its economy and jobs begin to flee the country's overpriced labor market.

The influence of the forces of the cultural baggage that accompanies them is most evident in those areas that reflect the expansion of the West's participation and influence in China over the course of the past three decades. China's regions most exposed to Western capitalism were also exposed to Western ideas of individuality and modern social mores, which run counter to the traditional patriarchal behavioral patterns and ocial expectations of the CCP. In other words, rising or falling, China's middle class isn't "down with the old ways." The CCP is definitely part of the old ways in China.

These forces are proving difficult for the Chinese ruling elite to control, but at the same time, are not manipulated by any politically organized opposition. There is no doubt, however, that it is proving to be more difficult for China to cope with the corrosive influence of both Western and CCP policies that inspired this brand of materialism and individualism than they may have anticipated. But involving the West in their economy and society was a choice that the CCP made of its own accord; it also happened to be the only realistic choice for the CCP's survival at the time.

The leaders realize, or will shortly, that development through direct foreign investment and technology transfers of its trading partners, primarily the United States, Japan, and Europe, and not through the organic development of a knowledge-based economy by China itself ultimately hamstrings the economic development of a nation. Most of those transfers have occurred either through purchase, joint venture, or theft. This situation is especially disadvantageous in difficult economic times, however, because relying on foreign investment and manufacturing to drive your economy means relying on foreign demand. The problem, of course, is that demand shrinks in a global economic recession or depression. And that, too, is happening already.

By contrast, an advanced knowledge-based economy, like that of the United States, for example, is able to create new markets by innovation and creativity. China's manufacturing-based economy is already struggling with low global demand and falling foreign investment; it is also suffering from tremendous contraction of its domestic consumption rates.

Thus, even as China's growth accelerated over the past 25 years, the state capital model has created critical structural and social problems related to corruption, demographics, middle-class expectations, imminent social safety net shortages, and insufficient domestic demand. These structural and social difficulties are not easily or quickly resolved—and quite likely are impossible to resolve—within the existing political and economic framework of China's state capitalism model. The CCP has not yet been able to even remotely approach a solution to these issues.

Finding the balance between the demands of exclusive power and long-term domestic economic sustainability has been elusive and with good reason. The two cannot exist together indefinitely. The demand from foreign markets has provided the Chinese economy with tremendous expansion and given the CCP valuable time to address the imbalances that threaten that economy and their own continued existence. However, they have yet to do so and still remain in power. But as the groundswell of civil unrest continues, these social and structural problems cannot bear being ignored for very much longer.

The marriage of Western capital and Chinese communism has created a monster of an economy and a society that is at war with itself, as the state seeks to devour not only the fruits of its capitalist enterprises, but the enterprises themselves, in an orgy of avarice, political corruption, and paranoia. The contradictions between the two forces in China are great and irreconcilable; in the end, between the CCP and capitalism, there can be only one dominant force in China. Both cannot continue to exist indefinitely. As we will see in Chapter 4, the Beijing Model that China is so proud of is not only well on its way down the road to oblivion, but is taking the CCP with it.

Taxation Imbalance

The tax issue is important as well and is both an apparent structural component of China's economy and a political one. By political, I mean another means of corruption. China's inverted tax structure, whereby the tax burden is largely put on the lower and middle classes rather than on the upper class, is based upon political cronyism and corruption. It's not that there are no taxes on the wealthy in China; there are. The highest tax rates in China are, according to *Forbes'* tax misery index, at 45 percent. The problem is that the wealthy are allowed to avoid paying taxes through political connections and bribery. As previously noted, China's tax authorities report that the lower and middle classes pay two-thirds of personal income taxes.

By not taxing the wealthy, political allegiance is maintained among the very powerful. But by overtaxing the middle and lower classes, the masses are spending more money to support the government, rather than spending it on consumer goods. This is not a sustainable condition in the long term, either politically or economically. As noted, the contrast with U.S. tax policy is unmistakable. The U.S. derives 80 percent of its tax revenue from the top 20 percent of its earners. The American middle class on the other hand, with its high consumption levels, drives the domestic economy.

Thus, China's inverted tax policy, a political necessity at the top, is another weight holding down the growth of its consumer economy and has prevented China's economy from moving up the value chain. It also underscores the point that in China, privilege and corruption come with the CCP. But not only does taxation imbalance inhibit China's economic development; the negative synergistic effects described above worsen its impact. The forces of each magnifies the impact of the others, causing greater harm to the economy as time passes. Again, this represents an internal structural and political contradiction that, if not corrected, will destroy the economy and with it, national stability and any remaining legitimacy of the CCP.

Weakening Political Legitimacy

Does the CCP still control the political, economic, and social activities in China? Most of its control remains in the political realm; China is still a one-party state. But the growing protests against government corruption can't mean anything except a challenge against the CCP's political monopoly. Does the CCP still retain the aura of legitimacy in China? Or, put another way, do enough Chinese still view the CCP as the legitimate government?

What do the current economic and political conditions look like to the Chinese? It depends. Let's look at a few hypothetical circumstances that are certainly reflective of realities in China for different strata of society:

• If, for example, you're a Communist Party member living in Beijing with a nice apartment, a late model BMW, top-level health care, a fat pension, and a passport, then CCP rule is indeed very legitimate. Really, what could be better?

- Or, say you're a middle-class family with a business that has brought you out of poverty and given you the opportunity for material wealth you never imagined could be yours, but the past several years have seen your business taken over by a state-owned enterprise. As a consequence, your income and wealth have both decreased. You're not certain of the future, and you're now starting to question the legitimacy of a government that can steal from you everything you've spent your whole life building.
- If, however, you happen to be a farmer living a hand-to-mouth existence and you've just had the farmland that supports your family seized by the local CCP authorities so that they may resell it to developers, the current regime may not seem legitimate.
- Or, say your family has just been forcibly relocated to perform factory work in some six-day-a-week, 12-hours-a-day industrial hell scenario a thousand miles from your village, where you soon discover that, according to China's *Hokou* system, you really don't qualify for government health care since "you're not from around here," then, quite possibly, the current regime may not seem so legitimate to you after all.

The real question that the above scenarios present is one of ratio and tolerance. What is the ratio of alienated Chinese to satisfied ones, and what are the tolerance levels of the alienated masses? How long before the distraught population says *enough* to the façade of wisdom and legitimacy behind which the CCP hides?

The Taiwan Problem

Chinese leaders from Mao Zedong through Deng Xiaoping, and the most recent leadership of Hu Jintao and Jiang Zemin, have all recognized that the free, democratic, and highly prosperous Republic of China on Taiwan is a huge threat to the continued existence of the CCP. As the economic inequalities and hardships increase for most of the Chinese people, the appeal of a relatively more stable and unquestionably freer Taiwan grows wider in China. Indeed, by its very existence, Taiwan mocks the CCP for its repeated failures and vast abuses of its people.

Just how big of an ideological and political threat is Taiwan to the CCP? Consider that before his death, Deng Xiaoping recorded a *political will* to the future leadership of China, warning of that very outcome. In that recorded message, he explained the great threat that Taiwan poses to the CCP:

> Over the past years, advocates of freedom in the bourgeois class within and outside of the CCP are itching to follow the so-called "Taiwan experience." There are even people who advise us to learn from Jiang Jinggou and end the ban on political parties. This political news should alert us to be much more vigilant. We must clearly educate the party members that the Taiwan problem has exceeded beyond our grudge against the KMT. . . . Settling the Taiwan problem directly affects the existence of the CCP and Socialism in China. . . .We must create conditions to quickly solve the Taiwan problem. Taiwan is different from Hong Kong. Hong Kong had a lease, so after 100 years we could still resolve the situation. Taiwan does not have a lease. If we continue prolonging the situation, the problem will become more disadvantageous and difficult for us to solve. . . .The Taiwan problem must be resolved by the end of Comrade Hu Jingtao's second term. Do not exceed the year 2012. I hope that the 18th Congress will also be the celebration for solving the Taiwan problem. . . . Comrade Jiang Zemin, do not fight for power or act rashly. You must steadfastly create optimal conditions for Comrade Jiang Zemin to settle the Taiwan problem. Chairman Mao, myself, and many other elderly comrades have been preparing the conditions for solving the Taiwan problem for decades. Comrade Hu Jintao will be the one to represent our party and consummate our efforts.[13]

There is no question that the Taiwan problem grows larger with China's own growing string of crises. But even Hong Kong is not as *solved* as the late Deng Xiaoping may have thought it to be. Fifteen years after returning to Mainland control, Hong Kong still retains its own identity, much different from that of Mainland Chinese. With hundreds of years of British influence, a free press, free elections, and a capitalist pedigree as the financial center of China, Hong Kong—like Taiwan—is an example to the rest of China of how life goes on, and is better, without the CCP having its hands in everyone's lives and wallets. Furthermore, unlike many Chinese under the CCP, both Taiwan and Hong Kong understand and remember Tiananmen Square and its true meaning and observe its anniversary.

Hukuo System and Urban/Rural Conflicts

A quasi-apartheid-like system, which limits the ability of rural workers relocated to the urban areas to receive government benefits like healthcare and education, causes not only class resentments but also retards the ability of the masses flooding into urban areas—whether by choice or not—to become integrated into the greater, more prosperous urban economies.

What does this mean from a socioeconomic standpoint? Among other things, it means that rural transplants are non-persons in urban society in terms of upward mobility, economically or socially. Thus, the inability of masses of urban workers to access the middle class government-provided benefits, keeps them perpetually *in their place*. They are effectively prohibited from becoming members of a consumer class and remain in limbo status as workers without a home. This rural-to-urban migration is thus a source of both cultural and economic conflict as jobs disappear due to the slowdown or from other reasons, and the migrant workers put additional stress on urban resources and are looked down upon by the more sophisticated urban natives. It is also a source of rising crime in urban areas.

Although the *Hukuo* system has diminished somewhat since the Mao era, it's still a powerful economic and political impediment to the 'harmonious society' that the leaders hope to engender, at least through the Party rhetoric if not through policy. The Chinese leadership has tinkered around the edges of this problem with minor adjustments to the *Hukuo* system, but has not yet found a way to successfully address the issue.

One suggestion by researchers at China's finance ministry was to "start returning land to the peasants, both to spur consumption and to help defuse growing rural unrest."[14] But the dilemma in that solution is to diminish Party control over the land as well as delegitimize the Party's reason for existence as the people's custodian of the people's land. Land reform, after all, and the slaughter of millions of private property landlords, was a major part of the CCP's policies in the past. What would it tell the Chinese people about the wisdom of the Party if private land ownership were to return on a large scale?

Nonetheless, conflicts and tensions between the rural and urban populations and with the CCP continue to rise. This is not only due to the *Hukuo* system, but also to the systematic seizure of land from the peasant farmers for more profitable development and greater land for farming. Peasants are packed in like sardines in hastily built apartment complexes with no yards, few facilities, and overcrowded conditions in order that the land upon which farmers' personal residences sit may be used for farming or other more productive uses. There is usually no due process involved, and little compensation is given for the seizures. This practice and condition is a source of pervasive discontent without any easy political or economic remedy on the horizon. Rather, it is the promise of continued civil violence.

One-Child Policy and Pension Crisis

China's One-Child policy, which was put in force in 1979, is exacting enormous strain on the taxation of today's generation to support their aging parents. China has 200 million people over the age of 60 already, and that number will skyrocket to 400 million by 2033. The oft-repeated warning that "China must get rich before it gets old" is true; the smaller numbers of workers from the One-Child policy means that fewer workers will have to support more people in the coming years. By 2050, the ratio will be 2.4 workers supporting each pensioner.

But the CCP need not worry about the problems of the year 2050; China's pension crisis is already here. In 2013, China's pension plan for seniors faces a $2.3 trillion deficit. How to make up for the shortfall? The CCP will have to increase tax inequality, raising taxes where it is politically most feasible: on the middle and lower classes. This policy has many negatives associated with it, which are noted above. Furthermore, there is little doubt that much of the taxes would not reach their intended target. The more likely scenario is that those revenues would find their way into the offshore accounts of Party leaders.

A secondary impact of the One-Child policy has been a preference for boys, leaving a sociologically dangerous imbalance between the sexes. Today, there are 30 million more men than women in the younger generation, which will come of age in 2020. That imbalance means a generation of surplus males with limited opportunities for marriage, or perhaps even sexual partners. Furthermore, those males for whom there is little or no prospect for a wife and family may become aggressive in their behavior and outlook in society. This portends dramatic increases in violent crime to be committed by wifeless men, or those without the economic means to attract a mate, who literally will have nothing to lose.[15] Clearly, this is a disaster waiting to happen in terms of crime and social stability.

A tertiary impact from the One-Child policy is the millions of forced abortions imposed by the state upon young families wishing to have more than one child. Such invasive, state-imposed barbarity is a trauma that is not easily forgotten or forgiven, and is its own condemnation of the Orwellian state that rules China. Of course, this kind of intrusion begets deep hatred amongst the people against the CCP, and fosters an aura of illegitimacy that is not easily or likely to be erased in the minds of the people even in the best of times.

When one combines the rising crime rates and declining social stability with rising labor costs and a falling job market in China, especially for the millions of recent college graduates, there will be earthshaking consequences for the ruling class. As noted earlier, roughly 40 percent are without jobs, and those with jobs are often in blue-collar positions beneath their education and status. These failures are creating deep tensions within the educated unemployed and the underemployed younger generation of today and a cynical and angry generation. The negative impacts of these factors are already being felt and widely expressed and will not simply go away.

As socioeconomic conditions continue to deteriorate, China's one-party political system is proving to be clumsy at responding to the needs of its people and even worse in adjusting to new economic demands and market realities. Its corrupt nature and preference for the brute efficiency of the bullet and imprisonment to political compromise and the ballot box make the prospect for long-term stability highly questionable.

Political and Economic Contradictions

The split between ideology and economics widens every passing day as China's growing-yet-shrinking middle class see the outdated strictures of a political system that cannot by itself provide the means for development. The economic vitality of capitalism in China has been warped and distorted in its forced marriage to a communist political system.

The defenders of the CCP who view it as a source of stability for China argue in much the same way apologists of the former Soviet Union once did. That is not to say that the external events affecting its demise are similar to what China faces today, but some of the internal economic parallels are evident and quite damning for the future of China.

What do I mean by this?

By the mid-1980s, economic vitality in the Soviet Union was on life support. The Soviet leaders found that most of their technological innovation came by way of transfers from the West, either by purchase or theft. The communist political and social structure was one of privilege for a few and hardship for the many, and stifled the energies and creativity of the people. And those innovations that were developed 'in-house' had no way of getting to market and being leveraged for any kind of mass financial benefit. The political system was corrupt, and corruption, or *blat*, was the currency of the realm.

By the time Mikhail Gorbachev came to power as general secretary, he fully realized the decrepit condition of the Soviet economy and the stifling impact it had on its people. Gorbachev's dual initiatives, *glasnost* (openness) and *perestroika* (reform or restructuring) were designed to bring new life and creativity into the oppressive, ossified Soviet economic system. Of course, the Soviet system could handle neither openness nor restructuring; without the Party's monopoly on information and power, the Soviet system collapsed.

A similar point can be made with regard to China. Undoubtedly, Deng Xiaoping saw the effect of *glasnost* and *perestroika* on the Russians' fate and wished to avoid it. He also clearly recognized the danger for deteriorating conditions in China in the late 1970s. He certainly understood that the legitimacy of Communist Party rule was based upon it being able to deliver development to China. The flip side of that was the understanding that continued economic deterioration represented a clear threat to the current political order, that is, to CCP rule. In spite of the radical transformation and accumulation of wealth that has transpired in China since those days, that very threat of illegitimacy remains today.

But for 30 years, through engagement with Western capitalist nations, Deng was able to forestall the inevitable outcome of ossification and internal conflicts that would ultimately cause the demise of communist command economies. However, the slow but constant growth of influence of capitalism in Communist China has performed its own gradual version of *glasnost* and *perestroika* in Chinese society at large. That is, the reform and openness that spelled the death of the Soviet Union's political economies will result in the same end for the current Chinese system.

That is because the CCP is, by definition, a product of exclusivity, tight structure, and secrecy. However, much of Chinese society is deeply riven by the openness and awareness that technology has brought to it, as well as by the politically reformative impulses of self-determination and individual independence that come with material comfort and knowledge of those conditions and rights that exist not only in the West, but also in Taiwan and Hong Kong. The leadership's answer has been a combination of devouring the wealth and profitable businesses of the middle class while at the same time allowing expansion of new entrepreneurship that will, in time, provide additional wealth for the CCP to expropriate. It's like a business farm, run by the state; when a business becomes wealthy enough, it is absorbed by the state, stripped of its wealth, and run into the ground as a state-owned enterprise with endless sources of capital to keep it going.

This *market-Leninism*, as China's economic model has been called, works only as long as there is sufficient demand—whether from trading partners or self-created by infrastructure projects—and sufficient health in the country's financial sector to support it. But the swollen level of state-owned enterprises has created a financial black hole that sucks in capital in the form of recurrent debt without returning profit to justify the loans. Hence, there is a terminal point in this process because financial health is necessary for sustaining an economy. Where that terminal point is remains to be seen. On the other hand, any sort of *glasnost* and *perestroika* openness or reform would certainly spell doom for the CCP. The notion that the authoritarian structure of the CCP has the ability to rectify the socioeconomic problems it has imposed on the society is an ill-conceived one at best.

The beginning of a cure to these problems would be to dismantle the most intrusive aspects of government, cease state seizure of businesses and lands, and expand personal freedoms and rights, all of which would strip the CCP of its power and drive it out of existence. Is this likely to occur? Probably not—at least not all at once. But neither is the idea that China's authoritarian system has the answers that beset the country or is resilient and creative enough to steer the country away from the disasters of financial collapse, famine, and civil unrest that loom ahead. The assumptions that business and the middle class are the CCP's dependable political allies are far from set in stone. It is more likely that the theft of profitable private businesses is creating political enemies rather than allies.[16]

As noted earlier, given the effect of the conflicts within the system, the middle class is at odds with the long-term goals of the CCP. Middle-class Chinese see the CCP's self-serving policies for what they are and are coming to regard their leaders and policies with suspicion, cynicism, and resentment.

How Will the Recent Transfer of Power in China Affect Stability?

It is true that the ruling elite in China seem stable in that the Party is so well entrenched in power, but it is also true that China's communist party finds itself threatened by both the economic and technological progress that have come to China in the past 25 years, as well as by the economic slowdown that now plagues most if not all of the world's largest and most advanced economies.

The reality is that the transfer of power in China has rarely been smooth. Mao Zedong spent the last 10 years of his life avoiding assassination from his political rivals within the Party, and the power transfer after his death in 1976 was treacherous as well. And as mentioned previously, political survival was Mao's overriding reason for instigating the Cultural Revolution. That such tragedy can be caused by the power lusts of one man is incomprehensible, but yet, it happened—twice.

Is such behavior an aberration? Or does the structure and political culture of the CCP cultivate, engender, and reward such personalities? According to Xiao Qiang, director of the Berkeley China Internet Project at the University of California, Berkeley, and editor of the *China Digital Times*, such behavior is *sine qua non* in the "dark politics" of the Chinese leadership.[17] The CCP attracts and rewards ambitiously ruthless people.

Power transitions in China are actually quite dangerous and potentially destabilizing as one dictatorial group hands power over to another. Scandal, criminality, and political intrigue are all part of that process. The scandal-plagued transfer of power in 2012 was, therefore, anything but smooth; of course, it was not out of the ordinary, either. The arrest and prosecution of the would-be ascending leader of the CCP, Bo Xilai, for high crimes, including collusion with his wife in the murder of a British businessman, provided high drama in the power transition within the CCP and an insight into the nature of the political system of China and the characteristics of its power elite.

The Bo Xilai scandal not only discredited the CCP as being able or qualified to provide legitimate leadership in China, but any illusion that may have existed of the CCP as an organized, stable, and well-functioning political body in China has been shattered. The deadly scandal has irretrievably shown China's communist leadership to be what they have always been: nothing more than a small cluster of vicious mobsters, scheming to get at each other's throats in their own individual quests for political power, wealth, and influence.

In fact, Xiao Qiang said in his April 26, 2012, interview with *PBS NewsHour* that it wasn't murder, wiretapping, or even secretly transferring $6 billion to foreign accounts in the United States and elsewhere (which has its own damning implications) that was Xilai's downfall. He stated unequivocally that all of the members of the Chinese leadership have similar skeletons in their closets. Rather, it was Bo Xilai's *public* campaign for leadership of the Communist Party, parading himself amongst the masses like he was the second coming of Mao, that led to his political demise.

But that is not the only reason. Bo Xilai's wife's conviction for the murder of British businessman Nick Heywood was, literally, about skeletons in the closet. Apparently, the Party decided that one Mao is quite enough, thanks, and took old Bo out to the woodshed to get re-educated. However, there is little reason to believe that the power struggle within the CCP has ended with the official transfer of power.

Why would this be?

This is because power within the CCP lies in political alliances, and the battle between the two most powerful ruling groups within the Party continues. These two groups not only compete for power, but they also bring conflicting ideas as to what China's direction and identity internally, and on the world stage, ought to be. The objective here is not to elaborate on the many differences within competing factions of the CCP, but rather, to focus on the much larger issue of how the new leadership will handle the crises that are already coming about in China, and which will become much more urgent in the very near future. The conflict is readily visible. The personal and commercial close ties that the Politburo Standing Committee has with the 145,000 state-owned enterprises leaves little room for reform without damaging their political support base and their own financial interests.[18]

Those interests align with both of China's competing political factions in the fifth generation of CCP leadership. Xi Jinping, a CCP legacy or *princeling* and Li Keqiang, from the ostensibly more populist and reform-minded wing of the Party, though they have competing interests, both share the interest of self-preservation. This prime objective was reaffirmed by Hu Jintao in his speech opening the Communist Party's 18th Congress, where he outlined the Party's main goal of preserving power.[19]

There is little doubt, however, that preserving the Party's grip on power is at odds with any major reforms. Even so, if there is a new direction in which the new leadership will take China, it has yet to materialize, other than as an anti-corruption campaign. Perhaps this is because there remains tremendous intra-party competition between the two factions. Consequently, whatever direction China's leadership takes will have an enormous impact with very serious implications. Not only is the world in a very unstable period, but China is as well. It is quite possible that a divided party is the enduring consequence of the two competing factions, regardless of the perception of consensus that the CCP likes to show the world. The last time there were such deep divisions in the party was during the Tiananmen Square crisis.

Another of the great dangers of the recent power transition is the fact that it is from one generation to another. This can easily involve a potentially dangerous gap in perspective and wisdom, which is especially critical in challenging economic times. However, it is also crucial with regard to internal and personal security as well as political power consolidation issues.

This spells out several implications, tendencies, and challenges for the new leadership. The fact is that the younger generation of Chinese leadership lacks personal experience—and therefore, perspective—on China's horrendous past, through which they did not live. The Cultural Revolution took place just past the living memories of most of the new generation of China's leadership cadre, who were born in the late 1950s up through the mid-1960s. They have matured politically in an age of a rising China in the world, which may have fostered their own set of unreasonable and unwise expectations, such as preferring confrontation to cooperation both domestically and in foreign policy.

For example, their fathers grafted a capitalist system onto a totalitarian political regime based upon Party connections, not merit, and they became very rich men. Therefore, the overriding factors in the Party's decision-making and its reactions and alliances are primarily politically driven, not economically driven. Today's generation of leaders in China are accustomed to China's development, prosperity, and global rise to power. They are mainly political animals steeped in a deeply corrupt system and therefore adept at working that system, which rewards graft and the leveraging of influence, and they are notoriously comfortable with state violence. At the same time, many are incompetent when it comes to real market economic policy or problem solving. It is entirely possible that those at the top with regard to leadership have little idea of how bad things really are in the economy as a whole or what needs to be done to remedy the country's current woes.

Furthermore, although the leadership succession has taken place, it is a mistake to assume that the younger leadership is fully secure in its position. The purge of the princeling Bo Xilai and his wife's murder trial in 2012 proved that fact beyond any doubt. But even with the leadership question officially *settled*, there remain great rifts in the ruling elite and power is by no means consolidated or ensured, and as the economy continues to decline, the legitimacy of the ruling class will rapidly decline with it, as it is declining to some degree already. The need amongst the masses for answers and for someone to blame will come to the fore.

Within the Party and the Politburo Standing Committee, fingers of blame will be pointed at each other, as both the princelings and the *tuanpai* leadership cadres look to blame each other. As the effects of China's slowing economy and growing instability worsen, there will be a need for scapegoats. First, someone in power will need to take the fall. If the past is prologue to how this will play out, it will likely be a high-ranking Party member, with a group of his political allies—most likely those who are reform-minded. They will become the internal political scapegoat, perhaps publicly prosecuted for corruption and theft, and accordingly punished.

There will also be a social scapegoat, which will probably come from a group within the Chinese society that is well known throughout the country as having a history of anti-communism. This will likely be a religious group such as Falun Gong, Christians, or both. A less likely group might be the Buddhists in Tibet or the Muslims in Xinjiang. As in the past, followers of the guilty parties will be prosecuted and publicly humiliated before being executed. A third scapegoat will be from outside, as a means to both unify the country and to focus blame on an external, foreign enemy. The West, and the United States in particular, will be the likely suspect. All of this will only heighten the competition for political survival in China.

In the international sphere, the new leadership in China has only disdain for the West, and for the United States in particular. They view the United States as a weakened hegemon, which it is indeed. But at the same time, the new generation of Chinese leaders possess a grand sense of entitlement and optimism, with a deep sense of destiny. The new Chinese leadership has no qualms about purveying nationalism to the people. Many truly feel that China is entitled to take up the mantle of world leadership and should push against the Americans for Chinese dominance in the Asian Pacific region and on the world stage.

Although a rabid nationalism is not the only motivational trope that will be in play, it may well be where the new leadership seeks refuge as the economy crashes and chaos returns to China. There appears to be little appetite for diplomacy in China's policies toward its neighbors. Chinese regional domination is a given of the new leadership's foreign policy posture. The tone and viewpoint of the new generation of leaders in the CCP and in the military are already evident. China has threatened war with both Vietnam and the Philippines over contested islands, within which oil has been discovered. China's growing bellicosity is well understood by Japan, which has already made major adjustments in its military forces in response to China's approach to the disputed islands.

Does this mean that the new leadership is any better or worse equipped to handle international affairs than the prior leadership? This is particularly relevant with regard to China's relations with the United States. Will the new leadership be more willing to work with the United States, or more apt to challenge it? Will they be able to respond to internal challenges any more appropriately and effectively than their predecessors? It doesn't seem likely, given that there has been no reduction in government-sponsored anti-U.S. propaganda, which continues to be a daily presence in all forms of government-run communication in Chinese society. In fact, it appears that the new Chinese leadership may use antipathy toward the United States as both a domestic and foreign policy scapegoat whenever it suits them.

Looking back on this chapter, it is apparent that China faces multiple challenges in the socio-economic and political realms. The status of each is fluid, but all are trending negatively. Furthermore, the prospects for those challenges to be met successfully are in doubt. A hardline response from the CCP seems to be in China's near future, although this conclusion is arguable. China bulls would vigorously defend against these conclusions, noting correctly that every country faces similar challenges in one form or another, which to one degree or another is true.

Is China's leadership more capable and adaptable than is portrayed herein? Is it a mistake to think that their communist regime is an inherently instable one? The answers to these questions remain to be seen. But as we explore the Beijing Model in Chapter 4, we will come to understand why it is a self-terminating process that will ultimately, and in the very near future, bring great ruin upon China.

Notes

1. Edward Friedman, "Understanding China's Global Impact," *The Diplomat*, February 19, 2011, http://thediplomat.com/whats-next-china/understanding-china%E2%80%99s-global-impact.

2. Suisheng Zhao, "Political Reform," *The Diplomat*, February 19, 2011, http://thediplomat.com/whats-next-china/political-reform.

3. Ding Qingfen and Li Jiabao, "FDI Falls Amid Slowdown," Chinadaily.com.cn, January 17, 2013, www.chinadaily.com.cn/china/2013-01/17/content_16128881.htm.

4. Chris Devonshire-Ellis, "The Pressing Need for Religious Guidance in China," 2point6billion.com, October 18, 2011, www.2point6billion.com/news/2011/10/18/the-pressing-need-for-religious-guidance-in-china-10313.html; Dr. Dao Wen, Ph.D., "China Moral Crises," www.createspace.com/3756711.

5. Helen H.Wang, "The Chinese Middle Class View of the Leadership Transition," *Forbes*, November 9, 2012, www.forbes.com/sites/helenwang/2012/11/09/the-chinese-middle-class-view-of-the-leadership-transition.

6. Jane Hardy and Adrian Budd, "China's Capitalism and the Crisis," *International Socialism* 33, January 9, 2012, www.isj.org.uk/?id=777.

7. Nathan Gamester, "The Legatum Institute Survey of Entrepreneurs: China 2011," www.li.com/docs/surveys-of-entrepreneurs/2011-survey-of-entrepreneurs-china.pdf, 13.

8. William de Tocqueville, "George Orwell's China?" *The Diplomat*, http://thediplomat.com/whats-next-china/george-orwell%E2%80%99s-china.

9. Alan Taylor, "Rising Protests in China," *The Atlantic*, February 12, 2012, www.theatlantic.com/infocus/2012/02/rising-protests-in-china/100247; and Daniel Wagner and John Margeson, "The Rise of the Chinese Urban Militia," *Huffington Post*, October 8, 2012, www.huffingtonpost.com/daniel-wagner/the-chinese-urban-militia_b_1946099.html.

10. Deng Jingyin, "Beijing Police Crack Down on Black Jails," *Global Times*, December 2, 2011, www.globaltimes.cn/NEWS/tabid/99/ID/686788/Beijing-police-crack-down-on-black-jails.aspx.

11. Associated Press, "China Targets Energy, Health Industries to Boost Slow-Growing Economy," *Oregon Live*, July 30, 2012, www.oregonlive.com/business/index.ssf/2012/07/china_targets_energy_health_in.html.

12. Minxin Pei, "China's Bumpy Ride Ahead," *The Diplomat*, February, 16, 2011, http://thediplomat.com/whats-next-china/chinas-bumpy-ride-ahead.

13. "Excerpts from 'The Taiwan Crisis'—Banned in China," China Uncensored, www.chinauncensored.com/index.php/banned-books/497-excerpts-from-the-taiwan-crisis-banned-in-china-3.

14. Chen Xiaoqiang and Liu Ling, "Urbanisation: Where Do You Live?" *The Economist,* June 23, 2011, www.economist.com/node/18832092.

15. Rob Brooks, "China's Biggest Problem? Too Many Men," CNN Opinion, November 15, 2012, www.cnn.com/2012/11/14/opinion/china-challenges-one-child-brooks.

16. Cheng Li, "The China Paradox and American Misperceptions," The Brookings Institute, October 21, 2011, www.brookings.edu/research/articles/2011/10/21-china-li.

17. Xiao Qiang, *PBS NewsHour,* April 26, 2012, www.pbs.org/newshour/bb/world/jan-june12/china2_04-26.html.

18. "Political Reform or Nationalist Regression for China's 'Team of Rivals'?" *Democracy Digest,* November 13, 2012, www.demdigest.net/blog/?s= Chongqing.

19. Cheng Li, "New Challenges in Predicting China's Upcoming Political Succession," *China Business Review,* November–December 2010, www.chinabusiness review.com/public/1011/commentary.html.

Chapter 4

Is China's Economy Sustainable?

A s noted in earlier chapters, today, many observers and policy makers regard China as the heir to the United States as the world's economic leader and the Beijing Model as the best way toward creating a healthy, wealthy economy. In the wake of the 2008 financial meltdown in the Western nations, the Beijing Model has not only been lauded as the economic model of the future, but China's authoritarian, state-run capitalism is supposedly replacing the liberal and open democratic market capitalism of the United States as the preferred model for developing nations. This is based upon the false assumption that since China *seemed* to be much less affected by the meltdown, its system must be superior to the ones that were, with the U.S. economy particularly in mind.

We will take a closer look at these assumptions in this chapter. *If* they are in fact true and the Beijing Model really is the path toward rapid development and a rise in national power, then the twenty-first century would certainly appear to belong to China. As a consequence, the rest of the world should abandon the underlying assumptions of liberal democracy and capitalism in a quest to mirror the success that the Chinese evidently have realized in only a few brief decades. After all, only the most dynamic, sustainable, and creative economies lead the world, don't they? But that's a pretty big "if" concerning the Beijing Model, and it's not an uncontestable fact by any stretch of the imagination.

The Beijing Model: The Path Forward or Cannibal Capitalism?

In order to understand why and how it got there, let's take a brief look at how both market capitalist and command economies allocate resources, goods, and services. Then we will closely examine some of the more egregiously fatal flaws of the Beijing Model as it has metastasized throughout China.

In a command economy, major economic policies are made at the top levels of government while many other decisions related to implementing the economic policy are made by Party bureaucrats at the provincial and local levels, according to criteria provided by Party authorities up the food chain. Resources and finished goods are therefore allocated by decree by state planners rather than by the price mechanism of the market. There are variations of this, of course, but this is essentially how a command economy works—and to varying degrees how China's economy functions.

Because of these features, command economies are always plagued by shortages and overages, fraud, graft, and corruption. Not sometimes; all the time. At all government levels and in those industries that work closely with government authorities, bribery and fraud are the ways in which resources get redirected, how businesses get contracts, and how people stay alive and get what they want and need. Ironically, in command economies, where the market forces of supply and demand and the price mechanism are misapplied or ignored, graft and bribery can be viewed as a sort of shadow price mechanism to get goods and services where they need to go.

Conversely, capitalist economies rely much more upon the price mechanism for distribution of goods and services. The profit motive, open competition, and a free flow of ideas and information make capitalist economies less prone to waste and much more efficient in putting the right factors of production in the right industries, as well as meeting the demand for the right goods. All of these attributes lead to greater levels of innovation and invention, allowing the people's innate creativity to flourish. There are excesses as well, of course—especially when the profit motive is misapplied in government contracts, for example—but in the big picture, wealth, innovation, creativity, invention, and abundance are hallmarks of capitalist economies.

The profit incentive and price mechanism also militate against widespread fraud within the capitalist system. At the producer level, for example, you are either making money or you're losing it. At the consumer level, a poorly made product or under-delivered service eventually costs the supplier business in the form of shrinking profits and expensive and often public lawsuits. Fraud, waste, and abuses occur, of course, but they tend to be much less part of the integral functioning of the economy. Shareholders of public companies, for example, demand accountability, as do the Internal Revenue Service and the banks lending to businesses.

There are also regulatory bodies in place to monitor the quality and safety of products and services, as well as a vigorous legal system to punish offenders and compensate victims. Are there imperfections, injustices, and other flaws in capitalist economies? Of course there are; after all, we're talking about human beings. But the degree is much less than in command economies and the standard of living and the level of humanity also tend to be much higher.

Identifying China's economy as a command economy is not to say that China's economy doesn't function at all; it does, but its functioning is greatly distorted. Its distortions come from many sources, both within and without. There are private business owners and landowners, but there are also no private property rights, the price mechanism is ignored as much as it is followed, information flows are very limited, and again, command economy style corruption is the way anything gets done.

China also leverages price advantages, economies of scales, and lax pollution laws to compete on the world market and attract foreign investment. Internally, however, the Chinese economy is at the disposal and command of the Party leaders to abuse and absorb the private sector at every turn, as well as the public financial sector, in the interest of enriching themselves and maintaining their monopoly on power. Thus, waste, fraud, corruption, and other distortions occur because command economies are inherently inefficient at allocating resources and finished goods, or even determining which goods and how many of each are needed and desired by the economy at large.

The historical experience—even in China from 1979 to 1989—shows without question that capitalist economies produce greater wealth, innovation, and rising standards of living for more of society faster, than any other economic system. History also shows that capitalism is most effective in a free and open society, with a free flow of information. Free-flowing information and its widespread access within a free and democratic society improve market efficiencies and therefore lead to greater productivity and wealth for the society as a whole.

That is not to say that capitalism is perfect. It is, after all, a system derived from the imperfect mind of mankind, with imperfect information and social concerns that often do not get addressed as quickly as one would prefer. There are also market disruptions, delays, and distortions due to some political or social values that the democratic society has decided are necessary or desirable. In the main, however, market capitalist economies, when they're allowed to function reasonably unhindered, are the most effective of economic systems and have generated the world's greatest levels of wealth wherever they have been tried, be it the United States, Hong Kong, Europe, Taiwan, Chile, Japan, or elsewhere.

By contrast, command economies of all stripes are invariably twinned with a lack of individual rights and liberties. And, because people usually chafe at the bit of oppression that occurs when a state tries to tell them what they should do, when they should do it, and how and for how long, authoritarian political systems usually require a robust and aggressive internal security force to enforce the will of the state upon the people, thereby squelching the natural resistance that people have to living under such conditions. The party in power must constantly reward itself and its supporters with wealth and perks, as well as perpetuate the illusion of economic control and success by punishing producers and buying off those it can't imprison or otherwise do without.

Of course, shortages can't be publicized, so with the right amount of bribery, theft, and manipulation of figures, shortages become surpluses. Furthermore, low, flat, or negative economic growth becomes double-digit gross domestic production (GDP) growth and the world marvels at the country's success and obvious economic brilliance expertly guided by the ruling class. Corruption and shortages only exist in the minds of those who are not pulling their weight or who do not have the connections to get their fair share of the spoils. Those who complain of shortage and corruption usually don't do so for very long.

That is the profile of the Beijing Model.

The Beijing Model's abuse of the people and the thwarting of human beings' natural inclination for self-determination are also yoked with a lack of respect for their natural resources and the health of the environment. Thus, although pollution of the environment occurs to some degree in all economies, the level of pollution and widespread abuse of the natural environs are consistently much worse under command economies. We will further explore the reasons for this later in this chapter.

As noted and verified by history, command economies in the industrial and technological arenas only thrive or, for that matter, *survive* in the long term with outside help from capitalist economies. And by survive, I mean achieve actual sustained growth over the long term. Yes, Castro's Cuba still exists after the collapse of the Soviet Union, but then, so do the decrepit 1950s vintage cars that wheeze and limp down Havana's *Malecon*, along with chronic shortages and a stifled and broken Cuban society. The idea of a "Cuban economy" is as much of a contradiction in terms as it is a pitiful legacy of the late USSR.

The Soviet Union itself is an even better example of the bankruptcy of command economies. Belorussia was the breadbasket of Eastern Europe before the revolution. After enduring Soviet collectivization for only a few years, Soviet Russia was never again able to feed itself and relied upon grain imports from the United States, Canada, Argentina, and elsewhere to avoid starvation among its people. Furthermore, vast swaths of forestland and even some suburban areas throughout the old territories of the former Soviet Union are no longer habitable by human beings due to the level of toxicity and pollutants that the state dumped or otherwise allowed to exist there.

These same symptoms of fraud, waste, corruption, oppression, and environmental damage that existed in the Soviet Union are present in China to an undeniably high and pervasive level. Fraud is so great and ever-present that no official numbers can really ever be trusted. It remains to be seen what will be worse: the absolute hollowness of China's numbers or what will transpire when their effects meet reality. Each time they have done so, calamity has befallen China. This time, however, the consequences of China's fraudulent and corrupt economy will affect the entire world when it collapses, and not just those within its control. This eventuality will have been brought on China care of the latest incarnation of CCP madness, the Beijing Model.

What Is the Beijing Model?

Is the Beijing Model really a new and better path toward successful and sustainable development? Is it really the newest, most dynamic, and effective economic "model" in the world today? Let's examine it and see.

To begin with, certain aspects of the Beijing Model are "new" only in that they are new to communist China. Recall that the Beijing Model began with the United States and the West providing capital and technology to China via joint ventures to Chinese firms. But achieving development—or redevelopment, as the case may be, from outside capital and technology—is a not a new concept *per se*. The United States did essentially the same thing in the Marshall Plan to rebuild war-devastated Europe as well as rebuilding Japan after World War II. There were some differences, of course, in that Europe and Japan were both already among the most highly developed, industrial regions in the world, but the fact is that China's Beijing Model began with the Open Door Policy of inviting foreign money, foreign firms, and foreign technology into China. This was solely because the CCP had proven itself to be an utter failure, from stem to stern, at developing the country over the preceding three decades.

But as for the Beijing Model being a *new* economic model? That's complete nonsense. Again, there are perhaps new twists here and there, but nothing revolutionary or even innovative is present. Rapid development of an Asian country had been done before. One hundred years earlier, Japan made the conscious decision to develop itself along a Western style industrial model and within three decades, it defeated the Russian navy, a major European power, in the Russo-Japanese war in 1905.

In China's case, at its essence, the Beijing Model is just another variation on the European fascist models of the 1920s and 1930s, where the state had the upper hand in directing the economies with established capitalist foundations and firms. China's new twist is its "farming" of private businesses, where it allows private companies to develop and grow. When they reach a certain level of prosperity, they are then likely to be taken over by state-owned enterprises with CCP affiliation of one kind or another. But, like the fascists of the past—and the Russian communist regime, for that matter—civil liberties and civil rights remain in very limited supply in China today amidst rising political corruption and moral decay in Chinese society at large.

Is the Beijing Model Self-Sustaining?

Given that assessment, is the Beijing Model a self-sustaining system that leads to not only greater long-term economic growth, but also *contributes to the long-term improvement of Chinese society and the general well-being of the country*?

There are two parts to this question, and for good reason. With regard to the first part, no one can argue against sustainable and steady economic growth being a desire for any nation, large or small. Without it, a nation loses its self-determination. Political and social instability result, as do human suffering and deprivation, which is not a beneficial outcome for anyone, except perhaps the few at the top wishing to hold onto power.

That is why the second part of this question is also included; it is just as important as the first. There is no good reason at this stage of human history to pretend that all styles of leadership and political organizations are of equal worth or validity. The criteria and standard for any political and economic system ought to be about how well the nation does economically of course, but also, how a given system treats its people. That includes civil liberties, how well it treats the natural environment and manages the natural resources upon which the society relies, and the political culture that it engenders. We will address this second part in Chapters 6 and 7, but it is worth keeping in mind as we look deeper into the Beijing Model.

Remember, when China's rise began, it was just coming out of the Mao era; there were party purges and show trials following decades of misery and brutality throughout the country. And amidst the show trials and purges, there was also widespread hunger in the country and deep discontent with the government. But most of all, there existed a profound lack of economic development throughout the country.

Quite rightly, Communist Party leader Deng Xiaoping was very worried about a legitimacy crisis within China and open revolt among the people against the CCP. So, in the beginning years of the Open Door Policy, it was actually quite effective in raising economic activity, liberalizing Chinese society, and enabling millions upon millions of the Chinese people to materially improve their lives. The Open Door, however, let in more than just money and know-how; as much as the CCP tried to prevent it and control it, the Open Door let Western ideas into China, as well.

Later on, however, as the Open Door Policy brought rapid growth and wealth into China, the CCP leadership increasingly felt the need to re-assume ownership over the economy as a way to reassert their control over the country and the commercial class. Therefore, today, the benefits of the Beijing Model are not as cut and dried as they were before. That is not to say that there are not a great many more wealthy people in China today than there were even a decade ago; there is no doubt that there are. But there are also many negative facets to consider.

Hence, even with the happy reality of new wealth in China, there is also a rapidly growing instability. It can be seen everywhere; one only need look for it. As we saw in Chapter 3, the reports and statistics of protests and rising civil violence are there for all to see. A short list would include political recklessness; rampant economic deceit; civil unrest; unsustainable debt levels; a real estate bubble; extreme pollution of the air, land, rivers, and seas; a growing distrust of the moneyed classes; widening wealth gaps in both rural and in urban areas; and falling domestic consumption.

These and many others are the symptoms of a distorted economic system that is not self-sustaining, and is instead a process or policy of

Cannibal Capitalism. That, for lack of a better term, is where the various parts of the economy—rather than synergistically growing and expanding the GDP and wealth-creating processes of a nation—actually feed upon one another, destroying the wealth-creating factors in the economy through waste, neglect, graft, and corruption at the highest levels.

Thus, rather than the economic forces of China being allowed to thrive and develop organically, they are distorted through corrupt government policies, official theft on a grand scale, and abuse of the financial sector and the currency to the short-term advantage of the very few at the top echelons of power—at the expense of the long-term prospects of development. China's economy today is one where the CCP greedily feeds off the wealth-creating aspects of the country in every way possible. The Beijing Model is best described as an orgy of warped capitalism and corruption gone amok, which is why even at this writing, China's economy has begun its descent into disintegration.

The Beijing Model itself is also illegitimate as far as models are concerned; and has proven to be more of an abusive process of theft and political advantage and oppression for the CCP rather than a sustainable model. And, as we enumerate below, its negative effects are felt throughout Chinese society. Therefore, rather than being the path forward as it is advertised to be, we will see that the Beijing Model, like the self-cannibalistic process that it is, is not only unsustainable, but it is also approaching a self-terminating point in its process with an astonishing velocity.

How can we know this to be the case with the Beijing Model? What are the most problematic attributes of it that lead to this conclusion? Let's take a look.

The Beijing Model has the following attributes:

- A means for the CCP to maintain power
- Authoritarian political structure
- A culture of corruption
- State control of banks and capital based upon cronyism, resulting in a debt crisis, which is creating triangular debt, *zombie* industries, and a real estate bubble
- Dependence upon foreign investment, foreign demand, and cheap labor
- Low and false domestic demand

- Demographic crisis via the One Child policy
- Extreme environmental degradation

Let us examine each of the above attributes of the Beijing Model to better understand this "new economic model." We will see why it is not what the Chinese and much of the rest of the world think it is, and why it and China's current political economy face a very difficult road ahead.

A Means for the CCP to Maintain Power

First and foremost, the Beijing Model—or whatever else China's current economic path may be called—was never intended to be a path to liberalization or the democratization of China. Though many in the West and in China believe that liberalization will eventually be the result of the adoption of capitalism (although it was somewhat true from 1979 to 1989) the reality is a different matter altogether. Liberal or moderate forces within China's CCP have been effectively purged before, and it is most likely that any others that show themselves to have liberal inclinations—that is, anti-collectivist, anti-CCP power monopoly inclinations—will also be purged.

The fact remains, after all, that without the excuse of collectivism and CCP leading the nation to wealth, the Party has no pretext to exist. The CCP exists because of and off of the collective masses. Collectivism and the delivery of economic growth allows the CCP to retain its power and ostensibly act on behalf of the collective people without having to explain its actions. Collectivism works for those who are at the top, and those at the top are in the CCP.

From the CCP's perspective, the Beijing Model is and always will be a *policy*. It was always employed primarily as a means for maintaining political power in China, and then for enriching the Party elite and growing China's economy. All three of these objectives are linked together. It was no coincidence that at the time Deng Xiaoping initiated the Open Door Policy in 1978, he also articulated the Four Principles of China, which were:

1. We must keep to the socialist road.
2. We must uphold the dictatorship of the proletariat.
3. We must uphold the leadership of the Communist Party.
4. We must uphold Marxism-Leninism-Mao-Zedong Thought.

The obvious question in the shadow of the Open Door Policy is, "Why did Deng feel the need to issue these Four Principles?" There is only one reason: He knew the risks that the Open Door Policy would bring. That is why the principles were presented to the country; they gave the CCP justification for any future crackdowns.

In 1982, likely anticipating the Tiananmen Square-type of demonstration to come about eventually, Deng changed the second principle to "upholding the people's democratic dictatorship." This allowed Deng and the CCP to justify and approve the military slaughter at Tiananmen Square of democratic protesters in 1989 to be described, regardless of how perverse it sounds, as a "defense of democracy," while at the same time crushing the threat to the CCP's legitimacy. To understand just how much the Beijing Model is *not* a formula for liberalization in China, to this very day, the discussion of the massacre in any form is forbidden and punishable by prison or worse.

China's Open Door Policy allowed for two developments that were directly responsible for developing the Chinese economy, which, in turn, strengthened and enriched the CCP.

1. Western capital and industry were given access to the extremely low-cost Chinese labor market. This was a profitable deal for both sides. Money and know-how flowed into China, along with newly built factories and supporting development. This activity injected capital, high labor demand, and innovation and innovation into China that simply was not there before.

2. Private Chinese companies were allowed to form and profit from their joint ventures with Western firms. That, in turn, spurred an explosion of suppliers, distributors, and numerous other privately owned support industries, beginning mainly in Eastern China, but spreading west as well. This massive entrepreneurialism, along with the necessary liberalization policies of CCP leader Hu Yaobang, spurred a rapid rise in Chinese GDP, in living standards, and in political expression for the newly emerging commercial class in China.

There is no doubt that the first decade of the Beijing Model was a resounding success, both economically and politically, for China. In fact, according to the work of Yasheng Huang, professor in international management at the MIT Sloan School of Management, "The most liberal period in Chinese politics and economics—from 1978 until the 1989 crackdown—coincided with the greatest improvements in Chinese welfare. And that period of growth was entrepreneur-driven rather than state-led. From 1978 to 1985, Chinese people in rural areas created up to 10.5 million privately owned firms."[1]

That period of time was crucial in the economic development of China. Note, however, that it was not the state-run economy that thrived and developed China the quickest, but rather, it was the private sector that was allowed to flourish under the liberal leadership of Hu Yaobang. The opening of the economy combined with the requisite relaxing of intellectual and political rigidity by Hu allowed China to grow rapidly for the first time in three decades of CCP rule. At the same time, it encouraged the Chinese people to expect more of the same, with an added expectation among the younger generation of the possibility of the establishment of democracy in China.

The internal and external political contexts of the times are very important in understanding what drove the CCP to massacre its young people on the particular occasion of Tiananmen Square. Less than three years earlier, in 1986, Taiwan, the ideological thorn in the side of the CCP, allowed the establishment of the Democratic Progressive Party (DPP) for the first time, a huge development in Taiwan's political culture on the road from martial law to democracy.

In fact, there was some very powerful symmetry in the liberalization processes taking place in China, led by Chinese Party General Secretary Hu Yaobang, and in Taiwan, with the legalization of a competing political party in the same time period of the mid-1980s. The CCP could see where things were headed, and it didn't look good for them. By 1987, China was experiencing widespread student protests and Hu's political opponents in the CCP successfully blamed his *bourgeois* liberalism for the protests and removed him from power.

It is important to also mention that the CCP was in no way oblivious to the fortunes—or misfortunes—befalling the Soviet Union. Soviet Russia, especially, was undergoing rapid changes. The ruling Communist Party under Gorbachev was losing control of the country and the economy through his *glasnost* and *perestroika* policies of openness and reform. The CCP leadership could see where those policies were leading the Soviet Union. It is no exaggeration to say that the CCP viewed

Hu, with his liberalization efforts and desire to make the CCP more transparent, as the Chinese Gorbachev, if you will. The CCP was having none of it. Not only was Hu Yaobang removed from power, he was also publicly humiliated and his policies were repudiated in the Party before his death in April of 1989.

In fact, it was in response to Hu's death that the students at Tiananmen Square were prompted to protest against the ruling leadership and demand more of the democratic reforms that Hu had put into place. The Party was deeply divided on the course to take, but ultimately, self-preservation ruled the day and the democracy movement in China was crushed. Since the Tiananmen Square protest for democracy and its heavy suppression by the CCP, there has been a dramatic shift in the economic policies that China initially adopted. From that day forward, the CCP has taken a greater role in the economy and stolen the greater share of wealth from it, as the ownership of the means of production has progressively shifted away from private firms to public or state-owned enterprises.

Of course, with the West's participation since before 1989 and continuing and growing even deeper thereafter, China's economy has continued to grow. The growth rate, however, is difficult to know, but certainly nowhere near what the Chinese say it is in any given year, as it has been proven beyond doubt that Chinese statistics are utterly unreliable. In fact, Chinese GDP statistics are so distorted as to be unbelievable altogether.

Why would this be? Perpetually fraudulent high growth rates are reported for several reasons. One reason is the need to justify the Party's nationalization of the private firms that lifted the economy so quickly in the decade from 1979 to 1989, and of course, to further justify the unspoken slaughter of the protesters against CCP rule. Going forward from there, the CCP needed to be consistently seen by the people as indispensable in guiding China correctly to justify its dominance and heavy intervention in the economy from 1989 through today. What better way than yearly GDP numbers that lead the world and are almost always better than the year before?

Essentially, it is crucial to understand that the CCP's GDP numbers are first and foremost political propaganda tools, not economic tools, as they are in the West. Continuing along that line of reasoning, inflated GDP statistics also allow the CCP to *keep up* with the real growth rates of Taiwan. Remember, a rich and democratic Taiwan represents an alternative to the Chinese path, which the CCP is rightly very sensitive about. Recall that before his death, Deng Xiaoping instructed his protégés to "take care of the Taiwan problem by 2012." Even today, with China's inflated economic statistics, the GDP in Taiwan is 10 percent of China's but with only 1/58th of the population. And the per capita GDP rate in Taiwan still outperforms China at a 5-to-1 ratio.[2]

The Beijing Model: A Two-Step Process. Thus, in broad terms, the Beijing Model can be described as having been a two-step process in China. Step One was the Open Door Policy from 1979 to 1989. Again, looking to the West for help was a calculated move by the CCP and Den Xiaoping to save the CCP from facing revolt from the Chinese people, as well as from facing possible bullying from the West; nothing more. It is perhaps more accurate to say that the real Beijing Models were the ones that emanated from the corrupt and twisted minds of the Party from 1949 to 1979, and from 1989 to the present.

Step One of the Beijing Model was very successful. The Chinese economy blossomed as never before. As the private firms multiplied and became profitable and rich, the children of the emerging commercial and manufacturing classes began attending universities. As the children of entrepreneurs, they had first-hand knowledge of the power of private ownership and capitalism. Many understood that the two worked best together.

The students became ever more tuned into political ideas and democracy, and Hu Yaobang's liberal policies gave students a hunger for more freedom. Under Hu, they could express that hope in the form of more protests. They were able to differentiate between the old system and the new and concluded that the new way was better. Who could blame them? After all, when you're not scratching for your food day in and day out, you have the time and the means to obtain an education, which allows you to make judgments about things and to entertain new ideas.

Step Two of the Beijing Model began in the aftermath of Tiananmen Square. By that time, economic failure was no longer a threat to the CCP, but both the demands for democracy and the massive economic successes of private Chinese firms certainly were. The Tiananmen

Square pro-democracy protest, which was witnessed by the whole world, showed the CCP just how big of a threat the private wealth that capitalism produced, as well as the Western ideas of individual freedom and political expression that accompanied it were to their legitimacy.

The CCP made the simple calculation that in order to maintain power, they must not only crack down on liberalization and political expression, but also on the commercial class that spawned the democracy protest. To accomplish this, the CCP began to shift the wealth and ownership of private firms into state-owned firms. There is no doubt that the shift from privately owned companies to state-owned ones was initiated by the CCP out of both fear and greed.

The CCP feared with good reason that the merchant class would become powerful enough to challenge their authority. Indeed, that is exactly what the Tiananmen Square protests were all about. Again, with an opposition party recently allowed in Taiwan, and the USSR being brought to its knees by reform and openness, the CCP made a conscious decision to regain control of the economy and the political culture of the country in no uncertain terms.

The greed aspect was simple as well. The CCP has always been about power and self-enrichment, and these two objectives were accomplished through the decades by wholesale violence and unlimited corruption. By absorbing the wealthy, privately owned firms, the CCP was able to maintain its grip on power while stripping the value from the firms and award it to themselves. That policy has been successful beyond the CCP's wildest dreams. The leaders of the Party are all enormously wealthy, with many having gained personal fortunes in excess of several billions of dollars.[3]

Of course, the Beijing Model doesn't work for everyone. It certainly doesn't work for those whose wealth and livelihoods have been stripped from them by the state. Nor has it worked for those hundreds of millions of Chinese in the lower class, who the *Hukuo* system keeps impoverished for life because upward mobility is not a possibility. In fact, for the Beijing Model to work at all, one must have connections to the Party to gain the spoils. This builds resentment toward the privilege of China's politically elite families who are absorbing the bulk of the wealth in the country, which has created great problems of instability for the Communist Party that grow more dangerous every day.

Consequently, one big problem of the Beijing Model is the growing income gap throughout China. With a growing economy, you would expect to see a growing middle class in China. That is what occurred rapidly from 1979 to 1989, and even for the 15 years after that, but that is not what is happening today. Since about 2005, domestic consumption has been falling. In its place has been the growing absorption of the economy by the state and state-owned enterprises, which resulted in a rapidly growing income inequality gap between a thin layer at the top and an expanding lower class whose property and wealth are stolen through inflation and state confiscation.[4]

This process of impoverishment of the middle class has approached an astonishing velocity of late and is responsible for the shrinking middle class—and the rising instability it is bringing to China—that we talked about in Chapter 2. In fact, the wealth gap in China has proceeded at an astonishing pace: "The income gap in urban China has widened more than in any other country in Asia over the past 20 years, according to the International Monetary Fund."[5]

The Beijing Model is simply a way or a process for the CCP to cannibalize the nation's assets to enrich themselves, pay off their co-conspirators like the People's Liberation Army (PLA), keep the Party cadre satisfied and in line, as well as diminish the power and steal the wealth of the private sector. Of course, as that shift from private ownership to state ownership has progressed, profitability has shrunk and corruption has expanded. This is another reason why the GDP statistics are virtually worthless.

It might be wise to recall that similar fairy-tale statistics were the hallmark of the old Soviet Union, before it collapsed in upon itself. Similar statistical whoppers are told in the form of returns on equity of Chinese state-owned firms. On the surface, they seem to be outperforming private ones, but when scrutinized, are not doing well at all. State-owned firms lag far behind their privately owned peers, yielding negative returns of 1.47 percent from 2001 to 2009, in effect destroying wealth while capturing greater shares of the market and capital resources.[6]

Thus, the Beijing Model isn't really a model at all—at least, not in any useful sense of the word. It is, as noted earlier, *cannibal capitalism*, a one-way path to oblivion and certainly not something to be copied or emulated by other countries if they want to have a sustainable economy for longer than, say, 25 years. And even that time frame is probably no longer realistic.

Authoritarian Political Structure

The Beijing Model is commonly referred to as *state capitalism* for a reason. The Chinese Communist Party runs the Chinese economy through heavy state intervention, even though it is, for the most part, running it into the ground. This is a key point to bear in mind in order to understand the thinking of the CCP and the reason for the Beijing Model.

The name *Beijing Model* itself is a bit of propaganda for the CCP. After all, in 1979, they were worried about mass revolt in China from 30 years of grinding poverty and catastrophe brought about by the CCP. But today it's a different story—at least for a little while longer.

The term Beijing Model is meant to underscore the abilities and wisdom of the geniuses in Beijing who occupy the highest seats in the CCP. And, as noted previously, it is likewise useful for the justification of the CCP's intervention in the economy in order to obtain *the highest level of development*. There is just one slight problem. There really is no Beijing Model; it means different things to different people within China and around the world:

> "Is there a China model?" was the theme of a round-table meeting of about a dozen academics, journalists and foreign-policy experts, convened in February near Paris by the Glasshouse Forum, a think-tank set up to conduct critical analysis of capitalism. To pose the question is in part to answer it. Like Tinkerbell in "Peter Pan," the model exists merely by dint of people believing it does.[7]

But regardless of reality, the CCP has laid claim to a new capitalism as the way to go forward in the future. It may be akin to the British boast that "America may have invented rock and roll but the British perfected it," only it rings much less true. Nonetheless, as the CCP pushes the Beijing Model boast throughout China to support its claim to legitimacy, and with strict censorship and continuous anti-American rhetoric emanating from the government, who's to argue with them? Certainly no one in China—except the hundreds of thousands of protesters who now plague the CCP on an almost daily basis.

China talks a similar game throughout Asia and to the world at large as it wags its finger, informing us that the Beijing Model is the model that all nations should adopt, particularly the West. Its admirers, like Wei–Wei

Zhang of Fudan University in Shanghai, smugly predict that the Beijing Model will replace the West's liberal democratic capitalist model:

> China had the capacity to learn from the West, but the West does not have the capacity to learn. We need new thinking, and China can humbly offer some wisdom.[8]

China has learned much from the West in terms of technological know-how, but has adopted very little with regard to market economies. It has broken basic economic laws because the primary goal of the Chinese leadership is not development for its own sake, but for the sake of keeping power. Thus, the CCP only truly cares about appearances, not market economics *per se*. It uses the market like it uses its people and its natural resources, with inherent disdain and gross disrespect. But, like any essential natural or economic law, when it is broken often enough and long enough, the law eventually catches up—and breaks the offender.

The Beijing Model, however, is also a calling card for China's regional foreign policy, a mantle of economic primacy and one to be emulated. China supports other hardline, authoritarian regimes in the area like North Korea, and at the same time is viewed by some as a true alternative to the sometimes clumsy and contentious U.S. model of open market and open democratic societies. (The irony here is that despite the unparalleled wealth that market capitalism has brought the United States, a cluster of ideological zealots at the highest level of power has succeeded in moving the country more toward a state-managed economy in the past decade, to the great misfortune of the country.) The Beijing Model, even as a non-entity, gives legitimacy to every authoritarian urge from statist, power-hungry monsters like the late Hugo Chavez in Venezuela to crypto-fascists like Vladimir Putin in Russia.

In whatever way one might wish to regard them, China's statist organs of authority and oppression are what have *created* the Beijing Model and its destructive distortions. Like Chairman Mao before it, the Beijing Model, or more to the point, the CCP, is hailed as China's savior, having lifted the country from poverty into great power status. It is true that capitalist cooperation with the West has done all of the above, but it is hardly true that this is due to the exercise of authoritarian power over the economy by the CCP; rather, it is *in spite* of that exercise of power.

The Chinese leadership would have the people—and the world—believe that they possess a new insight into market capital economics as well as special knowledge with regard to the peculiarities of China. They also seek and demand full credit for bringing China into the modern era. All of this, of course, is absurd.

Does China have economic experts trained at the best universities in the world? Yes, it does. But when sound economic policies challenge the political power of the CCP, it is a sure bet that the CCP does not lose the argument. This was clearly defined by the Tiananmen Square massacre, and is abundantly evident in the abuse and corruption of the financial and legal systems throughout China today. It seems apparent that political advantage and personal gain trump economic laws whenever necessary.

That is not to say that some wise decisions are not made by the CCP, because there certainly are from time to time. Nor does this mean that there do not exist some advantages to ruling an economy by fiat, because there are some definite advantages there as well. For example, because there are no labor unions, electorates, or courts to obstruct policy, economic decisions and policies can be implemented or changed quickly as needed. Or, if there are changes in the marketplace, a reallocation of resources, regardless of cost, can be ordered and carried much more quickly in some cases, where market forces have little ability to indicate that a change may be needed.

Of course, the ability to make quick changes in policy does not mean that the right decisions will be made. Furthermore, this kind of power also lends itself to grand abuses on a scale possible only in the all-encompassing power of an entrenched Communist Party. Authoritarian rule of the CCP is *a necessity* for the Beijing Model as it is run today, and nearly vice versa. Remember—as the CCP saw—that with the liberalization of the country in the 1980s came a loss of Party prestige and a restless population full of hope and expectation for democracy; neither of those outcomes were tolerable then and they are not tolerable today. The biggest flaw or weakness in the CCP is its intolerance for openness, which, therefore, also means an inability to adapt to the needs of its own economy. Indeed, as the economy begins to fall in upon itself, the government will turn to more oppression and theft in order to maintain its wealth and power.

Culture of Corruption

The Beijing Model certainly did not invent corruption in China, but corruption is certainly a central part of the Chinese command economy and the Beijing Model, especially post-1989, when the state took a much greater hand in the economy. Because there is such uneven enforcement of laws and contracts and a very murky legal and justice system throughout China, there is very little long-term risk planning in the economy. This means that few if any small businesses are willing or able to invest in or take risks for long-term endeavors.

As noted earlier, in the Chinese command economy, major economic decisions are made by Party bureaucrats at the state level according to reporting criteria by political leaders and authorities down the food chain. Because of this, China's command economy has always been plagued by inefficiencies, shortages, and overages, which are partially caused and addressed by fraud, graft, and corruption. Therefore, corruption in China is not a sometime proposition, but rather, it is a chronic condition and necessity.

At the government level and in industry, bribery and fraud are how people stay alive and get what they want and need. As China expert Jeremy Hurewitz observed, "You cannot be in the government in China without being corrupt. You'll starve." Again, in command economies, where the market forces of supply and demand and the price mechanism are not used well, if at all, graft and bribery can realistically be viewed as a kind of "shadow price mechanism" to get goods and services where they need to go.

This is especially relevant when the state is scooping up profitable, privately owned businesses whenever it feels like it. Today, the commercial and political classes in China are in a period of wealth accumulation under the general assumption of "get it while you can." There is the underlying understanding among many Chinese that what corruption has built is certainly not built to last, but curiously, at the same time, many are anxious for China to ascend to its "rightful place in the world." The culture of corruption engenders short term-oriented thinking; the business culture that has emerged is one built upon graft and immediate gratification rather than trust in the system itself over the long term.

This attitude is seen at the highest levels of government, and it doesn't bode well for China's future. CCP members now routinely are moving hundreds of millions—if not billions—of dollars overseas, into "safe havens" such as the United States and Europe. That includes not just the recently disgraced and purged former CCP leader Bo Xilai (who had transferred $6 billion out of China) but also *all of the CCP leadership.*

Isn't that interesting? China's elite and ruling class are transferring billions of dollars out of their own country. Why would Party members—*those who rule China*—be moving what amount to kings' fortunes outside of their own country, which is purportedly the greatest, most successful economic story for the twenty-first century? Remember, we are talking about China here, the world's example of how to become rich in a few short years, and the next superpower to dominate the planet. That the Chinese leadership is hedging their bets against their own country is hardly a stout endorsement of the Beijing Model or of China's future, is it? And they would know, wouldn't they? By mid-2012, cash outflows from China had reached all-time highs, even as Europe and the United States continue to struggle with their own economies. There is no reason to expect this to abate, either. Some estimates put the money outflows at $1.05 trillion in 2011 and 2012—some of it legal, but much of it not.

But it's not just the political elite who can see the writing on the wall. Ultra-wealthy business people are also moving billions of dollars out of China, as are even the moderately wealthy. Again, why would this be? For one simple reason: They know that China's future is not what the world thinks it is. The fact is, hundreds of billions of dollars, if not trillions, are leaving China. The Chinese government is fearful of the outflows being contagious and leading to greater, and more dangerous, levels of instability and turmoil in China than those that already exist.[9]

Mr. Shi (a rich writer) is considering emigrating to the United States—one of a growing number of rich Chinese either contemplating leaving their homeland or already arranging to do it. "Things are real there," says Mr. Shi, who has been trying to learn English by listening to language CDs in his car. He goes on:

> Here you don't know what to believe. . . . The elite exodus (from China) is a potentially troubling development for Party leaders, many of whose relatives have long since chosen to live or study overseas. . . . (W)hile the party touts the economic

success of the "Chinese model," many of its poster children are heading for the exits. They are in search of things money can't buy in China: cleaner air, safer food, better education for their children. Some also express concern about government corruption and the safety of their assets.[10]

Of the roughly 1 million millionaires in China, an inordinate amount of them want to leave rather quickly:

> Among the small proportion of Chinese who have the means to do so, many have already taken the plunge and many more are making plans. A study issued jointly last October by the Bank of China and the Hurun Report, a wealth-research firm, found that among survey subjects with assets worth at least 10m yuan ($1.6m), *14% had already emigrated or started on the paperwork.* An additional 46% said they were considering it. In March, a Beijing newspaper said that the study *probably underestimated the flight of Chinese wealth.* Foreigners in China—to flee or not to flee?[11]

The simple fact is that insiders always know more about the conditions in their country than outsiders do, and the trend of large amounts of cash and the elite of Chinese society leaving China tells a story that has yet to be heard or understood by most observers: China's fantastic economic run is coming to an end and the time to abandon ship has arrived.

Of course, defenders of China will say that fraud and corruption in any economy are a fact of life. This is certainly true, but as noted earlier, it's the *degree of corruption* that matters. In China's case, like the late Soviet Union, fraud and corruption run throughout its edifice and have permeated the entire Chinese culture. It is a very sad fact that fraud and corruption are, without question, an integral part of Chinese social norms. That is why Wen Jibao, former premier of China, lamented the morality crisis in China:

> By highlighting cultural reform at the end of its annual plenum last week, China's ruling Communist Party both drew attention to the country's moral crisis and demonstrated its own ideological bankruptcy.[12]

The world may know that China faces a moral crisis but it may not realize how serious the problem really is. The morality crisis has not been caused entirely by the corruption of the Chinese Communist Party, but the degree to which it afflicts all strata of society is a direct result of the corrupt ways in which their policies have hardened Chinese society. This is a systemic crisis that is growing worse, not better, as China grows more powerful.

Not only are religious minorities persecuted and slaughtered for their beliefs, but also their organs are harvested—often while still alive—for a bustling human organ smuggling industry that thrives in China today. It has even been credibly asserted that the Bo Xilai incident may well have happened not because of his political corruptions, but because his political rivals in the CCP knew not only that he and his wife were involved in the murder of British businessman Nick Heywood, but they also suspected that he and his wife were deeply involved in human organ trafficking.[13]

Thus, the examples of cheating, fraud, theft, abuse of innocent children, persecution of religious minorities, forced abortions, and a host of other deep moral failings occurring on a daily basis in Chinese society are endless. The CCP has led the country by example, and the grotesque abuse of China by the CCP has resulted in a similar treatment of the Chinese people at the hands of their own leaders.

Of course, that is not to say that China's economy doesn't function at all in the midst of its morality crisis and corruption; it does with the assistance of foreign investment, but which economic sector, or even which company, gets which goods and at what price are all determined at the government level, more often than not from a political rather than a market context. Who gets what in China really depends upon the strength of one's relationship with the authorities and the level of bribery one can bring to the best-positioned government authority. This starts at the bottom and goes all the way—*all the way*—to the top echelons of power on an unbelievable scale of ambition:

> The range of frauds is both impressive and ominous: Chinese-made fakes have included everything from Apple stores and police stations to foreign banks and high-tech components used in U.S. military gear. Another extreme practice that has developed

is the hiring [of] substitutes to bear criminal punishment for the offenses of others—something that has been suspected, though not proven, in the recent trial of the wife of fallen Communist Party leader Bo Xilai.[14]

With fraud and corruption such a major part of Chinese life, the carryover into GDP statistics is not only a certainty, but it should call into question the viability of China's claims for real, organic economic growth. Whatever numbers are given, whatever statistics are paraded forth by the Chinese government, it is vitally important to understand the motivations behind the numbers, rather than to be taken in by the numbers themselves.

> Doubts about the reliability of China's GDP data do not come from nowhere. In 1998, with the Asian financial crisis in full swing and China's neighbors Thailand, Korea, and Indonesia sliding into economic chaos, the National Bureau of Statistics (NBS) boldly proclaimed that China's growth was bowed but unbroken at 7.8 percent year on year, little changed from 9.3 percent in 1997.
>
> That number is wildly at odds with evidence of much slower growth from output of cement and electricity, imports and airline passenger numbers—all data series that should closely track GDP. Some independent economists have concluded that growth for the year was probably close to zero. . . . Calculations by Professor Harry Wu, an expert on accounting GDP calculations for China's growth, suggest that GDP growth in 1998 fell to −0.1 percent year on year.[15]

As Li Keqiang, then head of the Communist Party in the northeastern Liaoning province, was quoted as saying in diplomatic documents leaked by WikiLeaks, "Those numbers (GDP statistics) are not real; they're for reference only."[16] He is dead right.

But the extent of corruption levels goes even further than that. On any given morning, a Western CEO may visit a company factory in China and find that the gates are locked, that the factory has been taken over by their joint venture partner, and that all capital equipment, technological techniques, intellectual property, and market customers are now the exclusive property of the Chinese joint venture firm. China now steals whole factories from Western companies, without legal recourse. They are grabbing from the West what they can, while they can.

This is not a rare occurrence in China, but a growing epidemic, as pointed out by House Subcommittee Chairman Don Manzullo (R-IL):

> There is a growing number of similar trade cases involving American companies. I see China going backwards. I have never seen so many complaints over outrageous stealing of intellectual property and making folly over the rule of law. It is seizing entire U.S. companies without due process or recourse.[17]

Even big multinational corporations are not safe from wholesale theft of intellectual and technological property at the hands of their Chinese *partners*. The Volkswagen situation referenced previously is a prime example, but there are thousands of others.

In China's business culture, fraudulent representations know no limits. This includes Chinese companies of any kind, even those listed on the New York Stock Exchange. With the deep complicity of Chinese state-owned banks, they have been able to reap billions of dollars from investors in the United States and around the world by providing false revenues and false cash balances, thereby creating a mirage of value and stability, which only upon close inspection is found to be nonexistent. As John Hempton, the chief investment officer of Bronte Capital, an Australian hedge fund, said in a 2011 article in the *New York Times*:

> This means the Chinese banks were in on the fraud, at least at branch level. . . . This is no longer a story about Longtop, and it is not a story about Deloitte. . . . Given the centrality of Chinese banks to the global economy, it's a story much bigger than Deloitte or Longtop. . . .
>
> The audacity of these frauds (Chinese CEOs and banks providing auditors with false numbers), as well as the efforts to intimidate auditors, stand out. If investors such as Goldman Sachs and Hank Greenberg cannot fend for themselves, something more needs to be done if Chinese companies are to continue to trade in American markets.[18]

The coming China crises won't just leave China in a world of hurt; they will also cause the stock values of Chinese companies anywhere in the world to sink like a stone. Hundreds of billions of American investors' dollars will be lost in the United States alone, with Europe, Japan, and other trading partners greatly affected as well.[19] The culture of corruption, of cheating and taking shortcuts regardless of who or how many people it hurts, has reached unimaginable levels in China. But that is not the only consequence. The number of inferior, low-quality products that China produces threatens the well-being of millions of people around the world every day.

Take the construction industry, for example. Inferior steel manufacturing techniques are rendering buildings, bridges, and other infrastructure unsafe in China and in the United States and Canada as well. Bridges collapsing after only a few years into their lifespan are not uncommon in China and a recent train disaster caused rioting in China as people are fed up with the shoddy construction standards of state-owned firms, which cost the lives of the people when their products fail.[20]

But callous fraud and corruption are present throughout almost any product you can think of. Recent examples of toxic products coming out of China include:

1. Radioactive drywall containing phosphogypsum, a radioactive material that—among its other unpleasant effects—may put people at higher risk for lung cancer.
2. Toxic dog food containing melamine—a chemical that causes kidney failure—intentionally added to boost the appearance of protein in product tests. More than 4,000 Americans reported the death of a dog or cat due to the tainted food.
3. Dangerous sweets sold in America at many Asian markets contained deadly melamine. Formaldehyde was also found in the same brand of candy.
4. Toxic toothpaste containing diethylene glycol, an industrial chemical used in anti-freeze.
5. Dangerous ginger containing high levels of the pesticide aldicarb sulfoxide.
6. Carcinogenic fish found to contain traces of anti-fungal and antibiotic drugs known or suspected to cause cancer. Chinese fish farms,

many located in highly polluted waters, use the products to boost harvests.

7. Tainted toys containing lead paint which can harm brain development in children. Among the most notable were some of the immensely popular Thomas & Friends wooden train engines and cars.[21]

Lawlessness and brazen behavior have become the norm in China's trade relations, just as it is in every stratum of the economy and every part of its social structure. The behavior of its leaders and those with means is instructive, as it shows us that they see the world in a zero-sum context and know that deep trouble lies just ahead.

A good example of this is when China promised to get rid of rare earth export controls when it joined the World Trade Organization (WTO) way back in 2001. It gave in a little along the way, but in 2011 it returned to its initial posture. It has 30 percent of the world's supply but 90 percent of the world's exports. The WTO has ruled against China, but, over a decade later, China has yet to comply with the ruling.

Whether it is stealing U.S. firms' factories, building phony Apple stores, stonewalling on trade issues, ripping off U.S. technology, illegally burning DVDs, or poisoning children at home and abroad, theft and corruption are a way of life and business as usual for China.

State Control of Banks and Capital

The Chinese banking system is not like the United States or any other major developed nations. In China, the government owns all the banks and compels them to lend to state-owned businesses and local party governments regardless of the collateral involved—if any at all—or the performance or profitability of the business. Credit is not a function of the market or credit worthiness, but rather, is based upon Communist Party relationships. Qualifying for a loan in China is like getting invited to a nice dinner party in Beverly Hills; it's all about *who* you know.

Although state-owned banks are *not allowed* to lend to local governments directly, local governments cleverly formed *investment companies*: straw man firms set up to receive loans from the state-owned banks. This is a recipe, of course, for broad and deep abuses, as it causes and reinforces corruption on all sides of the deal. These investment companies have themselves been collateralized by land that has usually been seized illegally by local governments from farmers. This trick has contributed to artificially driving up land values to astronomical levels, which has allowed ever-larger loans to be made and received. As land values have risen, the loans against them have also gone up. This not only feeds a massive real estate bubble, but also sets up the Chinese economy for total financial system failure, the beginning of which we are seeing unfold today. The symptoms of financial system failure are many, but some of the main ones are noted in this section.

Domestic Debt Crisis.   China's debt crisis is directly related to China's state ownership of all banks and the real estate bubble, but it is also a result of the massive fraud and corruption in China between banks and state-owned enterprises and local governments.

But where did all that money go?

As noted previously, it has gone into all kinds of fake companies selling seized land at ultra-high prices, or into the stock of state-owned firms, artificially driving up the values of those companies, or into the pockets of the political class. This is not a mystery; it's just that not many really want to talk about it because the ending is not a happy one. But even China's former prime minister, Wen Jiabao admitted in 2009: "Structural problems are causing unsteady, unbalanced, uncoordinated, and unsustainable development."[22]

Those "structural problems" include but are not limited to the corrupt relationships between state-owned banks and state-owned firms. State-owned firms are a big part of it. *The Economist* observed that all but 3 of Mainland China's 42 global Fortune 500 firms are owned by the government. These firms receive large amounts of money with no accountability and earn no profits.[23]

The bottom line is that economists now see a tremendous domestic debt bomb waiting to explode in the faces of China's state-owned banks. A major default on domestic debt is inevitable and has already begun.

Is this any worse than the U.S. debt crisis?

Yes, because *the scale of China's debt crisis is so much larger*. Relative to total reported GDP, China's debt is more than twice the size of that of the United States. Estimates put it from 25 to 80 percent of China's GDP, which makes the U.S. debt problem seem somewhat less dire in comparison.

Triangular Debt. Like the false values in real estate, fraud and corruption abound in the financial sector across the spectrum of Chinese state-owned companies. Since all sides of the deal are corrupt, loan contracts are not enforced; they are just rolled over. This means that debts are not being retired or paid off by productive enterprises, but rather, bigger loans are issued to take out the current non-performing loans to shore up firms struggling to make a profit in a contracting domestic economy that has yet to be acknowledged as occurring.

This cycle runs between state-owned enterprises themselves, as one loans to another, and between state-owned banks and state-owned enterprises. Thus, Company A owes money to Company B, which owes money to Company C, which owes money to Company A, which has also borrowed money from Bank A and has rolled over that debt several times. Every firm owes money to the other, and as the economy continues to slow down, no firm is paying any other firm any money. The "solution," of course, is for these firms to get more loans—larger loans—and repeat the cycle. The astonishing part of this is that the Chinese government has no idea how much of a crisis triangular debt really is because, of course, no one tells the truth.[24]

Land and other collateral and business values are inflated not only to show that profit or production goals have been met, but also to line the pockets of officials and corporate officers. False reporting, waste, and fraud are rampant in China and have caused the real estate bubble that is now collapsing. But government bankers, municipal authorities, and state-owned firms got very, very rich. Today, China faces an avalanche of bad debt that it is trying to hide, misplace, and otherwise wish away.

Triangular debt is not only unsustainable, but its collapse will be felt throughout the entire Chinese financial system.

Zombie Corporations. Closely related to triangular debt is the emergence of "zombie corporations." China is creating these zombie companies as the economy continues to slow and banks are compelled to continue funding failing businesses. Andy Xie, independent economist and Morgan Stanley's former chief Asia-Pacific economist, warns:

> The Chinese banking system doesn't pull money out of businesses that are failing. A lot of businesses in China are going to be zombies. . . . This is an Asian thing because they (banks) don't enforce credit agreements.

The trend could become more pronounced as the country's slowdown sends ripples across the corporate sector. Already, the current earnings season is shaping up to be arguably the worst in history, with major firms in sectors ranging from banks to airlines posting double-digit profit declines. . . . (The) zombie phenomenon is especially prevalent in the real estate and financial sectors, where local governments have been known to actively lend financial support.

While putting companies on life support can preempt disruptive bankruptcies, Xie says it comes at the expense of economic stagnation. In a bid to counter slowing growth, Xie says local governments across China are pressuring lenders to keep businesses funded, regardless of profitability, perpetuating the so-called "zombie firms." These are companies which are on the brink, but continue to operate with state support.[25]

As more of China's profitable private companies are taken over by the state, the proliferation of fraud and zombie firms is rapidly expanding. With the full political backing of the state and the privilege that comes with such support, there is no effective regulatory body to spot the zombie firms or to correct the problem.

Again, only with state-owned banks that can print money at will and compel banks to lend for whatever reason can such zombie firms come about and continue to stay *in business*. But the question is, for how long?

Real Estate Bubble.   Like the real estate bubble in the United States and in Europe, China's has come about through its addiction to excessively easy money policies or *stimulus* infusion of liquidity into its economy. In the West, it was lax or nonexistent loan qualifying standards, but in China, state-owned enterprises and local authorities colluded to confiscate farmland from peasants, drive up the land values, and then reap the fantastic profits that real estate speculation brings as values skyrocket from artificially induced demand. Real estate development also served the dire political need to maintain employment. China's employment need is such that domestic real estate development is one of the few forms of economic demand that it can, at least in theory, control through its own financial policies and not through relying on foreign trading partners.

But this charade has not gone unnoticed. Noted hedge fund manager Jim Chanos, who alerted Wall Street to Enron's flawed model, and Harvard University's Kenneth Rogoff both warn of a crash in China:

> China is "on a treadmill to hell" because it's hooked on property development for driving growth, Chanos said in. As much as 60 percent of the country's gross domestic product relies on construction, he said. Rogoff said in February a debt-fueled bubble in China may trigger a regional recession within a decade.[26]

The Euro Crisis has perhaps taken attention away from that reality, but it is there nonetheless, and as it worsens in China, it will have an enormously negative impact upon the rest of the world.

Analysts for *Foreign Affairs*, are saying the same thing, and worse:

> For years analysts have warned of a looming real estate bubble in China, but the predicted downturn, the bursting of that bubble, never occurred—that is, until now. In a telling scene two months ago, Shanghai property developers started slashing prices on their latest luxury condos by up to one-third. Crowds of owners who had recently bought apartments at full price converged on sales offices throughout the city, demanding refunds. Some angry investors went on a rampage, breaking windows and smashing showrooms.
>
> Shanghai homeowners are hardly the only ones getting nervous. Sudden, steep price reductions are upending real estate markets across China. According to the property agency Homelink, new home prices in Beijing dropped 35 percent in November alone. And the free fall may continue for some time.

Centaline, another leading property agency, estimates that developers have built up 22 months' worth of unsold inventory in Beijing and 21 months' worth in Shanghai. Everyone from local landowners to Chinese speculators and international investors are now worrying that these discounts indicate that "the biggest bubble of the century," as *it was called earlier this year*, has just popped, with serious consequences not only for one of the world's most promising economies—but internationally as well.

What makes the future look particularly bleak is the lack of escape routes. If Chinese investors panic and rush for the exits, they will discover that in a market awash with developer discounts, buyers are very hard to find . . . Instead of developing a more balanced, consumer-based economy, an entire regime of Beijing technocrats—drunk on investment-led growth—let the real estate market run red hot for too long and, when forced to act, lacked the credibility to cool the sector down. That failure threatens to undermine the country's continued economic rise.[27]

Even Ge Zhaoquiang, senior researcher at China Merchant Bank, recently warned of ". . . serious risk of an economic downturn unprecedented in the past 30 years with possibly damaging consequences for China's social and political stability."[28]

Japan is watching China's economy very closely and sees similar dangers, as well:

Even as China promises to maintain a "firm grip" on real estate, many are still concerned about a property bubble and hard-landing, in terms of a slowdown and financial crisis.

At a speech delivered in Sydney, Kiyohiko G. Nishimura, deputy governor of the Bank of Japan said China is now "entering the danger zone" that could lead to a financial crisis.

Looking back at Japan's experience in the 1990s, and the American experience in the 2000s, that triggered "malign" as opposed to benign bubbles and led to financial crises, Nishimura says: "it is clear that not every bubble-bust episode leads to a financial crisis. However, if a demographic change, a property price bubble, and a steep increase in loans coincide, then a financial crisis seems more likely. And China is now entering the 'danger zone'."[29]

With property prices grossly inflated, Chinese demographic changes afoot, and seemingly *endless* lending cycles finally beginning to come to an end, the bubble is bursting. Many real estate offices have closed due to low demand and falling prices. These are all factors that indicate a serious crash is imminent.

Foreign Investment, Foreign Demand, and Cheap Labor

A fundamental and irreplaceable factor in the Beijing Model is its dependence upon massive foreign investment to drive its economic development. For 30 years, the Western nations invested hundreds of billions of dollars —if not trillions—into China, building factories, supply lines, and transferring technological know-how to China, effectively leading to the creation of the China we see today. The broken, hungry, and backward bicycle kingdom China of 1979 is the China that the CCP created. The wealthy, developed China of today is the one created by the financial and technological assistance of the West.[30] Without it seeking help from the West, China would never have developed as it has. Rather, it would have remained what it truly was under the autarkic communist rule of Mao: North Korea on a gargantuan scale.

The problem with foreign investment and the Beijing Model is that without continually growing foreign investment in China, there is no Beijing Model. With the world's major economies slipping in and out of recessions—and looking more like *in* than *out* for the foreseeable future—direct foreign investment in China is falling and will continue to fall.

Closely related to China's main foreign investors dropping off are the shrinking foreign markets for Chinese goods. Again, the Eurozone is China's largest trading partner, and with the Euro Crisis dragging on without a clear or permanent resolution—one that doesn't result in falling demand for Chinese goods or any other imports—Eurozone demand continues to fall. The effects of falling demand are clearly evident in the unclaimed shipments of iron ore and copper that are piling up on the docks in Shanghai, in granaries, in car parks, and elsewhere.[31]

Also, major mining companies have scaled back production based on falling demand from their main customer, China.

> This week, the world's biggest miner, BHP Billiton (BHP.AX) (BLT.L), said it was putting on hold a China-centric plan to spend $80 billion over the next five years to expand its iron ore, coal, energy and base metals divisions.
>
> The slowdown has hit hard some of the small and medium-sized manufacturers and traders who form the bulk of China's metals business. Some steel traders have committed suicide and owners of faltering factories have skipped town to escape creditors, according to local media reports over the past year.[32]

A key point to bear in mind with regard to falling foreign investment and demand for Chinese products is the changing nature of the global financial system itself. The entire world has run on a credit-based economy in one way or another since the end of World War II, and the pace of debt expansion among the developed nations of the world really picked up in the mid-1960s, and continued to dramatically increase going forward. Credit-based U.S. and Eurozone economies were sustainable while global economic growth was reasonable and sustainable. U.S. debt was rolled over year after year, as demand for American bonds steadily rose. Another factor was the developed economies continuing to create wealth with their economic activity and concurrent debt levels remaining well below the threshold of their respective GDPs. There are other factors related to this as well, but for this discussion, it is enough to say that the world has run on a credit-based system for over 60 years.

But since the Financial Crisis of 2008, that credit-based assumption has been shaken, and by 2012, after several rounds of easing in the United States, Europe, and China, economic growth had become less attainable or sustainable in the face of a continued fall in demand and the specter of crushing debt service on ever larger amounts of borrowed money. This means continued falling demand as incomes fall in the Eurozone, the United States, and in China, and as credit becomes tight and stays relatively tight (even as the People's Bank of China provides more stimulus) while interest payments on debts consume greater proportions of nations' wealth.

As direct foreign investment in China continues to shrink, China will need to find a replacement in order to keep the economy running. So far, the People's Bank of China (PBOC) has been filling that role by lending money to whomever has the right connections, driving up land prices, creating greater levels of debt without real repayment schedules, only rolling over debt into greater debt, as discussed in the debt crisis section of this chapter, and creating false demand in a shrinking domestic market on an unprecedented scale. Such over-lending in the face of shrinking domestic demand is less useful or effective than before because it drives prices higher, further shrinking domestic demand.

The consequences of falling domestic and foreign demand and falling direct foreign investment in China are crystal clear: The money flows that helped China expand into its current state as a warped, bloated economic behemoth are rapidly slowing down; the Chinese government has its hands full trying to keep demand—and employment—at levels that will not trigger revolt. But falling demand for Chinese goods is not just a function of the financial crises we are living through; there are other reasons, as well.

One advantage that China once had that now is going away is its relatively cheap cost of labor. As its middle class has emerged, labor costs in China have risen steeply, diminishing China's cheap labor advantage over the West.

(T)he era of cheap China may be drawing to a close. . . . Costs are soaring, starting in the coastal provinces where factories have historically clustered. Increases in land prices, environmental and safety regulations and taxes all play a part. The biggest factor, though, is labour. On March 5th Standard Chartered, an investment bank, released a survey of over 200 Hong Kong-based manufacturers operating in the Pearl River Delta. It found that wages have already risen by 10% this year. Foxconn, a Taiwanese contract manufacturer that makes Apple's iPads (and much more besides) in Shenzhen, put up salaries by 16–25% last month.

"It's not cheap like it used to be," laments Dale Weathington of Kolcraft, an American firm that uses contract manufacturers to make prams in southern China. Labour costs have surged by 20% a year for the past four years." Joerg Wuttke, a veteran

industrialist with the EU Chamber of Commerce in China, predicts that the cost to manufacture in China could soar twofold
or even threefold by 2020. AlixPartners, a consultancy, offers this
intriguing extrapolation: if China's currency and shipping costs
were to rise by 5% annually and wages were to go up by 30% a
year, by 2015 it would be just as cheap to make things in North
America as to make them in China and ship them there.[33]

There are those who think that even with rising labor costs, China
will still remain the world's greatest manufacturing center, citing its supply lines, improving per capita productivity, and flexibility. It's true that
China can muster thousands of workers out of their dormitories at mid-
night to answer demand for the latest version of the iPhone, but that
advantage won't offset rising labor costs, rising social demands for better
treatment of workers, higher taxes, demands for pensions, health care,
and other costly social safety nets that are rare in China today.

Nor will China's ability to keep its labor force captive like beasts of
burden last forever. How ironic is it that a society allegedly built upon
protecting the working class can roust thousands out of bed and force
them to work through the night? As noted earlier in this book, social
unrest and political instability are added risks that will drive up the costs
of doing business in China more rapidly than they are already rising.
In fact, many firms, seeing that trend already coming into play, are now
looking outside of China to build factories. Some U.S. firms are even
returning home to *reshore* their manufacturing base in the United States
where labor costs are comparable, shipping costs are minor, and where
productivity, quality control, and predictability is better.

A combination of economic forces is fast eroding China's
cost advantage as an export platform for the North American
market," says Boston Consulting Group in a report issued last
summer, which forecast that by sometime around 2015, it will
be as economical to manufacture many goods for U.S. consumption in the United States as in China. BCG points to seven
industries that are nearing that break-even point: electronics,
appliances, machinery, transportation goods, fabricated metals,
furniture, and plastics and rubber—all products with relatively
low labor content and high transportation costs.[34]

China's State Council affirmed in 2010 that rising labor costs were becoming an issue for China's economy, as well as affirming many other rising problems:

> Foreign companies have increasingly felt unwelcome in China because of what they believe are discriminatory government policies, inconsistent enforcement of laws and increased protectionism restricting foreign investment in certain sectors. Also, rising labor and logistics costs, lack of available land and surmounting levels of pollution in Eastern China have prompted regulators to create rules to further optimize foreign investments.[35]

Low and False Domestic Demand

A self-sustaining economy is certainly a requirement for any would-be superpower, and that means an economy with a domestic market strong enough to provide demand for its industries. For instance, as a country grows wealthier, domestic consumption should rise as a percentage of GDP. In China, this has occurred, but it has also reversed course the past seven years. China's Beijing Model has been fueled largely by ever-larger amounts of foreign investment into China for the past 30 years. But over-reliance on foreign investment has badly warped China's economy. Demand has slowed to 2008 levels as China's main investors in the Eurozone and the United States cut their investment levels. In the past five years alone, overall domestic consumption as a percentage of GDP in China has dropped by 20 percent or more—falling from 55 percent in the early 1980s to 34 percent in 2011—even though labor costs have doubled, or more, in the same period.[36]

But what about that middle class that has emerged in China? Is it not large enough to raise domestic demand? After all, many of the world's millionaires and billionaires, not to mention a big chunk of the world's luxury spending, are all in China. Will China's middle class rescue the economy?

Not likely. China, as noted earlier, has more wealth going to the top of Chinese society—the political elite—and more Chinese are becoming impoverished. *The middle class is growing in number, but also growing poorer.* Thus, domestic consumption falls along with the falling fortunes of the middle class. China can only run its economy this way for a limited period of time; and that time is running out. As the era of seemingly "unlimited" foreign investment and cheap labor comes to an end in China, as noted above, China will try to make up its own demand with loose money policies to support domestic demand and keep employment stable.

We have already talked about the way Chinese firms do not pay back loans, but rather, the loans are just rolled over. But how is China creating its own "false economic demand" in real estate if prices and incomes are both falling? Part of the answer is in the financing and building of vast construction and infrastructure projects. Many are not necessary, and others are simply unaffordable to most Chinese. Thus, much of China's domestic demand is based on projects that nobody uses or can afford. An example of this is the hundreds of "ghost cities" that now have been and continue to be built in China. These ghost cities are complete urban areas with high-rise office buildings, condominiums, luxury mega shopping malls, parks, rail systems, and utilities.

These ghost cities are called such because they are empty—with few if any people living in them—and can be found all over China. These ghost cities are financed by excess Chinese liquidity, factored into calculations for GDP, employment and natural resource needs, and are symptomatic of how distorted the Chinese economy really is. In fact, there are around 64 million vacant luxury apartments in China right now. For the sake of scale, that's twice the total number of apartments in all of Britain. At the same time, tens of millions of Chinese workers live in slums, 10 to a room, and work 10 hours a day, 6 days a week for slave wages.

This is what is happening today, and will continue to happen going forward, until, at some point, when the bubble economy can no longer sustain itself, the Beijing Model will meet its end. The aftereffects will be quite bad for China. Factories will close. Massive layoffs will occur. Civil unrest will rise among the hundreds of millions of Chinese factory workers throughout the country.

These conditions will only worsen with China's economic slowdown. But as economic conditions in China worsen, shouldn't this make China weaker? Yes, it should and it is. If desperate actions are a sign of desperation, then the great theft that the CCP is perpetrating upon the people of China, sucking wealth from the people and then sending it out of the country, can be easily described as an act of desperation. Those at the top who are moving billions of dollars overseas understand that the whole system is failing.

That's also the reason why China grows more lawless in its relations with foreign firms, brazenly stealing their technologies. Weakness begets recklessness. Such weakness explains why China now steals whole factories from Western companies, without legal recourse. They are grabbing from their people and from the West what they can, while they can, before their economy, based upon the Beijing Model, self-terminates.

One Child Policy

China's One Child policy was implemented in 1979, the same year as the Open Door Policy, as a means of slowing the population growth rate to allow China to develop with the help of the West. This policy has helped China in some ways, but has had devastating impacts in others.

Culturally, since boys are preferred over girls in China, infanticide rates jumped in the aftermath of the One Child Policy. This has not only led to a coarsened view of human life as abortions of females have been widespread, but it has also been enforced with the typical brutality of the CCP. Those women without birthing permits are often forced by the state to abort their babies and fined for breaking the law. In 2007, for example, state enforcers apparently took sledgehammers to several dozen towns and threatened to break holes in the homes of people who had too many children or had not paid fines for the offense. Not surprisingly, riots broke out, government buildings were burned, and some fatalities may have even occurred as a response to the state exercising its "legitimate control" over the people. This also includes forced sterilizations by government doctors and forced examinations of women to determine if they are pregnant, which has resulted in elevated rates of suicides among women who are forced to abort their children.[37]

The One Child policy has had other negative impacts, as well, such as a huge gender imbalance. This not only means that many Chinese men will go through life unmarried, but that, as noted in Chapter 3, there will not be enough workers to support the workers entering retirement now through the next few decades. The net result is a retirement crisis added on to the current $2.3 trillion pension crisis because of the shortsighted population control policy.

There is also the impact that a generation of single children will have on shaping Chinese society's norms going forward. Because there are fewer women to marry, China is seeing an increase in the importation of prostitutes, which of course does little to promote healthy family values in Chinese society. On the other hand, neither do forced abortions or infanticide.

Another impact is in social behavior of children without siblings. Some sociological studies indicate that only children often lack the social networking skills, sharing, and empathy for others that children with siblings normally develop in the multiple child family setting. An only child is necessarily very coddled and protected by the family, which may translate into the *little emperor syndrome*, a sense of entitlement in the children of the One Child policy.

This has implications for a Chinese society that values narcissism over the welfare of others, and may indeed be already reflected in Chinese society today. (See China's Morality Crisis, previously discussed.) To be fair, other sociologists counter that argument with the socialization that children receive in school from kindergarten onward in China being sufficient to their proper social development.[38]

There is no question that with the gender imbalance of 120 boys born to every 100 girls, and the changed nature of child rearing due to the One Child policy, behavioral and perceptual changes may well be a part of the social makeup of Chinese below the age of 30. Furthermore, the pressures of not only providing for their own immediate family's welfare, but quite possibly the well-being of two sets of parents in their declining years are also formidable burdens for the One Child policy generation. This is especially true today, as the Chinese economy contracts and the middle class and domestic consumption rates fall. Providing for two generations will be a challenge, to say the least.

Like the other facets of the Beijing Model, the One Child policy has created more problems than it has solved, and like the other policies of the CCP, it has left the Chinese economy distorted beyond easy repair. China's child limits essentially gave it one generation to get rich before it gets old, and the reality is now setting in that it is not happening. The vast majority of China is growing poorer as it gets older, with no safety net whatsoever to rely on. At some point, such abuses are liable to become the stuff of rank civil dissent, if not outright revolt from the masses.

Extreme Environmental Degradation

Another factor—or symptom—of China's distorted economic development through the Beijing Model has been an unmitigated disregard for the environment of the country. This ought to come as no surprise, since for all intents and purposes, China's economy is a command economy, with firm political control in the hands of the CCP. Command economies, history shows, have consistently proven themselves to be the worst offenders of environmental degradation. In the old USSR, for example, whole forests were rendered uninhabitable due to the extreme pollution levels from toxic waste dumping, slipshod pollution standards, shoddy construction and production processes, and nonexistent industrial waste handling procedures.

Unfortunately, but with utter predictability, there has been no improvement in environmental concerns with the Chinese Communist Party in power. We will take a more in-depth look at the true cost of extreme environmental degradation that China is now facing in Chapter 6. But for this section, it will suffice to simply point out the reasons why extreme environmental degradation is a fundamental part of the Beijing Model.

By the way, it is also important to point out that environmental degradation did not originate with the Beijing Model. As I point out in the following list, environmental degradation is not new, but is certainly a key aspect or symptom of command economies. Today, extreme environmental degradation has become synonymous with China's development and poses a full-scale threat to the well-being of the Chinese people under the development process of the Beijing Model. There are four basic reasons why extreme environmental degradation has become what it is in China.

1. Because command economies like China's and the old USSR necessarily rely on graft and corruption to remain in power, there is little motivation—in fact, no motivation, but rather great danger—in whistleblowing on polluters since those polluting are doing so with the blessing of some Party authority.
2. Because legitimacy is largely based upon the control of violence and the lack of political opposition, those who point out the environmental degradation are, *de facto*, in opposition to the Party and risk official reprisal in one form or another.

3. Because China's legitimacy is also based upon economic viability, their concern for the environment is way down the list of importance. In the production cost cycle, there are additional production costs in developing more environmentally sound production processes and the processing of industrial waste materials. Bribing the right party official lets the offenders avoid all of those costs and increase production.

4. A fundamental disrespect for the nation as a whole. If the Party is willing to slaughter hundreds of millions of its own people, and imprison millions more for speaking out, or force abortions on its women, or use its citizens for organ harvests, or numerous other atrocities, why would it care about the environment? This basic lack of decency is seen in China's moral crisis discussed earlier in this chapter, which manifests itself in every aspect of Chinese life.

A fifth reason that is also a consequence of command economies is the Tragedy of the Commons theory, which we go into further in Chapter 6, where we will explore China's great problem of environmental degradation.

Structurally, the Beijing Model has put China on a manufacturing track, to make use of its hundreds of millions of poor laborers. This policy has not only kept China from moving up on the development scale and transitioning from a manufacturing-based economy into a knowledge-based economy, but has also indirectly contributed to the degradation of the nation's natural resources. This is simply because, with economic growth as the primary economic goal and manufacturing the means to that goal, regard for the environment on a policy level has not been a part of the agenda. Employing more environmentally-safe manufacturing methods is costly and disruptive to the status quo, and there exists no effective legal recourse to remedy it. Consequently, degradation becomes part of the development-at-all-costs policy.

Has the Beijing Model succeeded in growing China? It has indeed, much the way that steroids grow an athlete: size and strength are both increased, but potentially fatal damage is visited upon the vital, life-sustaining internal and reproductive organs. It is sufficient to say that the Beijing Model has been a process of creating conditions in China for wealth to be both created and destroyed. It has both structurally and demographically changed China in ways that have allowed it to develop rapidly as a society, but at the same time hobble it in so many ways that will cost it dearly. It has also defiled the nation's environment, set up the nation for massive food shortages, and skewed the natural social reproductive rhythms of the country in vile, brutal, and quite possibly irreversible ways.

The Beijing Model is no more of a useful economic model than bone cancer is a recommended health condition. Both live off of the host, weakening the host from the inside out, until there is no more to feed off of, at which point the host dies. Thus, the Beijing Model is not an economic system, but rather is more akin to a degenerative process, where the parasitic state devours the rest of the nation at an advancing rate as the process nears its end. And that is, more or less, where China's Beijing Model is today. In Chapter 5, we take a closer look at China's financial system, how it functions, and why its weaknesses are so dangerous to China itself and to the global economy as a whole.

Notes

1. Dan Blumenthal, "The 'Beijing Model' Bubble," *The Weekly Standard*, March 19, 2012, www.weeklystandard.com/articles/beijing-model-bubble_633427 .html.

2. "Taiwan Country Report," *Global Finance*, www.gfmag.com/gdp-data-country-reports/166-taiwan-gdp-country-report.html; "China GDP Per Capita," *Trading Economics*, www.tradingeconomics.com/china/gdp-per-capita.

3. "China's Billionaire Lawmakers Make U.S. Peers Look Like Paupers," *Bloomberg News*, February 27, 2012, www.bloomberg.com/news/2012-02-26/ china-s-billionaire-lawmakers-make-u-s-peers-look-like-paupers.html.

4. Victor Shih, "China's Highly Unequal Economy," *The Diplomat*, February 2011, http://thediplomat.com/whats-next-china/china%E2%80%99s-highly-unequal-economy.

5. "Xi Jinping Millionaire Relations Reveal Fortunes of Elite," *Bloomberg News*, June 29, 2012, www.bloomberg.com/news/2012-06-29/xi-jinping-millionaire-relations-reveal-fortunes-of-elite.html; and "China's Billionaire People's Congress Makes Capitol Hill Look Like Paupers," *Bloomberg News*, February 27, 2012, www .bloomberg.com/news/2012-02-26/china-s-billionaire-lawmakers-make-u-s-peers-look-like-paupers.html.

6. "The Long Arm of the State," *The Economist*, June 23, 2011, www.economist.com/node/18832034.

7. "Beware The Beijing Model," *The Economist*, May 26, 2009, www.economist.com/node/13721724.

8. Ibid.

9. Gordon G. Chang, "The Great Chinese Stampede: Hot Money Leaving the Country," *Forbes*, October 28, 2012, www.forbes.com/sites/gordonchang/2012/10/28/the-great-chinese-stampede-hot-money-leaving-the-country; and Malcolm Moore, "China's Communist Party Cadres Launch Property Fire Sale," *The Telegraph*, January 21, 2013, www.telegraph.co.uk/news/worldnews/asia/china/9815998/Chinas-Communist-party-cadres-launch-property-fire-sale.html.

10. Jeremy Page, "Plan B for China's Wealthy: Moving to the U.S.; Europe," *Wall Street Journal*, February 22, 2012, online.wsj.com/article/SB10001424052970203806504577181461401318988.html.

11. "To Flee or Not to Flee," *The Economist* (*Analects* blog), August 22, 2012, www.economist.com/blogs/analects/2012/08/foreigners-china.

12. "China's Moral Crisis: From Maoism to Daoism?" *Democracy Digest*, October 31, 2011, www.demdigest.net/blog/2011/10/chinas-moral-crisis-from-maoism-to-daoism.

13. Wang Yiru, "The Real Reason Gu Kailai Murdered UK Businessman Nick Heywood," *The Epoch Times* (English Edition), August 13, 2012, www.theepochtimes.com/n2/china-news/british-businessman-neil-heywood-divulged-too-much-276439-all.html.

14. Stanley Lubman, "Fraud, Culture and the Law: Can China Change?" *Wall Street Journal*, August 4, 2012, www.law.berkeley.edu/14074.htm.

15. Tom Orlik, "Chinese GDP Data: How Reliable?" *China Realtime Report* (blog), June 10, 2011, http://blogs.wsj.com/chinarealtime/2011/06/10/chinese-gdp-data-how-reliable.

16. Ibid.

17. Richard McCormack, "A Cautionary Tale of Outsourcing to China: You Could Lose Everything," *Manufacturing & Technology News*, April 15, 2011, www.manufacturingnews.com/news/11/0415/Fellowes1.html.

18. Floyd Norris, "The Audacity of Chinese Frauds," *New York Times*, May 26, 2011, www.nytimes.com/2011/05/27/business/27norris.html.

19. Satyajit Das, "Fake Goods, Fake Growth: Will the Chinese Feast End?" *Daily News & Analysis*, March 23, 2012, www.dnaindia.com/money/report_fake-goods-fake-growth-will-the-chinese-feast-end_1666143.

20. Christina Larson, "The Cracks in China's Shiny Buildings," *Bloomberg Businessweek*, September 27, 2012, www.businessweek.com/articles/2012-09-27/the-cracks-in-chinas-shiny-buildings.

21. "Made in China: Seven Toxic Imports," *The Week*, December 11, 2009, http://theweek.com/article/index/104062/made-in-china-seven-toxic-imports.

22. Christian Caryl, "Why Bow to China?" *The Daily Beast*, May 15, 2009, www.thedailybeast.com/newsweek/2009/05/15/why-bow-to-china.html.

23. "The Long Arm of the State," *The Economist*, June 23, 2011, www.economist.com/node/18832034.

24. "Triangular Debt: An Unknown That the Chinese Government Seems to Worry About," *Also Sprach Analyst*, August 24, 2012, www.alsosprachanalyst.com/economy/triangular-debt-an-unknown-that-chinese-government-seems-to-worry-about.html.

25. Ansuya Harjani, "'Zombie Firms' a Growing Risk for China, Says Andy Xie," CNBC.com, 29, August, 2012,www.cnbc.com/id/48823041/lsquoZombie_Firmsrsquo_a_Growing_Risk_for_China_Says_Andy_Xie.

26. Shiyin Chen and Haslinda Amin, Bloomberg, "China May Crash in Next 9-12 Months: Marc Faber," *The China Post*, May 4, 2010, www.chinapost.com.tw/business/asia-china/2010/05/04/255060/China-may.htm.

27. Patrick Chovanec, "China's Real Estate Bubble May Have Just Popped," *Foreign Affairs*, December 18, 2011, www.foreignaffairs.com/articles/136963/patrick-chovanec/chinas-real-estate-bubble-may-have-just-popped.

28. "Beware the Middle Income Trap," *The Economist*, June 23, 2011, www.economist.com/node/18832106.

29. Mamta Badkar, "China Is Entering a Danger Zone," August 21, 2012, *Business Insider*, www.businessinsider.com/china-entering-a-danger-zone-2012-8.

30. *The Economist*, May 26, 2009, www.economist.com/node/13721724.

31. Fayen Wong and Randy Fabi, "Update 3—Chinese Buyers Default on Coal, Iron Ore Shipments—Trade," *Reuters*, May 21, 2012, www.reuters.com/article/2012/05/21/china-coal-defaults-idUSL4E8GL1BS20120521.

32. Fayen Wong and Jane Lee, "Analysis: China's Towering Metal Stockpiles Cast Economic Shadows," *Reuters*, May 18, 2012, www.reuters.com/article/2012/05/18/us-china-commodities-idUSBRE84H09E20120518.

33. "The End of Cheap China," *The Economist*, March 10, 2012, www.economist.com/node/21549956.

34. David Conrads, "As Chinese Wages Rise, US Manufacturers Head Back Home," *The Christian Science Monitor*, May 10, 2012, www.csmonitor.com/Business/new-economy/2012/0510/As-Chinese-wages-rise-US-manufacturers-head-back-home.

35. "China's New Policies for Promoting Foreign Investment," Sidley Austin LLP, China Update, June 8, 2010, quoting 2010 Business Climate Survey Report, Chinese American Chamber of Commerce, www.sidley.com/files/News/e946b17a-36b7-4576-aa84-21faee960312/Presentation/

NewsAttachment/b706e423-ed11-401a-b046-27cba9f50d4a/China_
Update_06.08.10.pdf.

36. Yuhan Zhang and Lin Shi, "Low-Consumption China Needs Serious Reforms,"
East Asia Forum, November 22, 2011, www.eastasiaforum.org/2011/11/22/
low-consumption-china-needs-serious-reforms.

37. Alan Sears, "China's One-Child Policy: The Culture of Death on Steroids,"
TownHall.com, October 27, 2011, http://townhall.com/columnists/alan
sears/2011/10/27/chinas_one-child_policy_the_culture_of_death_on_ster
oids/page/full.

38. Xuefeng Chen, "The Social Impact of China's One-Child Policy," *Harvard
Asia Pacific Review*, Summer 2003, http://web.mit.edu/lipoff/www/hapr/
summer03_security/CHEN.pdf.

Chapter 5

China's Quiet Crisis: Financial and Economic Meltdown

I n Chapter 4, we examined the notable and mostly negative aspects of the Beijing Model and China's distorted economy of triangular debt, a real estate bubble, and a political economy based upon fraud and corruption. But there is much more to learn about China's financial system. Upon closer examination, we find that it is not only distorted in its functioning, but that it also faces several grave structural threats to its continued existence in its current form. Those threats are now being noticed by observers and recognized as having the potential to trigger a level of disaster in China's economy that even the former premier of China knows can spell the end for the CCP and China's economy.

A Perception of Strength

The perception has been that China's economy was growing steadily regardless of what the United States or Europe were going through in the aftermath of the 2008 Financial Crisis. Even though the United States, the Eurozone, and much of the rest of the world were deeply affected by it and fell into recessions, it seemed from its Gross Domestic Product (GDP) reports that China had come through it relatively unaffected, with reported growth rates of 9.6 percent in 2008, 8.7 percent in 2009, and 10.4 percent in 2010.[1] But did China escape the global financial crisis unscathed?

For most of the prior 20 years, China's economy had experienced—or at least, reported—significant growth. Hundreds of thousands of millionaires, or more, and many billionaires have been created by China's expanding juggernaut of an economy. Manufacturers from around the world have relocated to China to capture the cost advantages that its labor force offers. Corporations saw their profit margins increase and China has seen tremendous levels of foreign investment quickly transform their agrarian landscape and failed economy into a rapidly developing manufacturing monster.

With its population of 1.3 billion, China has successfully leveraged its massive market before foreign manufacturers for decades. The lure of the largest potential market in the world has proven to be an irresistible enticement that no foreign firm can ever truly penetrate without a Chinese partner. Indeed, the Chinese market has proven to be a major source of global market share for many of the world's top corporations, like Microsoft ($100 million in annual earnings), Volkswagen (35 percent of their global market), Apple, Boeing, and many others. Of course, all have also found that the Chinese would eventually try to steal every business and technological advantage they could from them. Undoubtedly, it's simply become a cost of doing business.

Still, all of this activity and productivity in China made its economy appear to be a better, stronger, and more resilient economy than the aging—and ailing—economies of the United States, Japan, and the Eurozone. And in some ways, it is true. Where no infrastructure existed only a few years ago in many places in China, the latest technology has been put in place. Communication technology is a good example of this. High-speed web connections and the most advanced cellular technology have connected China rapidly and more completely than outmoded technology that remains in place in many parts of the United States and Europe. And the skylines of China's great cities of commerce have come to quickly rival and in many cases surpass the most developed and wealthiest cities in the West.

Contrast this with the well-documented crumbling infrastructures of the United States, Japan, and even Europe and their respective excesses of unsupportable public and private debt and historically high levels of public spending relative to GDP. Such debt and spending levels year after year helped bring about the crisis that Europe is still reeling from today, and which the United States still seeks to avoid as it searches for a viable long-term solution. The global notoriety of these very dangerous problems has taken much of the world's attention away from China and its still relatively closed and politically straightjacketed society.

In contrast, China's liquid cash reserves and portfolio of U.S. treasuries had steadily grown, and by 2006, China became the United States' largest sovereign creditor. By 2008, China's cash reserves were over $1 trillion, and its trade surplus with the United States was averaging over $250 billion per year. Its economy had surpassed Japan's to become second only behind that of the United States, and its profile around the world was that of a confident, capable, and well-run economic giant. To many observers, including many very confident Chinese economists, China's Beijing Model represents the twenty-first century growth model.[2]

It is certainly understandable why the perception of China's economic strength is what it is; it is the most populous nation in the world, with its seemingly limitless force of cheap labor, lack of unions, minimal social safety net expenditures, and wealth of cash stashed from years, even decades, of trade surpluses. China has appeared to be a much more dynamic and healthy economy than the United States, which in a good year will grow the GDP 3 to 4 percent, but since 2008, has been lucky to manage growth in the 2 percent range at best, and in *de facto* recession otherwise. At the same time, China has been claiming 9 to 12 percent growth in GDP, or even higher, almost every year for over a decade.

That is the picture the world sees and admires, and in the case of the Eurozone, it's to whom they look for help in getting through the crisis that continues there even at this writing. It is also no secret that the

United States depends upon China's purchases of U.S. Treasuries to keep functioning. This dependency is slowly falling as China gradually diversifies out of the U.S. dollar.[3] However, while China's economy has made enormous strides and its development has been moving at a fantastic pace, there are also glaring weaknesses that have been revealed in the 2008 Financial Crisis and in the years afterward that today augur for financial collapse much more than they do for continued financial stability. This applies to many aspects of the Chinese economy, and though it has been discussed earlier, another look at the question of China's GDP is helpful in understanding the impact of falsity in China's economic statistics, as well as putting the conclusions derived from them into context.

China's Quality of GDP

A big part of the picture in China's claims of economic strength is its GDP growth rate. However, a big part to the puzzle of China's impressive GDP statistics is the *quality* of its GDP. That is, what kind of economic activity in China is included in its GDP calculations?

Prior references in this book have pointed out China's false advertising regarding the strength of its economy and its GDP statistics over the years. We have also noted how China's claim of double-digit annual GDP growth doesn't jibe with flat or minimally increased electricity use; or as observed earlier, that China's GDP numbers are for *reference only*. These are all very valid points of concern and tell us that a closer look at China's economic activity will likely reveal many strands of weakness in the country's economic fabric.

It truly cannot be overstated that the pervasive culture of corruption, fraud, and graft throughout every aspect of China's economy and society creates enormous difficulties in accuracy regarding the country's growth or other national aspects. Behavior by those in authority as well as the Chinese public at large is a much more reliable indicator of reality than falsified official statistics. Behavior is the lens through which a certain clarity regarding the health of both China's economy and its society is most clearly viewed. And the view is a disturbing one.

Hu Jintao, China's most recent leader, said as much in his warning to the new leaders in his 2012 state-of-the-nation address to Party members:

In a state-of-the-nation address to more than 2,000 hand-picked party delegates before he hands over power, Hu acknowledged that public anger over graft and issues like environmental degradation had undermined the party's support and led to surging numbers of protests.

"Combating corruption and promoting political integrity, which is a major political issue of great concern to the people, is a clear-cut and long-term political commitment of the party.

"If we fail to handle this issue well, it could prove fatal to the party, and even cause the collapse of the party and the fall of the state. We must thus make unremitting efforts to combat corruption."[4]

Hu's warning to his fellow party members to "combat corruption and promote political integrity" goes to the heart of China's economic system, which operates along political axes, not from a demand-based context or a profit/market axis. Its state-directed economic activities like reckless lending, inflated profit claims, false revenues, construction projects like entire cities that remain unoccupied, and other stimulus-related economic activity that has little to do with actual demand or purpose in the economy is counted in GDP at some level. There is—or ought to be—great doubt as to what level of real value those activities inject into the economy. State-mandated activity, from lending to labor, may lead to a new construction project, but will the project add value to the economy past its construction period? Is it really productive and adding to GDP? Is there a verifiable return on capital? And is the reported economic impact even accurate?

As Mancur Olson pointed out in his classic book, *The Rise and Decline of Nations* (Yale University Press, 1982), greater infrastructure and well-built roads lead to increased trade and productivity. However, there has to be demand for traffic between point A and point B in terms of a functioning market and financial rewards for doing so. The same goes for building houses, factories, or wind farms. Building these things has some value in that it puts people to work, but unless there is a socioeconomic *raison d'etre* for the construction, the end result is wasteful spending on massive projects—cities, railways, steel mills, and such—that end up either overproducing or rotting from neglect and disuse while going into hundreds of billions of dollars in debt.[5]

The larger truth is that state-directed economic activity in China is politically connected and mandated, is rarely completed up to standards due to graft and theft, too often has to be redone at great added cost (which is also counted in GDP figures), and quite significantly often adds little or no value to the ongoing economy. Furthermore, state-run projects and investments often actually suck the value out of the economy by misallocating land, labor, and capital to projects where they are not needed or wanted. Developments are pet projects or otherwise directed by political fiat, not by market forces that would indicate whether a true demand for a given project actually exists. Counting the losses from rolled over loans on bad debts or not recognizing the loss of GDP from, say, a productive farm confiscated by authorities to make way for a new construction project that may not add any long-term value, for example, or lost productivity due to pollution, desertification, or abandonment, such as in the case of neglected wind farms, also fall into that category.

This phenomenon isn't about the occasional political pork barrel earmark project; it is, in the main, the way things are done in China. As Patrick Chovanec, a professor at Tsinghua University in Beijing, astutely points out, the method of counting productivity results, or the calculation of GDP, is much different from actual GDP in China. For example, Professor Chovanec notes that additional—and utterly false—GDP padding in China can be attributed to many activities, such as:

- Adding the value to GDP when profitable private firms are confiscated and become state-owned enterprises through Party authority.
- Frontloading long-term projects into shorter time periods to count value of the project today.
- Replicating projects.
- Funding failing businesses.
- Counting unused, surplus inventory.
- Funneling business loans into the stock market or into other unrelated projects.
- Supporting higher real estate values through rollover loans to prop up the real estate market to show continued demand.
- Counting finished goods as sales when they leave the factory, not when or if they are actually bought.[6]

Of course, there are certainly many other creative ways that make China's GDP seem much greater—and more meaningful—than it truly is. But the point, I think, has been rightly made here and elsewhere that China's reported GDP numbers and other results, economic or otherwise, are certainly not what they are portrayed to be and are neither sustainable in practice nor renewable in their processes. What must also be considered is that China's GDP numbers are not only deceptive, but also come at great expense and waste of human capital and natural resources that are not wealth-creating as much as they are wealth-depleting over the long-term.

China's development and its GDP are, in fact, quite paradoxical. China has become the manufacturer to the world and is the world's largest trading nation, according to recent statistics. But at the same time that it is building beautiful modern cities throughout the country, nobody is living in them. As its national wealth grows, so does the wealth gap. As private industry thrives, more of it is taken away by the state and it ceases to become profitable. The more China manufactures, the worse the quality becomes and the more it pollutes its environment, which reduces GDP by 8 percent per year. The more the middle class grows, the poorer it becomes.

Again, that is not to discount the great economic strides that China has made in the past 30 years, both in developing its cities and infrastructure and in the creation of a middle class. But when it's broken down into its components, the Chinese economic miracle is much more understandable, given a slave labor pool of over a billion people combined with the capital and technology of the most developed countries in the world at a time when communication, manufacturing, and information technology advances were light years ahead of the previous generation. These factors made rapid development a much easier task than it would have been at any other time in history. Add in the good fortune of Hong Kong—the capitalist financial center of Asia—reverting back to Chinese ownership in 1997 and the complete lack of any advanced economy expenses such as costly social programs, environmental regulation, unions, or inconvenient legal impediments, and the results are predictable. Finally, being admitted to the World Trade Organization under U.S. sponsorship in 2001 led directly to China transferring

over 2.7 million jobs—76 percent of which were in manufacturing—
our of the United States in the next 10 years.[7]

The reasons for this deception have been articulated well and clearly
enough. And, as identified before, when the price for failure to reach
an economic goal or production quota is harsh punishment—up to and
including heavy fines and imprisonment—and the culture of corruption
is as deeply engrained in society as it is in China, should it be surprising
that gross inaccuracies exist? The greater point is that economic growth
in China has probably never been all that it has been claimed to be. It
is doubtful that even Chinese authorities are truly aware of what their
actual GDP numbers are. What is important for the Chinese leadership is that the GDP figures reflect positively on the CCP and bolster
China's image in the world. As for the future, the Chinese economy will
not be the engine to rescue the rest of the global economy. Considering
the direction in which it is headed, it is doubtful that China will even
be able to rescue itself.

A Public and Private Stimulus Time Bomb

Like the United States and the Eurozone, China has constructed its own
stimulus time bomb as a result of the global economic slowdown, specifically in the United States and the Eurozone. (Japan enjoyed 40 years of
rapid growth before enduring economic stagnation for the past 20 years
through several rounds of stimulus.) China's response to the financial
crisis in 2008 was to inject 4 trillion yuan ($586 billion by 2008 conver-
sion rates) of stimulus money, the equivalent of 16 percent of the annual
GDP, into its economy to finance development projects and create jobs.
It is worth noting that China's method of stimulus differs substantially
from that of the United States. Because of China's high savings rate, it
has preferred to stimulate its economy via state-owned banks making
loans from existing reserves rather than the government directly injecting additional capital from debt into the economy.[8]

Regardless of the source of the funds or their qualitative difference,
like the United States, the stimulus money in China remained mainly at
the higher levels of the economy. It was available for larger corporations
and state-owned businesses, but it was largely absent from the lower and

much more populated parts of the economy such as the tens of millions of small business owners. Thus, as in the United States, the positive impact was less than anticipated in the small business economy.

The response in the small business community has been the expansion of an already vigorous community of private lenders in China. Private lending has always been a part of the Chinese small business community, so there is really nothing new there in that respect. But the lack of capital reaching the small business community greatly expanded the role of private investors and loan guarantors in recent years. A business owner may be someone who lends extra cash to another business owner or a private lending syndicate that pools its own and investors' funds into loans to small businesses or property developers. There are also other arrangements that allow small business owners access to needed capital that is not available to them through official banking channels.

As noted, private or mutual lending as it is called, is as much a cultural phenomenon as it is an economic one. Mutual lending relationships between many businesses have provided much needed capital for centuries in China, but they have been especially relevant in the past several years when banks in China tightened their lending. When the economy began to contract, even more money was borrowed and lent in China's shadow banking world. But today, the impact of the loans all coming due and none being paid back is growing to catastrophic levels with enormous deleterious effects on the small business economy throughout China. The city of Wenzhou is a prime example, as the following excerpt shows, but it is certainly not a unique scenario.

> (A)fter China began market reforms in the late 1970s, Wenzhou flourished. "The Wenzhou Model" of small, low-cost manufacturing operations was widely copied in China. Wenzhou now has some 140,000 companies, and its business folk have invested across the country in everything from real estate to mining. The city is the locus and symbol of private enterprise in China.
>
> But in recent weeks, the reputation of Wenzhou's entrepreneurs has taken a serious hit. Dozens of factory bosses have fled bad debts, and at least two have committed suicide. . . . The main cause of Wenzhou's ills is far more explosive, however, and lies in the local tradition of private lending.

The government estimated earlier this year that 60 percent of Wenzhou businesses and an astonishing 90 percent of households were involved in some form of private lending. Problems began to really emerge in late summer, when some large borrowers stopped repaying. In September, Hu Fulin, president of Xintai Group, another eyeglass manufacturer, fled to the U.S. to escape some $300 million in debts. He has since returned, but the situation remains dire—some 90 other company heads have absconded.

The Kid (a private moneylender) collected about $3 million in August and early September, but says he recovered a mere $50,000 between late September and late October. "Everyone is hoarding money," he says. "Once they get it back, nobody lends it out again—not even to their closest friends." The Wenzhou bubble has burst.

"Should the liquidity chain in Wenzhou collapse to spark either sell-offs in the property market or the cutoff of liquidity for manufacturing or mining, this local crisis could evolve into a national problem."[9]

The reality is that Wenzhou was a model of economic efficiency and success in China and, if not the canary in the coal mine, it is certainly not going to be the only city that finds itself needing a bailout from the state. It may well be the first of many. Also worth noting is that even a full government bailout will not provide a long-term solution to the falling real estate values or the liquidity and demand needed for industrial growth.

A similar lending crisis is occurring with the larger banks and their loans to the big Chinese corporations. A crisis of failing government banks is in the near future due to inflated and outright fabricated values of companies, falling revenues, and lax lending criteria that has little to do with profitability, and much more to do with political ties, graft, and waste. China's state-run firms and banks are reeling from the crashing values and cratering revenues from the global slowdown and their own fraudulent profits reports and debt rollovers. Certainly, development projects like housing construction, steel mills, and high-speed rail lines continue to be built, but the demand for those projects, like the ghost cities throughout the country, just isn't there.

Still, China funded those projects with another round of stimulus of 4 trillion yuan, or about $635 billion dollars, in 2012, which was also used to rollover even more bad debt. It is, as noted earlier, a profit-less activity that keeps people working and firms in business, but does not add real value to the economy—at least not in the classic Western sense of the word as it relates to economic growth driven by market demand.

In the shadow of China's official stimulus plan, shadow banking products known as Wealth Management Products (WMPs) that offer higher returns than the net-negative yields in banks, have exploded in number in China. These high-yield, often high-risk, and low-information investments have begun collapsing, as unscrupulous purveyors invest WMP clients' money in questionable enterprises that subsequently go bankrupt. How much damage collapsing WMPs will inflict upon the economy is unknown, but some experts foresee an escalation that could threaten the entire Chinese financial system.[10]

Development versus Economic Growth

Given that China's state-run banks continue to throw amazing amounts of money into projects and developments throughout the country, which, in so many cases, have not led to sustained economic activity or wealth generation, and have often despoiled the environment and destroyed or displaced profitable enterprises in the process, will there be a reckoning to face? Will China's economic miracle turn into another massive disaster, as previous economic policies have?

Or is China immune from the laws of economics that have been defined in the West? What will be the consequences of China's policies?

The banking crisis that looms on China's horizon can be viewed as a conceptual or political crisis as much as an economic one. Where actual profit is the defining objective in capitalism, it is not so in China's state-run banks and companies. Development for development's sake and for political reasons are the greater values over profit in the Chinese economy. There is therefore a great divide in China between develop-ment and economic growth. Building 20 steel mills and building an Olympic sports complex are both forms of development *per se*. However, the question of whether the construction of steel mills or an Olympic village contributes more to the economy going forward is quite another. There seems to be an epidemic of confusion in China between development for development's sake and economic growth. Infrastructure, steel mills, and sports complexes ought to become sources of wealth generation year after year, rather than just developments that provide a political clique quick profits at the outset, bragging rights, and nothing more. But managing appearances is the priority, and the economy suffers because of it.

Along with the economy, in many cases, the quality of what is built suffers because of this, too. The collapse of a high-speed rail line, due to poor construction because the builder cut corners to make more money, killed several hundred people and caused several days of violent rioting against the government. (Shoddy quality in finished products is becoming a constant with China's manufacturing and construction industries both in China and abroad.) Even the Olympic Village that hosted the Beijing Olympics of 2008 now sits unused and is already in the process of rapid decay.[11]

Is China really immune from the laws of economics and capitalism? Can true, economically beneficial development be separated from economic demand? Or is China's imbalanced and uncontrolled development just another way for the politically connected in the CCP to reap the wealth of the working and business classes and retain power?

How Much Was the Money Supply Expanded in China?

From 2008 to 2010, China's money supply increased by over 50 percent, mainly through lower reserve ratios in banking and loose loan standards at the local level.[12] This was also done in partial response to the U.S. stimulus program, as a means to keep the yuan devalued relative to the U.S. dollar, in order to keep Chinese products cheaper and thus more competitive in the global market. Therefore, China attempted to increase domestic demand through loans, as well as keeping the yuan affectively devalued relative to the dollar.

China's stimulus monetary policy has released inflationary forces throughout the country. But that stimulus-derived inflation was mostly transmitted through rising asset prices rather than consumables, so at first inflation wasn't felt by consumers, but rather by skyrocketing values in real estate development projects, for example. The Chinese government also dampened inflation for a while by having the People's Bank of China (PBOC) issue sterilization bonds, whereby they compel banks to maintain higher levels of reserve ratios as well as buy special central-bank bonds to absorb the undesired yuan liquidity. But the stimulus, as noted earlier, also enabled zombie companies which are not profitable to stay in business. In a nutshell, China's stimulus time bomb is poised to go off in two distinct ways: (1) inflation and (2) a banking crisis from the collapse of real estate values and a cascade of toxic debt.[13]

Inflation in China hit first in the asset classes such as real estate. Housing prices skyrocketed in 2009 and 2010 as investors and first time buyers scrambled to get in on the housing rush. The Chinese real estate boom, like its broader economy, seemed immune to the travails of the 2008 real estate meltdown that hit the United States and Europe. This was because of China's enormous stimulus program, which literally flooded China with more money than its economy could absorb. This led to not only rushed and shoddy development projects on a massive scale, but also to unnecessary infrastructure projects, many poorly constructed, and even more of the numerous ghost cities we talked about in Chapter 4.

Bursting Bubbles

The effect of this boom on the Chinese economy was predictable. A real estate bubble has emerged, as excess demand was created by easy money. Pent-up savings in China were tapped to invest in the real estate boom and make it big as prices leapfrogged their way up the ladder. There are many reports of Chinese buyers who would camp out for weeks at a time in order to purchase a condominium unit months or even a year or two before it was to be built. As in other places, the real estate boom in China had to end, and its crash has already begun. The Chinese leadership understood that loose money policies had to change, and it has done so, but it is not at all clear that they can control the economy as much as they say or think they can.

In fact, there are very rational reasons to believe that the Chinese have lost control of their economy. If China's control over other policies we have talked about herein are any indication, the road ahead looks awfully difficult for the people of China. Its overdependence on foreign investment and real estate development in driving its economy forward are major weaknesses. There is certainly no way for China to control or compel continued foreign investment from either Europe or America; both are flirting with another round of recession. Overheated levels of real estate development, as has been shown, in many cases add nothing of lasting value to the economy, and will collapse in upon themselves sooner or later.

The crash in China's real estate market has indeed begun, and is just in its beginning stages. From the New York Times:

> "Last year, when things were good, we had over 100 people a day coming into our office," said David Zhang, the sales director at the Honor-Link Investment Consultant Company, a real estate brokerage [in China]. "Now we have three or four a day, and no one is buying." . . . But the real estate downturn has only just begun, Mr. Zhang said, adding, "We are on the cusp of winter, and we don't know who will survive it and who will not."[14]

By late 2012, the real estate crash and waves of failing businesses in China were already having a major impact on China's state-owned banking system as well as the shadow banking system of private loan guarantors. As noted above, what has happened—and continues to occur—in the real estate sector also applies across the board in the business sector. Financial losses in myriad transactions involving real estate and businesses are coming in waves in China as corrupt lending practices have led to massive levels of triangular debt; and once collapse commences, this will have a domino effect on the whole economy. Just as the subprime mortgage bubble collapse rippled out into the economy as 50 percent of U.S. mortgages were classified as risky or subprime by 2007, leading to default, foreclosure, collapse of the residential real estate market, and deep recession, China faces a similar prospect. The problem is that the impending downfall is on a much larger scale relative to China's economic makeup, and not just limited to the real estate sector.

The assets that so much of the stimulus money went into via loose and reckless lending created asset bubbles—in residential and commercial real estate, overbuilt wind farms, overvalued solar companies, the stock market overall, and banks—all overvalued and underperforming, if not completely bankrupt. As noted earlier, as the loans become nonperforming, the banks have been rolling over the bad debt with more debt. But that can only last for so long. The debt/stimulus crisis in China is a structural defect in the system itself that will lead to a great unraveling of China's financial and economic pretensions much like it will in the United States and especially in Europe, which is further along in that process.

How Underperforming Are the Assets and the Loans Underlying Them?

China's economy is marked by enormous levels of waste that almost defy belief. One fundamental reason for this is that, although their economic planners can decide what is to be made and in what amounts, they cannot enforce the efficacy of what is produced nor control costs or engender efficiency. In fact, quite the opposite occurs.

Beijing's twelfth Five-Year plan, for example, determined that green energy was to be among "strategic emerging industries." Solar and wind power, electric cars, and other green technologies were funded with hundreds of millions of dollars, each with nothing to show for their efforts but tech failures and bankruptcy. Massive fraud schemes involving bond scams, embezzlement of funds by high level CCP officials, and bloated budgets on large projects like high speed rail systems that go unused are typical of the waste and false productivity of China's command economy that is losing hundreds of billions of dollars each year. Much of China's economic activity and GDP figures are holographic in nature and substance; across the spectrum of economic industries and sectors, there is so much less there than meets the eye.[15]

This is reflected in the level of non-performing loans in the economy. As far back as 2010, well into China's 4 trillion yuan stimulus program, Chinese banks were in trouble from making too many reckless loans:

(E)stimates leaked by Chinese bank regulators suggest that 23 percent of loans to local government-sponsored infrastructure projects are an outright loss, with another 50 percent at risk of cash default. If Chinese banks made appropriate provision for these losses alone, it would reverse the record earnings they have been reporting and eat into their capital base. Apply these estimates across other risky loan categories, such as real-estate development and business lending diverted to speculation in stocks or property, and their capital is in real danger of being wiped out. The loan-to-deposit ratio doesn't matter; they can have captive deposits and lots of cash, and still be bankrupt if they threw it all away on bad loans.[16]

Even with more money flowing into the economy from the government and some prices falling in the real estate sector, any bump in sales is reactive, but ultimately suffers from the same malaise: lack of real performance. Selling condominiums below construction costs may drive sales upward, but it does not result in a profit being made or a construction loan being repaid. Given the many years and decades of corruption and crony lending based on political connections and false balance sheets, should it be a surprise to anyone that China's banking sector, though carefully hidden by the CCP,[17] is at the beginning of its collapse?

And yet, the Chinese economy, the Beijing Model, is supposedly the new model of development for the twenty-first century. But what does China plan to do in order to prop up the country's failing banks? The answer is a combination of more stimulus, rolling over or transferring debt to other banking institutions, and hoping that growth solves the problem. Have the Chinese figured something out about capitalism and markets, what best drives development and industry, and how best to maximize the real estate market, that has escaped Western economists? Is China "different" enough that it can somehow avoid the looming economic consequences of its actions?

Some observers think that China's economy can indeed continue to perform as it has, even under more dire circumstances, given the iron grip that the CCP has on the political process and economic decision-making. But, as noted above, former premier Hu Jintao's warned that the system in place is in grave danger if reforms to address corruption are not made. That is the harsh reality. The Chinese leadership knows that their economy cannot continue operating as it has.

How do we know this?

Because the Chinese economy, its corporate world, and its banking sector (both state and private) are all showing signs of structural weakness regardless of what the official GDP numbers might be. An even bigger sign of this is the behavior of China's largest, most powerful banks. Seeking some relief from a cascade of bad debt in China, China's banks are now lending large sums of money not just to leading Chinese firms, but to some of the biggest names in corporate America.

China's Banks Looking for the Real Thing

Unlike the multitude of knock-offs for which Chinese firms are notorious—from Coach bags to entire Ikea stores—the Chinese banks realize that they can't afford to lend money for imitation profits forever. They want, and need, the real thing.

In extending loans to America's largest corporations, is China somehow riding to the rescue to bail out corporate America? It's an interesting question, isn't it? It is especially perplexing since:

1. The companies don't need the money. At this writing, corporate America holds an estimated $1.7 trillion in offshore cash. Plus, the Federal Reserve's quantitative easing policies have driven stock prices to record highs, giving the best of corporate America even more liquidity. Working capital is not an issue for most of corporate America.

2. Chinese banks are ranked as strong—or stronger—than many of the biggest U.S. banks:

   The increased syndicated lending by Chinese banks comes as their balance sheets compare favourably with U.S. counterparts. Standard & Poor's last year upgraded the long term credit ratings of Bank of China and China Construction Bank from A– to A. The credit rating agency maintained the rating of Industrial and Commercial Bank of China (ICBC) at A. At the same time, the long-term credit ratings of Bank of America, Citigroup and Goldman Sachs were cut to A–.[18]

The highly rated, very strong and solvent Chinese banks, including the Bank of China, the Bank of Asia, Industrial and Commercial Bank of China, and Chinese Construction Bank, are all lending money to corporate America. The names are the biggest in the country—Walt Disney, Caterpillar, Wal-Mart, UPS, Tiffany, Pfizer, Dell, and many more.

It's certainly no exaggeration to say that U.S. businesses are much more transparent than Chinese firms; they have no choice but to be so. That is not to say that there isn't a *fudge factor* in corporate America, because there is plenty of it. No one would deny that fact, and besides, accounting is a sick, twisted science any way one cares to look at it.

Having said that, the profits and revenues of corporate America are almost infinitely more reliable than what is on the balance sheet of any Chinese company you choose to examine. And again, the Chinese understand this fact better than anyone. They know how fraudulent their economy is. They also understand that, by and large, U.S. corporate balance sheets have to be based in reality; in general, revenue must exist to be called profit, otherwise share prices fall and corporate heads roll. This would explain the desire of Chinese banks to lend to corporate America.

Are Chinese banks saving U.S. businesses? Or is it vice versa?

There is ample evidence that the latter is the case. The Chinese banks—which are all state-run—are desperate for real returns on their lending portfolios. The lending environment in China in late 2012 was deteriorating rapidly as the global slowdown continued to hit China's export-based economy very hard. It put a spotlight on the very dangerous and widespread practice of loan guarantees passing from one company to another to form a daisy chain of dozens of companies guaranteeing each other's loans with none able to honor them or even make the interest payments. This triangular debt structure in China that we talked about in Chapter 4 is a virtual financial house of cards and the winds of global recession are showing just how fragile this system is and how deeply non-performing loans (NPLs) threaten the entire Chinese economy with collapse. Indebted business owners are fleeing rather than pay back their loans, and NPL ratios are beginning to rise, especially in the eastern province of Zhejiang's state-run banks. The great fear is that it is the beginning of a much wider systemic unravelling that will eventually affect the entire country.[19]

Concurrently, banks' collateral bases are diminishing as well. As more borrowers go bankrupt and property values continue to fall, the amount of damage to banks' balance sheets grows, making bailouts ever more costly to cover the worsening balance sheets.[20]

The practice of triangular debt has been widely enabled by loan guarantee companies. As Patrick Chovanec observed in his June 28,

2012, *Business Insider* article, "A Brand New Type of Credit Crisis Is Producing a Domino Effect in China":

> (T)he Tianyu story, along with Zhongdan and others, should finally put to rest the argument that last year's credit meltdown in Wenzhou (which is still going on, by the way) was a "unique" or "isolated" case. Shadow banking, and the risks it hides, are pervasive across China's economy. If you're still buying the line that what happened in Wenzhou has no relevance to the rest of China, I have a couple of high-speed rail lines I'd like to sell you.

The specter of China suffering through a banking crisis is not only real, but also a very dangerous possibility. That reality goes a long way to explain why Chinese banks would be so interested in loaning money to the biggest names in corporate America, as reported by the *Financial Times*. With that in mind, the picture looks more like this: China is already our biggest sovereign buyer of Treasury bonds; now, it lends money to the United States' biggest corporations, as well.

Why would they do this? Because they feel that they must do so. Why do they feel compelled to do so? Because they know that the country faces some very big problems in its own economy very soon.

At its most basic level, the majority of China's financial and economic problems redound from the economic and social repression imposed upon the people by the CCP. The levers of power that the CCP pulls to control economic development in the macro economy are the interest rates and the exchange rates. Like other parts of the economy, by not relying on the price mechanism to determine demand levels, which in turn identify the right pricing and allocation, the CCP's decisions are based on political demands, not economic ones. Furthermore, lack of a privatized financial market and capital freedoms also hinders proper development, and causes the great imbalance and wasteful development that is rampant in China today:

> The consequences of China's financial repression are easy to see: a sea of nonperforming loans; misallocation of capital, with overinvestment in the state sector and underinvestment in the private sector; politicization of investment decisions and widespread corruption; poor performance of stock markets even though economic growth has been robust; an undervalued real exchange rate; and stop-go monetary policy.

By suppressing two key macroeconomic prices—the interest rate and the exchange rate—and by failing to privatize financial markets and allow capital freedom, China's leaders have given up flexibility and efficiency to ensure that the Chinese Communist Party (CCP) retains its grip on power.[21]

The end result of this policy is that China's financial collapse is well on its way to becoming a reality. But apparently this economic collapse is a cost of retaining power that the CCP is willing to let the rest of China bear, seemingly indefinitely. But like all excesses, the cost will eventually prove unbearable to both the Chinese economy and to the people themselves, and ultimately, the CCP.

Currency Manipulation and the Domestic Economy

The argument is often made that China has manipulated its currency to the detriment of U.S. jobs. That has probably been true at various times in the past decade, although as of late 2012, the U.S. Treasury opted not to label China a currency manipulator.[22] However it is also true that at times China has kept the yuan artificially low relative to the dollar, and at other times, allowed the yuan to substantially revalue against the dollar.

Is currency manipulation a part of China's economic policy? At times, it certainly looks that way. But the more important question is what long-term effects will currency manipulation have on China's domestic economic structure? The answer is very little. Currency manipulation is not irrelevant when discussing Chinese economic and trade issues, but it is not particulary significant for our discussion.

But it is relevant to note that as the global slowdown continued through 2012 and on into 2013, China's loose monetary policy of 2009–2010, which resulted in price inflation for housing, among many other asset classes, has given way to a policy of tight credit as a means to bring prices downward and make homes and other products more affordable to the country's domestic market. Also, a ban on second home purchase aimed at reducing speculative buying and driving real estate prices lower to increase affordability has resulted in a crash in the construction industry and real estate marketing industry, which means lost jobs.

This boom-bust cycle is not the intended consequence, and is painful to an already slowing Chinese economy. Remember, China's domestic consumption as a share of GDP declined around 20 percent from 2005 to 2010[23]; it has continued to inch downward since. Add to that the result of tighter credit, which has been to exacerbate the slowdown in China's domestic consumption because domestic spending has fallen as well, and there is ample reason for economic concern.[24]

Thus, China's yuan devaluation policy is to stimulate foreign demand for Chinese exports. It's true that the value of the yuan has fluctuated over the years, care of the Chinese government—which carefully controls the exchange rate since the yuan is not openly traded in the world's currency market—and that the continued effort by the Chinese to keep the value of the yuan low relative to the dollar is a way to keep manufacturing jobs in the country.

Will the Yuan Devaluation Be Enough to Keep the Economy Going?

A cheap Chinese currency relative to the dollar and the euro means that Chinese products will retain at least some of their competitive advantage. But will it be enough? Or, put another way, do the Chinese people themselves have confidence in the economic policies to increase their consumption levels enough to make up for the lower demand from China's foreign trading partners like the Eurozone? The answer is "no", even though raising the domestic consumption level through rebalancing the economy is on the CCP's twelfth and newest Five-Year Plan, unveiled in 2011.[25] So far, however, domestic consumption as a percentage of GDP remains around 35 percent. Price wars among domestic manunfacturers on a glut of unsold goods intended for the domestic market are ongoing, as they try to unload their surplus inventories on the world market with little success:

> The glut of everything from steel and household appliances to cars and apartments is hampering China's efforts to emerge from a sharp economic slowdown. It has also produced a series of price wars and has led manufacturers to redouble efforts to export what they cannot sell at home.

The severity of China's inventory overhang has been carefully masked by the blocking or adjusting of economic data by the Chinese government—all part of an effort to prop up confidence in the economy among business managers and investors.

But the main nongovernment survey of manufacturers in China showed on Thursday that inventories of finished goods rose much faster in August than in any month since the survey began in April 2004. The previous record for rising inventories, according to the HSBC/Markit survey, had been set in June. May and July also showed increases.[26]

Even with a devalued yuan, there is simply not enough domestic demand to spur jobs and economic growth in China. Finished products and basic resources like iron ore sit piled high on docks unused, with no one coming to claim the shipments. As noted above, the Chinese domestic consumption rate is nowhere near where it needs to be to drive the economy, and it continues to fall. (We could just as easily say *stated* GDP because the numbers are not real). This is where state spending plays an enormous role in the Chinese economy, as it is greatly helped along by the very high Chinese savings rate of 50 percent of GDP, which is the highest savings rate in the world. The global average is 20 percent.[27]

Why does China have such a high savings rate? In a word: fear. The average working Chinese citizen fears not having enough to pay for retirement, for housing, for education, for medical care, for food, for a car, *ad infinitum*. Why do they have these fears? Most do so because they have no confidence in the government or the economy. And those fears and suspicions are well founded on past experience with CCP policies.

The high savings process works like this: Without social safety nets of health care or social security, the average Chinese worker must save to provide for his/her retirement income and medical care when they stop working; not to mention the additional expense of buying a house or paying for higher education costs for their children. But, the motivation for a high savings rate gets even higher with the One Child policy effect. With only one child, now grown, that child may well have to support his/her parents in their old age, or quite possibly, even two sets of parents. Those factors go a long way in explaining such a high savings rate. Of course, when people are saving money, they are, by definition, not spending it.

With such high national savings rates, and very few places in which to put their savings except for near-negative yield banks and insurance policies, people have to put away even more for the future. From late 2011 to late 2012, the Chinese government banned all gold exchanges except for two in Shanghai. Prior to that, people throughout China were buying gold as a hedge against the devalued yuan, falling real estate values, and falling interest rates.[28] Today, the Chinese government is encouraging individuals to purchase gold and silver again. And to add just a bit more vinegar into the wine, the aforementioned bulk of the tax burden is levied on the middle and lower classes. Is there any question as to why the savings rate is so high in China?

This world-leading savings rate means that the Chinese government has a large pot of very cheap money by which to put currency back into the economy for development and infrastructure projects. But again, the high savings rate (and buying precious metals) reflects a lack of confidence in the economy and in the future among many Chinese, and in their ability to get ahead and stay ahead. One very dangerous potential problem directly related to that is the inflation that goes with all that stimulus spending. Knowing that your currency will continually lose its value, and thus your savings will, too, will result in even more savings.

But eventually, when inflation has eroded enough of the people's savings and their ability to care for themselves and their families, civil unrest over loss of those savings to inflation most certainly will manifest itself. That fear is not lost on the Chinese people. Fear of losing everything to a devalued yuan has driven many to buy gold as a store of value until all but two gold exchanges were closed down by the Chinese government in late 2011.

To be fair, there are observers who point to the number of economic and financial areas where China leads the world. They often conclude that any speculation on the dangers that the Chinese economy will soon be in a world of hurt is simply a case of China envy, because China is 'beating the West at its own game,' or words to that effect. But the facts remain that China's manipulation of its market, its currency values, and its monetary policies have consequences, just as they do in the United States or anywhere else.

Unfortunately, China's domestic economy is so underperforming that it will take an enormous amount of stimulus spending over an extended period of time to delay their economy from collapsing. But at some point, even stimulus cannot spur domestic spending if the consumers lack confidence in the economy, the government, and the future.

How long will this continue?

It seems likely that China's high saving rate and government stimulus will continue until the global slowdown is over. The average Chinese citizen must wonder to himself, "How long will that take?" Or the average Chinese citizen may not wonder at all because the answer is that it doesn't matter. The CCP will be keeping its boot on the neck of the people for a long time to come—if they can manage it—despite the growing unrest in the country, or a growing economy or a shrinking one. The more likely outcome is a collapse in China's macroeconomy. Perhaps the ultimate irony is that China's best bet to spur real demand for its economy, short of lifting the heavy stone of economic repression from the back of its people, would be for the American economy to recover first.

Inflation and Deflation Dangers

Like other nations, China's policymakers face the dual challenge of addressing both inflation and deflation in different economic sectors at the same time. However, with its policies of economic and financial repression, its uncontrolled and distorted development path, and rising discontent among its 1.3 billion population, the latitude of options and time frame for success are less than they would otherwise be. The CCP has kept a close watch on the growing civil unrest in Greece and other European nations, not to mention the public uprisings in the Middle East known as the Arab Spring. The leadership knows that the specter of popular violence in China is not only real and growing but is easily ignited as both inflation and deflation bring greater hardship and uncertainty into people's lives.

The effect of the global slowdown has been to depress commodity prices. In China, as elsewhere, this means lower demand and fewer jobs. Deflation in producer prices was a fact of life in late 2012—and remains so today—and a danger that China will try to resist or at least minimize as much as they can through government stimulus spending. The problem is that as they pour more money into the economy to stimulate demand, housing prices rise, which will push domestic demand even lower than it already is, so there is a delicate dance, at least in the minds of China policy makers, between stimulus spending and inflation in the producer economy:

> "A renewed inflationary trend could prove to be a further complication to policy makers' growth-inflation trade-off," said Glenn Maguire, chief economist at consultant Asia Sentry Advisory Pty Ltd. in Sydney. "China will have enormous difficulties in crafting a policy response to these divergent price and activity trends."[29]

On the consumption side of the economic equation, inflation is quickly becoming a grave concern in the CCP. In an economic environment where people's savings are in a net negative interest rate, they have been restricted from purchasing other currencies for hedging purposes. Whenever they are allowed to purchase gold, they do so in record amounts.[30] This while the economy is contracting. Though jobs are less available, rising food prices are becoming a major source of discontent and could spark violence in China on any given day.[31] And the fact is, food prices throughout the world are expected to continue to rise going forward.

Food for Riots

Several factors do not augur well for China's ability to keep food prices under control, or even to continue to feed its population going forward. Not only is China destroying its farmlands through development, pollution, overgrazing, and encroaching desertification, but also, China's food consumption patterns have changed. Much of this change has to do with the rapid urbanization of China's population.

In the past three decades, as China has moved from a mainly agrarian society to a developing industrial one, the Chinese diet has changed along with its demography. With about half of its people now in its major cities, China's consumption patterns have changed from a predominantly cereal-based diet to a meat-based diet, which is more cereal intensive in the production of meat from the feeding of livestock. The country's meat consumption has become similar to that of other industrial nations:

> Unlike the traditional energy sectors, food energy efficiency has received little attention. As meat production now depends on grain as a key input, any increase in meat demand will result in an accelerated demand for farmlands and grazing lands. In 2008, at least 35 to 40 percent of the cereals produced was used as feeds for livestock and only 43 percent was used for human consumption, which was because of harvest and post-harvest distribution losses and use as animal feed.
>
> The shifts in per capita calories intake and food consumption patterns (in China) can result in water scarcity. Consequently, different food consumption patterns require different amounts of water resources. With economic development and improved living standards, the proportion of water-intensive foods, such as meat animal products, has been growing in food consumption patterns so that more water resources are required to meet human food demands.
>
> (T)he status of per capita calories intake and food consumption patterns have major impact on food security and water security, but control of food energy intake and shifting food consumption patterns trend are still most difficult problems, and need further research.[32]

Add to this higher demand for grain production major droughts in grain-producing regions of the world like Russia, North America, as well as China itself, and there is great potential for food supply disruption in China that is not only a very real possibility, but is actually a likely event on the horizon. Again, this is a near certainty as China's arable land disappears and desertification increases.

Another major factor facing China's food supply and distribution is due to its corruption in the food production process itself and in the related distribution inefficiencies and food safety issues. This is not a sideline issue in China today, as a Reuter's report tells us, but instead represents a fundamentally weak pillar in China's food supply problem:

One of the most dramatic shifts in public opinion was over food safety; respondents rating it a very big problem jumped almost 30 percentage points from 2008 figures, underscoring the impact of repeated food scandals on public confidence. Chinese media reports on food adulteration cases almost every day, including the scourge of old cooking oil dredged from gutters to be re-packaged and re-sold, and the regular tainting of dairy products with poisonous substances.[33]

It is difficult to overstate the level of public awareness of food scandals that involve life-threatening toxicity that can only be explained by a total absence of responsibility, quality control, or human decency:

> Rotten peaches pickled in outdoor pools surrounded by garbage are spiked with sodium metabisulfite to keep the fruit looking fresh and with bleaching agents and additives harmful to the human liver and kidneys. The peaches are packed in uncleaned bags that previously held animal feed and then shipped off to big-brands stores.
>
> Toxic preserved fruit is the latest item on China's expanding list of unsafe food products. Baby formula adulterated with melamine is the best known, but there is also meat containing the banned steroid clenbuterol, rice contaminated with cadmium, noodles flavored with ink and paraffin, mushrooms treated with fluorescent bleach and cooking oil recycled from street gutters. A 2011 study published in the Chinese Journal of Food Hygiene estimated that more than 94 million people in China become ill each year from bacterial food-borne diseases, leading to about 8,500 deaths annually.
>
> China's food-safety problems highlight both the collapse of the country's business ethics and the failure of government regulators to keep pace with the expanding market economy. Yet an excessive focus on poor government oversight often means that the much graver problem of disintegrating civic morality is neglected.[34]

As China's food problems persist and worsen while Party members eat only the very best, legitimacy again comes to mind. When basic

necessities like food and water are absent or are so toxic they are killing people, public revolt—such as is happening on a daily basis—can
only grow. Is there any wonder that internal security has become a top
budget priority?

For the moment, China can produce enough food to feed itself,
based upon the reported grain production figures and other official statistics, but for how long? Price inflation in food is a fundamental factor
in the legitimacy calculus of the CCP and stability in Chinese society.
The Chinese authorities are having great difficulty in addressing food
production and food safety problems today in any meaningful way. It is
a political time bomb and will only worsen as the weather and impacts
from China's extreme environmental degradation come into play. For
the moment, China can feed itself; but how long will that remain true,
given the threatening factors discussed earlier?

Financial Endgame

Regardless of one's perspective on China's growth path over the past
30 years, it is the years directly ahead that will determine whether China's economic and financial policy choices were the right ones. The
boom and bust financial policies and monetary policy manipulations are
not only reckless in and of themselves, but they have created long-term
distortions in China's macroeconomy. Real estate bubbles and nonperforming loans are pervasive throughout the Chinese economy, not just
in real estate, but in state-supported businesses and industries all the way
down to the micro-lending crisis of the tens of millions of small businesses that fuel China's economic activity.

Add to that the evil twins of simultaneous inflation in the consumer
sector, which are suppressing China's consumer economy, and deflation
in the producer sector, where commodity prices are falling and jobs are
going away, and the prospect of China stimulating its economy is only
a half-measure at best, and an exacerbating policy at its worst. There
is no one single financial or economic policy, or any combination of
policies, that the CCP can employ that will fix what is broken in the
Chinese financial and economic systems. Even with urgent advice of
the outgoing leadership to the new leadership to reform the political
and economic system, there is no reason to believe that it will come

about in any real or effective way. Not only is the graft and corruption so deeply engrained in Chinese society—especially in the political class—that it renders them unwilling to change, but for all intents and purposes, they are unable to reform themselves.

The reality of the day is that the political grip on power that the CCP enjoys and demands is dependent upon financial repression. The free movement of capital, the privatization of capital, and the opening up of the market for money and interest rates all mean a fatal loss of power and control for the CCP. The reforms necessary to change the financial and economic systems are, by definition, antithetical to the interests of the CCP and therefore will not happen in any measured way or neatly arranged, steady manner.

The day is near when civil disobedience and revolt over land theft, for instance, or pollution levels, or from any number of obscene acts by the ruling party in China, will become attached to other *causes belli*. The reaction to one of them will spill over into many others, such as astronomical food prices, devastation of people's savings through rampant inflation, and other such symptoms of financial collapse and economic breakdown. This is the path that China's financial policies are on and it can only lead to disaster.

Without a substantial consumer class to support the economy, the machinations from above have to become greater and more intrusive to maintain the perception of real demand and a functioning economy; the illusion of economic health through orgies of infrastructure construction and property development not only lay waste to a country's resources, labor, and environment, but crush the ability of the economy to provide organic demand. Government absorption of all productive labor and capital crowds out the organic economic activity of the small business person, and destroys the ability of the economy to find its footing on sound and real economic standards or certainty. Collapse and calamity are inevitable in China's economy; what remains to be seen is only the final straw to be laid upon that camel's back from above, or the spark of protest that immolates the entire system from below.

It is the world's great misfortune that this phenomenon is not just a major problem for China; it is one that all developed countries are facing. For seven decades, developed nations of the world have foolishly embraced the top-down destruction of their economies through the discredited-yet-statist-enabling policies of Keynesianism that have never resulted in sustainable robust economic growth, but rather, have consistently caused the rise of more dehumanizing bureaucracies and economic inequalities and inefficiencies, while at the same time, abetting the destruction of the human spirit along with the economies of those nations.

Notes

1. "GDP Growth in China 1952–2011," *Chinability*, updated November 5, 2011, www.chinability.com/GDP.htm.

2. Nake M. Kamrany and George Milanovic, "China's Growing Economic Strength in the 21st Century," *Huffington Post*, November 17, 2011, www.huff ingtonpost.com/nake-m-kamrany/chinas-growing-economic-s_b_1100416 .html.

3. Tom Orlick and Bob Davis, "Beijing Diversifies Away from U.S. Dollar," *Wall Street Journal Online*, March 2, 2012, http://online.wsj.com/article/ SB10001424052970203753704577254794068655760.html.

4. Sui-Lee Wee and Ben Blanchard, "China's Hu Says Graft Threatens State, Party Must Stay in Power," *Reuters*, November 8, 2012, www.reuters.com/ article/2012/11/08/us-china-congress-idUSBRE8A62LZ20121108.

5. David Stanway and Ruby Lian, "Analysis: China's Steel Mills too Big to Fail—or Succeed," Reuters, May 3, 2012, www.reuters.com/article/2012/05/03/ us-china-steel-idUSBRE84203620120503.

6. Patrick Chovanec, "China's Quality of GDP," *An American Perspective from China* (blog), October 26, 2009, http://chovanec.wordpress.com/2009/10/26/ chinas-quality-of-gdp.

7. Robert E. Scott, "The China Toll," *Economic Policy Institute*, November 23, 2012, www.epi.org/publication/bp345-china-growing-trade-deficit-cost.

8. China's stimulus package," *The Economist,* November 12, 2008, www.economist .com/blogs/theworldin2009/2008/11/chinas_stimulus_package.

9. Austin Ramzy, "When Wenzhou Sneezes," *Time*, November 28, 2011, www .time.com/time/magazine/article/0,9171,2099675,00.html.

10. Simon Rabinovitch, "Uncertain Foundations," *FT.com*, December 2, 2012, www.ft.com/intl/cms/s/2/7070ccdc-3ade-11e2-bb32-00144feabdc0 .html#axzz2JZnnah1s; Michele Cabruso-Cabrera, "Chinese Shadow Banking Endangers National Economy," *GlobalPost.com*, December 18, 2012, www.globalpost.com/dispatch/news/regions/asia-pacific/china/121218/ china-banking-credit-crunch.

11. Mark McDonald, "'Ruin Porn'—the Aftermath of the Beijing Olympics," *IHT Rendezvous*, July 15, 2012, http://rendezvous.blogs.nytimes.com/2012/07/15/ruin-porn-the-aftermath-of-the-beijing-olympics.

12. Keith Brasher, "On China Currency, Hot Topic in Debate, Truth is Nuanced," *New York Times*, October 17, 2012, www.nytimes.com/2012/10/18/world/asia/chinas-renminbi-has-strengthened-during-obamas-term.html.

13. "China's Real Monetary Problem," *Wall Street Journal*, September 17, 2010, http://online.wsj.com/article/SB10001424052748703743504575493120916038074.html.

14. Keith Bradsher, "Government Policies Contribute to Cooling of China's Real Estate Boom," *New York Times*, November 10, 2011, www.nytimes.com/2011/11/11/business/global/government-policies-cool-china-real-estate-boom.html.

15. Patrick Chovanec, "China's Solyndra Economy," *Wall Street Journal*, September 11, 2012, http://online.wsj.com/article/SB1000087239639044368600457763422014756802.html.

16. Patrick Chovanec, "Chinese Banks Are Worse Off Than You Think," *Wall Street Journal*, July 22, 2011, http://online.wsj.com/article/SB10001424053111190355490457645977407311473 8.html?mod=googlenews_wsj.

17. "Storing Up Trouble," *The Economist*, May 5, 2012, www.economist.com/node/21554234.

18. Kandy Wong, "Chinese Banks Step Up Lending in the US," *Financial Times*, August 29, 2012, www.ft.com/intl/cms/s/0/90cd25de-ec9b-11e1-8e4a-00144feab49a.html#axzz2JfkEy1qG.

19. Zhang Yuzhe and Zhang Bing, "China Banking Sector Sees Rise in Bad Loans," *MarketWatch*, June 25, 2012, http://articles.marketwatch.com/2012-06-25/industries/32407166_1_banking-industry-banking-sector-commercial-bank.

20. Ibid.

21. James A. Dorn, "Ending Financial Repression in China," CATO Institute, January 26, 2006, www.cato.org/publications/economic-development-bulletin/ending-financial-repression-china.

22. Kasia Klimasinska and Ian Katz, "U.S. Treasury Declines to Name China Currency Manipulator," Bloomberg, November 27, 2012, www.bloomberg.com/news/2012-11-27/u-s-treasury-declines-to-name-china-currency-manipulator.html.

23. Samuel Sherraden, "Putting China's Low Household Consumption in Perspective," *World Economic Roundtable* (blog), March 15, 2011, http://roundtable.newamerica.net/blogposts/2011/putting_china_s_low_household_consumption_in_perspective-46600.

24. "China Voice: Is China Economy Sliding into Dangerous Position?" *Xinhua* (English news), September 22, 2012, http://news.xinhuanet.com/english/indepth/2012-09/22/c_131867004.htm.

25. Michael Wines, "China to Unveil Its Strategy to Rebalance Its Robust Economy," *New York Times*, March 2, 2011, www.nytimes.com/2011/03/03/world/asia/03china.html.

26. Keith Bradsher, "China Confronts Mountains of Unsold Goods," *New York Times*, August 23, 2012, www.nytimes.com/2012/08/24/business/global/chinas-economy-besieged-by-buildup-of-unsold-goods.html.

27. Han Peng, "China's Savings Rate World's Highest," *People's Daily*, November 30, 2012, http://english.people.com.cn/90778/8040481.html.

28. Robert Wenzel, "China Bans Gold Exchanges," *EconomicPolicyJournal.com*, December 27, 2011, www.economicpolicyjournal.com/2011/12/china-bans-gold-exchanges.html.

29. Zheng Lifei, "China's Inflation Rate Heats Up," *Business Insider*, September 9, 2012, www.businessinsider.com/china-inflation-2012-9.

30. Kitco News, "Focus: China Gold Scam Could Translate Into Higher Demand," *Forbes*, July 20, 2012, www.forbes.com/sites/kitconews/2012/07/20/focus-china-gold-scam-could-translate-into-higher-demand.

31. "Chinese Gov't Urges Measures to Stabilize Food Prices," *Xinua* (English), January 29, 2013, http://news.xinhuanet.com/english/china/2013-01/29/c_132136326.htm.

32. Jian-ping Li and Zhou-ping Shangguan, "Food Consumption Patterns and Per-Capita Calorie Intake of China in the Past Three Decades," *Journal of Food, Agriculture & Environment* 10, no. 2 (2012): 201–206.

33. Ben Blanchard, "Chinese Increasingly Worried about Graft, Inequality: Survey," *Reuters*, October 16, 2012, www.reuters.com/article/2012/10/16/us-china-attitudes-idUSBRE89F1GU20121016.

34. Yanzhong Huang, "China's Corrupt Food Chain," *New York Times*, August 17, 2012, www.nytimes.com/2012/08/18/opinion/chinas-corrupt-food-chain.html.

Chapter 6

China's Extreme Environmental Degradation

O rdinarily, pollution alone is not counted as one of the more powerful factors that drive people to rebel against their government. Issues like starvation, economic impotency, overwhelmingly poor treatment of too large of a proportion of the society, growing economic disparity, divided elites, or other more stridently political and economic factors have driven people into the streets to riot and revolt against those in charge. And, as we have noted, most of those factors are actually present in China today.

Aside from those negative aspects, crucial levels of pollution and the impacts of it are yet another driving force with which the Chinese Communist Party (CCP) must reckon in China today. The pollution levels in China are of such an unimaginable—and *unmanageable*—magnitude that they pose a real and growing threat to the lives of millions. For that reason, pollution in all its forms threatens the social and political stability of China, and therefore, threatens the very legitimacy of the CCP.

Raging Environmental Crises

The unvarnished truth is that China has poisoned itself beyond all imagination. Air pollution in China, of course, is a well-known fact; during the 2008 Summer Olympic Games in Beijing, the air pollution was a major factor in the progression and scheduling of the Olympic events. But even though poor air quality is a well-publicized fact, it's just the tip of the proverbial iceberg in terms of how polluted and toxic the Chinese Communist Party (CCP) has allowed the once agrarian China to become. Not too long ago, China was known more for its bicycle traffic jams and the drab Mao attire of the masses, rather than for its millions of manufacturers, heavy industry, and world class wealth. Today, however, in addition to its industrial transformation and meteoric economic rise, China and the CCP own the dubious accomplishment of being the most toxic, polluted, and environmentally damaged country in the world.[1] Such facts raise very pointed and important questions.

For instance, why is pollution so much worse in China than in many other parts of the developed—or developing—world? What are the causes? And what, in specific terms, are the pollution levels in China today? And how widespread is it and what sort of environmental damage has occurred? Also, what kind of threats does China's pollution pose to the land, air, fresh water, and seas? And what of the Chinese people and the CCP? Of course, of prime importance are the prospects for China taking the right measures to reduce its pollution before the land, sea, air, and water are beyond restitution. How much of the environmental damage throughout China is reversible, and under the leadership of the CCP, is it even politically or economically possible to do so?

The answers to these questions are just as important—if not more so—than the questions themselves.

A History of Huge Mistakes

The primary cause of pollution in China lies with the CCP. As the historical records of both the Great Leap Forward and the Cultural Revolution have shown us, when the Party decides upon a policy, regardless of how idiotic it is, how damaging it might be to the country, or even how fatal it may be to its people, it pursues that policy all the way to the bitter end, and usually with disastrous outcomes. And, like all the other crises that China faces today, its pollution problems are nothing short of spectacular in their scope and utterly criminal in their impact upon the Chinese people and upon the environment of China, not to mention the rest of the world. The levels of pollution and scale of environmental degradation in every possible measure in China is figuratively—and quite literally—breathtaking.

As *The Atlantic* magazine noted in its July 5, 2012, issue:

> Few non-political issues in China garner so much attention today. The Chinese government does seem to be listening and at least trying to act. More and more local governments, under public pressure to publish pollution data, are starting to release data on the concentration of particulates in the air, as well as on pollutants such as NO_2, SO_2, and Ozone. The public is also getting more engaged, as bad pollution strikes lesser-known cities. In Wuhan, a city in central China, the sky turned brown on June 11 as the air pollution index registered an astounding 478 on a scale from zero to 500. The concentration of particles in the air that are smaller than 2.5 micrometers, the size at which they can penetrate the lungs, is on average 10 times higher in Beijing than in New York, according to our past three months of data collection.[2]

The tragic fact is that China's pollution problems are of such scale and magnitude that they not only pose a potent point of discontent and civil unrest in the country, but they also have reached fatal levels on an epidemic scale, causing an estimated 750,000 deaths every year.[3] Only an act of war, a pathogen outbreak, or a natural catastrophe could inflict more death upon China than its own pollution levels do today. Not surprisingly, as the level of environmental degradation increases, so does the level of civil dissent against the Chinese government. And the Chinese leadership is acutely aware of this, and while it is not denying it, it also has not shown itself to be willing or able to combat it.

After years of rapid economic growth, "China's environment has reached the most dangerous stage, affecting the health of many ordinary people," said Wang Yongchen, co-founder of non-profit Green Earth Volunteers. "We will keep having incidents like these" until the government gives ordinary people a voice in decision making," she said.

"I worry there will be more, and more violent, protests," said Beijing lawyer Xia Jun, who specializes in environmental litigation. "Many people will study Qidong and Shifang and copy them." Protest may be the only recourse. "Even if a judge feels he wants to help the people, many local governments do not allow courts to accept environmental lawsuits" against government-approved projects, Xia said.

Berkeley's Wang said he hopes Qidong is "a wake-up call" for leaders: "If they don't create genuine channels for engaging with the public before polluting projects are approved, they will inevitably have to deal with the much uglier aftermath when protests erupt."[4]

But the wholesale defiling of China hasn't happened overnight. It has, in fact, been the direct and long-term results of the policies of the CCP, the political culture of the command economy, as well as an attitude displayed by the CCP of what can only be described as deep contempt toward its own country, its people, and the collective future of the Chinese people. This deep contempt has been demonstrated time and again since the very beginning of the People's Republic of China in 1949, and in so many ways, many of which are mentioned herein. Having said that, why should it be any wonder that the CCP's attitude toward the environment is no different than it is toward its own people?

And lest anyone think that China's extreme environmental degradation has been a direct result of adopting its state capital model in 1979, or that it is somehow the sole result of reckless Western corporations violating the good earth of China, these are simply not the case. China's air, sea, and land pollution problems, its disregard for quality control, and its poor record of managing its resources, construction processes, and encroaching desertification have been a legacy of the CCP since its earliest days in power. Consider the fact that the leaders of the CCP, up to and including Mao Zedong himself, determined that the laws of science and nature did not apply to the Chinese under the *iron will* of the Communist Party leadership:

Mao Zedong's armies "liberated" Mainland China in 1949 and set to work immediately to build a new society. While China's newest rulers claimed to govern by rationality and "scientific socialism," in reality Mao and his acolytes believed themselves bound neither by the laws of men nor even by the laws of nature. They held that with will power, sweat and a superior ideology the rules of biology, chemistry and physics could be rewritten: according to their bizarre world view, infant piglets could be made to spawn litters, broken glass could fertilize crops and earthen embankments could be put to the same exacting use as concrete dams.[5]

Such self-delusional intellectual prostration by the leaders of the largest nation on earth sounds preposterous and impossible to believe, and yet such was the situation in Maoist China, and it cost the Chinese tens of millions of lives. During the Great Leap Forward, for example, over 80,000 dam construction projects were initiated, which included a dam on every one of China's major rivers. But by 1973, almost 3,000 of the completed dams had failed, that is, collapsed, leading to widespread flooding of farmland and homes. And in 1975, their efforts to dam the Huai River resulted in at least 80 dam failures and 80,000 deaths and left more than a million homeless.[6]

But the damage was far worse than that. The Great Leap Forward also impacted the native fish supplies to the point of eliminating fish from the national diet. Forests were also decimated and have yet to recover. The soil was made unproductive by becoming alkaline and toxic. The Great Leap Forward was more of a great leap of destruction and famine upon the land and rivers, and contributed greatly to the ongoing and seemingly unstoppable desertification process in China.[7]

Undeterred in its desire for power at any costs, the CCP has continued to consistently flout both economic and environmental laws over the decades to this day. Therefore, the great environmental crisis that China faces today is a result of the CCP's repeated violation of the laws of nature and economics since it first took power, and may well be the catalyst that causes the Chinese people to fully and completely rise up against the CCP and challenge its power. Rising protests against pollution are already the reality and are a source of deep concern for the leadership of the CCP.

And the truth is the CCP *should be* concerned. As the absolute leaders of the country, they have lost almost all of the credibility or legitimacy that they might have earned with the development of China; both the human and environmental costs have been unconscionably high. In fact, in early 2013, air pollution levels in Beijing were literally *off the scale*.[8] This heretofore unknown level of toxicity comes after years of official knowledge of the life-threatening levels of pollutants in the air and millions of respiratory illnesses and death attributed to it. To put it in the simplest of terms, the CCP has amply shown the world—and its own people—that it respects neither.

Consequently, China's leadership has chosen to follow a path of development without regard for the negative environmental impacts of its actions, and has proven itself to be just as bad, or worse, in its abuse of the environment than its former mentor and advisor, the late USSR. And by the way, that's really saying something. The late Soviet Union left behind a Russia and Eastern Europe devastated by levels of land toxicity, deforestation, desertification, poisoned ground water, dead zones in its sea coasts, and rivers and lakes unfit for human consumption and virtually unlivable for wildlife.

The key point to bear in mind in China with regard to policy and reality is that the CCP remains in firm control of which areas get polluted with what chemical. If corruption is tolerated and encouraged at the expense of stated anti-pollution policies or, in this case, at the expense of the environment, the CCP is fully responsible, as 90 percent of environmental regulations are not enforced.[9] Thus, as China simultaneously struggles with hundreds of millions still in poverty, an economic slowdown, and a pollution crisis, the political survival of the CCP is what remains the priority for the leadership—sustainability and the pressing needs of the environment be damned:

> Looking at sustainability issues in China today, it is important for outsiders to understand the following: China's issues of sustainability are not historically linked to private consumption as they are in the United States or Western Europe; they are linked to the industrial processes that are supporting China's economic development model. China does not see emissions as a problem that must be dealt with immediately. With millions remaining in poverty, economic growth is still the priority. . . .

For some, it is a strong central government that provides hope that China will make changes. Yet at times it is the system itself that hinders the process of identifying and solving problems. . . . China's problems are complex and growing. While historically the costs of fixing the problems may have been seen as too great, the country is running out of options.[10]

Note that China's "issues of sustainability are not . . . linked to private consumption," but rather, "they are linked to the industrial processes that are supporting China's development model." That is an elliptical way of saying that the CCP's industrial policies are what is driving China's pollution levels to the very edge of disaster. As we will show in the sections below, expecting a different path from a central government than the one that has brought the country from being a backward agrarian basket case to "a world class economic leader" in only a few decades and helped the Party to remain in power is quixotic at best.

Hiding the Truth

Of course, in dealing with official figures, a word about access to accurate information on pollution is needed here. Like other statistics that come out of the Middle Kingdom, the reports on China's pollution problems—as horrendous as they are—are more than likely underreporting the problem. Perhaps China's distorted pollution figures are not as manipulated as its GDP figures (because pollution is much easier to measure and therefore harder to hide), but there is ample proof of the CCP preventing, or trying to prevent, accurate information on pollution figures from ever seeing the light of day because they know how explosive the information truly is.

For example, in Beijing, the Chinese government routinely underreports the levels of particulate matter in the air:

The controversy has centered on PM 2.5, the fine particles believed to pose the largest health risks since their small size (less than one-seventh the average width of a human hair) can lodge deeply into the lungs. The Beijing Municipal Environmental Monitoring Center has collected data on such particulate matter for the past five years but refused to make it public, preferring to release the readings of the larger PM 10 particles—which make the air readings seem cleaner than they are.

This led to farcical situations where the government would declare the air "good" or even "excellent" when the opposite was true. After the U.S. embassy in downtown Beijing began releasing on Twitter hourly air quality measurements, including PM 2.5, from its rooftop monitoring station, the disparity between the two accounts was stark. In the first analysis of the embassy data on pollution, Steven Andrews, an environmental consultant based in Beijing, found in the last two years Beijing officials have announced good or even excellent air quality nearly 80 percent of the time, while the embassy has rated 80 percent of days with unhealthy levels of pollution.[11]

And it's not just air pollution statistics that are unreported; in every category of pollution, it is difficult to take the *official* statistics at face value:

The 2010 pollution census revealed that China's "water is far more polluted and its industry is producing far more waste than previously realized." For instance, in 2007, water pollution was more than twice as severe as previously shown in official figures that had long omitted agricultural waste.[12]

And, fearing a civilian backlash, Beijing successfully altered a World Bank report on pollution in China due to concerns that the truth of the number of premature deaths might provoke social unrest. As noted earlier, the report found that about 750,000 people die prematurely in China each year, mainly from air pollution in large cities. Such environmental damage and abuse was common fare in the old USSR, and has since been matched—and perhaps exceeded—only by the Communist Party of China.

Command Economies, Dehumanized Society, and Pollution

One obvious question is: Why does the CCP think that it can continue to pollute the nation as if there were no tomorrow? And why has it been able to recklessly destroy the very earth that the people rely upon to survive? The answer may sound simple and simplistic, but it's the truth: The rampant and careless levels of pollution in China are a direct result of the communist political system and the lower culture that it spawns in its citizenry. Both of these influence how people view the land, natural resources, the country, and society. A cynical and pervasive apathy toward society at large develops within the individual, and a narrow self-interest that is focused on the *now* instead of on the future becomes primary in people's minds. People's attitudes and perceptions take on aspects of a callous and deep-seated nihilism and an ambivalent despondency toward life.

This destructive and dehumanizing attitude engenders the phenomenon known as the *tragedy of the commons*:

> (T)he plundering of the environment in the socialist world is a grand example of the tragedy of the commons. Under communal property ownership, where no one owns or is responsible for a natural resource, the inclination is for each individual to abuse or deplete the resource before someone else does. Common examples of this "tragedy" are how people litter public streets and parks much more than their own yards; private housing is much better maintained than public lands . . . the national forests are carelessly over-logged, but private forests are carefully managed and reforested by lumber companies with "super trees"; and game fish are habitually overfished in public waterways but thrive in private lakes and streams. The tragedy of the commons is a lesson for those who believe that further nationalization and governmental control of natural resources is a solution to our environmental problems.[13]

For the sake of comparison, prior to the fall of the Soviet Union (the other major command economy of the twentieth century and the progenitor of the CCP), information was sketchy about the degree of environmental damage and how extensive it had become throughout Russia and the European countries in the Soviet Bloc. But shortly after its collapse in 1991, word rapidly spread of the degree of damage that Communist governments had inflicted upon their people through environmental despoliation.

This is important to understand because it is a lower part of human nature that comes predictably to the fore under certain political and social conditions of command economies such as socialism and communism, regardless of where they are tried or imposed. Russia and Eastern Europe were turned into ecological nightmares due to the same behavioral patterns of unbridled despoliation of their land, forests, waterways, air, and seas that plague China today. Dangerous and persistent toxicity levels in every form and in every environmental category mark Eastern Europe and Russia. The environmental scars of communism are huge swaths of naked, unusable, defiled, or irradiated land where forests once were, poisonous lakes and inland seas with water levels and life depleted from overuse, mismanagement, and persistently high toxicity levels. Decades of communism have left the former Soviet countries as some of the most polluted, infertile, and degraded places on earth.[14] Such environmental disasters are the USSR's legacy in Europe.

But it's not just the big command economies of communism that bring destruction upon the environment; even Cuba has suffered, and continues to suffer great environmental damage as a result of governmental mismanagement, abuse, and disregard for the natural resources (as well as its people) under its charge. Soil degradation, deforestation, water pollution, decline in bio-diversity, and deteriorating urban conditions are present in discouragingly high percentages in that small island nation.[15]

As is noted in the following excerpt, the similarities between the former USSR and China today are unmistakable, undeniable, and yet completely predictable. This is true not only in their propensity to poison the earth, but also in their inability to effectively remedy the situation. Thus, although recently there have been laws passed in China to protect the environment, by and large, as in the old USSR, the environment is subject to a political and cultural environment that values holding onto power (of which development is a means to that end) more than the health of the environment, and is suspicious of any report that makes them look bad as a challenge to their power, which essentially is the case.

Additionally, we will see that the pervasive corruption in China also prevents any major efforts at ecological protection from being successful or sustained in their duration.

In the Soviet Union there was a vast body of environmental law and regulation that purportedly protected the public interest, but these constraints have had no perceivable benefit. The Soviet Union, like all socialist countries, suffered from a massive "tragedy of the commons," (w)here property is communally or governmentally owned and treated as a free resource, resources will inevitably be overused with little regard for future consequences.

In China, as in Russia, putting the government in charge of resource allocation has not had desirable environmental consequences. Information on the state of China's environment is not encouraging. According to the Worldwatch Institute, more than 90 percent of the trees in the pine forests in China's Sichuan province have died because of air pollution. In Chungking, the biggest city in southwest China, a 4,500-acre forest has been reduced by half. Acid rain has reportedly caused massive crop losses.[16]

It is noteworthy that Thomas J. DiLorenzo wrote "Why Socialism Causes Pollution" in 1992; however, the depth and extent of China's environmental pollution has become much worse since then. Today, given the culture of corruption and economic challenges of a global recession, the prospect for real environmental recovery is not likely. The Chinese leadership views its only choice as being a tradeoff between continued economic development and maintaining high employment at the expense of the environment. On the one hand, China has said that lowering carbon levels is a priority, but most estimates say that China's GDP must grow at least by 8 percent per year just to maintain social stability. But even when supposedly meeting growth targets, they are still seeing over 100,000 strikes and demonstrations every year.

At the same time, a Chinese government-backed report estimates that environmental degradation inhibits GDP by almost a quarter in 2008. That means that even though the *official* GDP growth has been reported to be about 10 percent per year, the *real* GDP in any given year is 25 percent less than what is reported. The costs of poisoned water, air, land, and desertification are, of course, not counted. They do not *fit* with Beijing's official, politically necessary statistics. But as far back as 2005, Pan Yue, vice minister of environmental protection, predicted that the country's economic miracle would soon, end because of China's ravaged environment, noting that, "We are using too many raw materials to sustain this growth. To produce goods worth $10,000, for example, we need seven times more resources than Japan, nearly six times more than the United States and, perhaps most embarrassing, nearly three times more than India."[17]

The point is that the political realities in China are such that the CCP is not about to sacrifice economic growth, which is its main source of legitimacy, for a cleaner environment. Corruption throughout the system makes it highly improbable that any real improvements will occur in the foreseeable future. Thus, with the possible exception of the removal of the CCP from power, China's extreme environmental degradation will continue.

Pollution, Development, and Democracy

The above discussion on command economies and pollution is not intended to imply that pollution has never been a problem in the Western democracies or any other nations for that matter, because it certainly has. The reality is that economic development comes with pollution as a by-product, and there have been thousands of incidents of polluted rivers and lakes, toxic soil, and harmful chemicals in the food chains of every developed country. The creation of a modern world and the need for greater amounts of energy and technology simply come with those risks. The key, of course, is to minimize them as much as reasonably and economically possible. The best way to do that is with free and openly representative government. The developed nations with the highest pollution standards and the cleanest air and water and most innovative ways to reduce pollution and identify or develop clean technologies are all democracies.[18]

This fact does not preclude democracies nor advanced technologies from polluting the earth in horrible ways, but it does make it less likely. That said, the 2011 Fukushima nuclear accident in Japan is just one dramatic example of technology endangering the environment, but there are many others. And of course, there is no political element in a tsunami wiping out a nuclear power facility; it was a natural disaster (two, actually: the earthquake and then the tsunami) before it became a nuclear catastrophe. (Although, building nuclear power plants in a seismic zone might well have been a political decision.) Regardless, Fukushima-sized disasters are occurring in China every year as a result of China's development policies and unsupervised corporate polluters.[19]

The truth is that there is no perfection to be had on the environmental front in any industrialized society; modern human civilization is, by its very existence, invasive to nature. The issue, however, is the degree of pollution that each economy and government produces, and the steps that are—or are not—taken to alleviate the worst aspects of it, to minimize or eliminate it wherever feasible. The ability of a nation to adapt to environmental challenges is crucially dependent upon an open political and economic system that encourages and rewards innovation and punishes waste, fraud, cronyism, and environmental abuses.

In Western democracies, public criticism and response to private or corporate pollution occur via a free press, a vigorous and transparent legal system, and free elections. All of these tend to make the government and corporations somewhat more responsible and reactive in the long run, which has resulted in pollution levels declining to only a fraction of what they once were. But even at their worst, the pollution levels in the market democracies in the West were much less than those in the command economies. Even in the case of the 2010 BP oil spill in the Gulf of Mexico, as bad as it was (and in some ways, continues to be), and where there has been a massive clean-up effort, there was no question about where ultimate responsibility belonged, nor was there any dispute over whether the pollution would be addressed and remedied in some way.

As imperfect as that process may be in market democracies, it simply doesn't occur in China. Although the CCP fears a revolt from the people, it never has, and in all likelihood never will behave responsibly toward its people. To do so would require reform and a level of openness that would prove fatal to the CCP.[20] Furthermore, because it does not rely upon the market forces or freedom of information, the CCP and its state-owned economy can do to the environment and the people whatever it wants to do in its pursuit of power and wealth. That fact has been pretty well established. And power and wealth are the objectives above all else; the CCP leadership seeks to remain in power and to enrich themselves. And there is little or no respect for humanity or habitat in their pursuit of those objectives, with the degradation of the country and health of its population as apparently acceptable costs.

Such attitudes and behaviors also explain and reinforce just why the leadership of the CCP has been transferring so much wealth out of China; they must know what they are doing to the country, and understand that they may well need an *escape plan* at some point. And again, like the USSR before it, the CCP has proven that command economies are by a long stretch not only the very worst pollution offenders on the planet, but also the least capable of admitting it or changing the situation for the better.

China's Lose-Lose-Lose Proposition

The false choice that the CCP made between development and stability has come back to bite them, and the leadership is now faced with a horrible dilemma. Even though China seeks to continue on with its current behavior and development plans, the fact is the environment will soon be unable to support the country.[21] Indeed, China's environment is already failing under the current scorched earth development policies of the CCP. At the same time, as the economy begins to fail on several fronts, the CCP also faces internal instability that comes with economic slowdown. And finally, the CCP faces perhaps even greater levels of instability due to the widespread, ungodly levels of pollution throughout the country.

If the CCP seeks to even begin to remedy its environmental problems, it must begin with the closing of thousands of horrendously toxic enterprises as well as develop and enforce costly environmentally responsible production processes if it's to salvage what's left of China's environment. But both of those would increase the danger of instability that comes with an even steeper drop in the economy as workers are laid off from the polluting companies and revenues fall due to pollution controls. It's a lose-lose-lose proposition, but that is the reality the CCP faces today. As Peng Peng, of the Guangzhou Academy of Social Sciences, told the *Washington Post*, "Officials are thinking twice about whether to close polluting factories, whether the benefits to the environment really outweigh the danger to social stability."[22]

That is the tradeoff, but it's a false one. High polluting factories—from dye makers to steel producers—that have been or were supposed to be shut down have either been allowed to remain open or re-open without any reduction in their pollution levels. And China has no intention of shuttering any of its coal-burning energy plants, either, but rather, to build more of them.[23] Ultimately, China's development policies not only threaten their own environment, but the rest of the world's as well:

China's spectacular economic boom may be inflicting a terrible toll on the global environment, a new study warns.

China is becoming the sucking force, taking raw materials from across the planet, because it alone doesn't have the resources it needs to sustain its growth.[24]

Given China's rate of use and waste, the prognosis for the long-term effects the Chinese boom will have on the world's raw materials is not good. It is clear that China's own natural resources—its air, land, and water—are already suffering terribly.

As mentioned earlier, much of the air pollution stems from China's overwhelming reliance on low-quality, high-sulfur coal as its main source of energy. Coal makes up almost three-quarters of the country's energy needs. The acid rains that fall on one-third of China's cities are blamed on the burning of that coal and will only get worse over time. Ironically, China also leads the world in production of green technology, but its implementation and impact are underwhelming due to lack of grid access, graft, disuse, and conflicts with domestic policy.[25] From a policy perspective, public health and social stability are sacrificed daily in pursuit of growth and development. But as the levels and costs of pollution rise, they both dampen economic growth and exacerbate the already dire conditions of public health and social stability. It's a self-defeating process that the CCP cannot change.[26]

The facts and statistics, underreported though some may be, nonetheless paint a dire and deadly picture of China's pollution problems. The damage and toxicity of China's skies, its inland waterways, rivers, lakes, and streams, as well as its lands and coastal regions are not only in most cases the *very worst* in the world, but are manifestly on a truly biblical scale in terms of the devastation to China's environment in all quarters. The following are collected statistics, data, news article assertions, and reports of various stripes of eclectic provenance, which paint a harrowing and depressing picture of China today—and an even more frightening one of the China of tomorrow.

China's Air Pollution—Gasping For a Breath of Fresh Air

To say that China has an air pollution problem is to grossly understate the facts. Just how bad is China's air pollution? It's actually impressively worse than any one statistic or even any group of statistics can possibly convey; nonetheless, let us take a deep breath and jump right into an examination of the facts.

A poll by the Pew Research Center in 2008 found that 74 percent of those interviewed in China worried about air pollution—little wonder why. In major cities, blue skies are rare; the streets are difficult to see from only a few stories up, and "fresh air tours" to the countryside are commonplace. According to World Bank statistics, China hosts 16 out of 20 of the world's cities with the dirtiest air, with many cities' air smelling like sulfur or leaded gasoline. The Chinese government reports that about one-fifth of the Chinese urban population breathes heavily polluted air and that only one-third of 340 Chinese cities that monitor air pollution meet air pollution safety standards. As a comparison, the air quality in Beijing is 16 times worse than it is in New York City.

This is due to several factors. Predictably, with the explosion of automobiles in the past two decades, auto emissions accounted for 79 percent of China's total air pollution in 2005[27], which shows no sign of abating. This is because China is in the middle of the largest rural migration in human history[28], with millions of its rural people immigrating into mushrooming cities. With factories multiplying and car ownership surging, the cities' air quality has plummeted as, for the first time in the country's history, more people live in cities than in rural areas. [29] The country is now the second largest emitter of carbon dioxide after the United States.[30]

Another cause is that many of China's worst polluted cities are surrounded by heavy industry, coal-fired plants.[31] In cities like Shanghai, the air is so polluted that airports have been shut down due to poor visibility.[32] But it gets much worse than visibility problems. A study by the World Bank found that only 1 percent of the urban population of 690 million breathes air that is actually safe by European Union standards, and the World Health Organization (WHO) calculates that the number of airborne particulates in northern China is about ten times above a safe level.[33]

Just as one would imagine, the consequences of toxic air are getting worse as the toxicity level rises. Hong Kong researchers have identified a direct relationship between the rise in pollutant percentages in the air with a rise in the number of people taken to the emergency hospital.[34] One of the reasons for this is that China relies on coal for about 70 percent of its total energy supply (compared to the United States' 30 percent). As a consequence, China is the world's biggest producer of carbon dioxide, passing the United States in 2006, according to the Netherlands Environmental Assessment Agency.[35] And the future doesn't look any better. By 2030, China's carbon dioxide emissions could equal the entire world's CO_2 production today, if the country's carbon usage keeps pace with its economic growth.[36] Take the presence of automobiles, for example. In the 1980s, there were virtually no private cars in China. In 2003, there were 14 million. In 2015, China will have an estimated 150 million cars.[37]

China also has a significant impact on the regional and global environment. The burning of coal is responsible for about half of the world's sulfur dioxide emissions and causes acid rain throughout East Asia; and China is home to an estimated 56 underground coal fires that not only have been burning for decades—and in some cases, centuries—but consume up to 30 millions tons of coal per year and send huge amounts of carbon dioxide and sulfur dioxide into the air.[38] Huge brown clouds of sulfur actually cross the Pacific Ocean and impact the West Coast of the United States. The haze in Los Angeles is no longer just due to local sources; 25 percent of the particulates in Los Angeles air come from China.[39]

The world's most polluted city is Linfen, China; not surprisingly, China's State Environmental Protection Agency reported that it has the worst air in the country.[40] However, as noted earlier, Beijing has recently upped its game, with air pollution readings that are literally off the charts in January of 2013, with Beijing residents describing the level of air pollution as "post-apocalyptic," "terrifying," and "beyond belief."[41]

It is helpful, if not frightening, to recall that this is several years after the Chinese government admitted there was a problem with air pollution and claimed they were taking steps to reduce it. In any case, the real number of Chinese whose health is destroyed or lives are cut short by pollution-linked diseases is truly difficult to know because the government fears that the figures could trigger social unrest, which is absolutely true.

Bitter Water: China's Lakes, Rivers, and Streams of Poison

In addition to achieving the auspicious title of the world's worst air quality, the CCP has successfully poisoned the country's lakes, rivers, and streams to such an extent as to rival and even surpass the absolute worst polluted water sources in the world. With an industrious effort and official CCP blessings, Chinese industry has poisoned and otherwise tainted the country's water supplies and waterways to such a level of toxicity that in many of them, the possibility of sustaining life itself is well on its way to being completely eliminated.[42]

And like its air pollution, the CCP has only recently allowed somewhat accurate assessments of the damage to come to the surface. The 2010 pollution census revealed that China's ". . . water is far more polluted and its industry is producing far more waste than previously realized." For instance, in 2007, water pollution was more than twice as severe as previously shown in official figures that had long omitted agricultural waste.[43]

How could they understate the problem so much? One big reason is that China's first pollution census in 2010 revealed farm fertilizer was an even bigger source of water contamination than industrial runoff. It is now estimated that about 11.7 million pounds of organic pollutants are dumped into Chinese waters on a daily basis. This is over two times the amount in the United States (about 5.5), and almost three times the amount in Japan or India (3.4 and 3.2, respectively), and nearly five times the amount in Germany (2.3).[44]

How Bad Is the Water Pollution Situation in China?

It's difficult to overstate and impossible to enumerate completely the totality of China's water pollution, but some of the more egregious statistics are as follows:

43.2 percent of state-monitored rivers were classified as grade 4 or worse in 2010, meaning their water was unsuitable for human contact, according to data from China's Ministry of Environmental Protection.[45] Sadly, more than one-third of all the fish species native to the Yellow River are now extinct because of damming or pollution, Chinese officials announced in 2007.[46] But just as bad, or perhaps worse, is that up to 90 percent of China's urban groundwater is contaminated.[47] With such alarming statistics as these, one has to wonder: What level of contamination does the water have to reach before spontaneous and widespread revolution occurs?

The plain truth of the matter is that China's air and water is literally killing people—lots and lots of people. But it's not just urban water, tainted with industrial waste, sewage, and fertilizer runoff, that is causing these deaths. Water *shortages* and water pollution in China are such a problem that the World Bank warns of "catastrophic consequences for future generations." That is likely understating the problem of widespread famine that is likely to occur in China.[48]

But even if future generations will bear the brunt of the impact of polluted water, the horror stories of today seem bad enough. For example, half of all Chinese have no safe drinking water and two-thirds of rural Chinese—over 500 million—routinely have access only to water tainted by industrial and human waste. Carcinogenic chemicals are found in virtually all of the country's water supplies so that nearly 1 billion of China's 1.3 billion people drink polluted water on a daily basis, at least 600 million people drink water containing human or animal waste, and at least 20 million people drink water with high levels of radiation. Elevated rates of cancer of the liver, stomach, and esophagus have been traced back to excessive water pollution.[49]

What's more is that it is estimated that by 2030, China will have exploited all of the country's available water supplies, according to official Chinese government projections.[50] But today, many fish are grossly deformed, having only one or even no eyes and distorted skeletons. Also, a widely used paint chemical found in the Yangtze may be causing the extinction of the now rare wild Chinese sturgeon.

Cancer Villages and Insanity

But the human and environmental costs of China's water pollution are just starting to become well known, and the reports are as tragic as they are staggering. The following is just a sampling of the problems:

- Nearly 200,000 residents of the Hubei Province of central China lost their supply of water due to the contamination of the Han River by ammonia, nitrogen, and other heavy metals that turn the water into red "mud."[51]
- Water-borne pollution causes bladder and stomach cancer, and diarrhea, killing at least 60,000 people every year.[52]
- People living along polluted rivers in Henan Province have cancer rates 30 percent higher than the national average.[53] Drinking water has had to be brought in for over 1 million people due to toxicity levels caused by 1,111 paper mills and 413 other industrial plants, which had to be closed.[54]
- In many villages and towns, rivers and the drinking water are so badly tainted with factory effluents that ulcers appear on the legs of those exposed to it. High cancer mortality rates—in one case, 11 deaths out of 17 where cancer had once been rare—have given rise to the name "cancer villages" along many different rivers and tributaries.[55]
- In southern China, the toxicity is so widespread that brain damage, insanity, miscarriages, and death are all well above the national averages. In the village of Badbui, one-third are mentally deranged.[56]
- In many towns, villages, and cities, the air has such a sulfuric or *rotten egg* odor or distinct chemical smell that it makes one feel faint within minutes of inhalation.[57] In many such areas, the rates of cancer and birth defects are disturbingly high. Even in Beijing, as noted earlier, the air quality is horrid, with a toxicity level akin to smoking two packs of cigarettes a day, killing tens of thousands of children every year.

Why Has China's Water Pollution Gotten So Bad?

In addition to the industrial causes of water pollution, there are some very basic causes of China's water pollution that have little to do with industrialization. For example, more than 90 percent of household sewage is funneled directly into rivers and lakes *as is*, without any treatment whatsoever. It may sound hard to believe, but almost 80 percent of China's cities have no sewage treatment or water reclamation plants whatsoever,[58] nor do many have any plans to build them. Perhaps not too surprisingly, 90 percent of urban groundwater is contaminated, most of it "severely contaminated."[59] Add to that the water pollution caused by industrial waste and chemical fertilizers, and that represents tens or even hundreds of billions of dollars in pollution costs of the Chinese economy every year.[60] One can imagine that the spiraling health costs from China's water pollution disaster alone must be astronomical, and of course, will only get worse as toxicity levels continue to rise.

Like other imbalances in Chinese society, the water pollution problems are unevenly present in different parts of the country, but all regional waterways and water supplies are under siege, with far-reaching effects. Here are just a few examples:

- Northern China endures more serious pollution than the south. For example, more than 75 percent of the ground water in Northern China Plain is not safe to drink.[61]
- China's water pollution impacts the welfare of surrounding countries. Pollutants travel down China's rivers into the seas to Japan and South Korea.[62]
- Native fish populations in rivers and canals are nearing extinction in 70 percent of China's rivers, lakes, and waterways, as thick layers of trash, chemicals, and human and animal waste turn the water into liquid death zones unsafe for any life forms.[63]
- Rivers are routinely an abnormal deep green or red from the dumping of dye makers and paint manufacturers. Poisonous metals such as beryllium, manganese, nonylphenol, and tetrabromobisphenol are found in the drinking water of the Pearl River delta.[64]
- Routine polluters of China's rivers and waterways include drug and chemical makers, fertilizer factories, tanneries, and paper and textile

mills. Some close for a while, but quickly reopen in the same place or another location. Textile factories' hazardous, poisonous waste water dumped into China's rivers reaches 1 million tons in just two days.[65]

- It is estimated that 75 percent of all disease in China comes from its tainted water supplies.[66]
- All seven of China's river systems are polluted and the water situation in China is deteriorating.[67] At times, the pollution and the collection of garbage is so thick on some rivers that people can walk on them.[68]

These are just a few examples out of hundreds of thousands that occur every year in China. Any gains that might be made in one area or another are more than cancelled out in other areas, where untreated chemicals, sewage, heavy metals, dyes, plastics, radiation, and other pollutants enter China's water supplies daily, and in the majority of cases, with minimal legal or political consequences.

If there is a way to curb the levels of pollution in the country's water supplies, the CCP has yet to seriously implement it. At the rate they are poisoning their water and their people, the lasting legacy of the CCP is more likely to be the creation of a nation of pollution refugees rather than the world's next superpower.[69]

Lifeless Oceans

The costs of China's development policies are also borne in the depredation of its coastal areas because China is the world's largest polluter of the Pacific Ocean. Offshore dead zones—oxygen-starved areas in the sea that are virtually devoid of life—are not only found in shallow water but also in deep water. Dead zones are one of the main reasons China violates the coastal waters of its neighbors—there are no fish left alive in China's own coastal waters. That is because 50 percent of China's coastal areas are seriously polluted from untreated waste, industrial runoff, and shipping accidents, of which there were an astounding 733 in the decade from 1998 to 2008. In 2010 alone, China had 68 sewage-related red tides affecting 3.4 times the area affected in the 1990s.[70]

What life remains in China's offshore regions is toxic. Lead has been found in shellfish at 50 percent above safe levels, with levels of the pesticide DDT and cadmium at 40 percent above normal in China's oxygen-depleted coastal areas; and the toxicity is increasing. In 2009, 147,000 square kilometers failed toxicity tests, a 7.3 percent increase from 2008. Sadly, a 2010 China Marine Environment Bulletin found that 86 percent of China's five million hectares of estuaries, bays, wetlands, coral reefs, and seaweed beds were below what the SOA considers *healthy*. What's worse is that China's coastal wetlands are rapidly diminishing at an annual rate of 20,000 hectares.[71]

Although there continue to be pronouncements about the importance of getting pollution under control in all of China's rivers, lakes, streams, canals, wells, water tables, and coastal regions, it has not happened. Despite the well-documented dangers China's vast and pervasive pollution poses to human life and the environment, actions taken by the CCP have not been nearly adequate. As a result, the poisoning of China continues unabated. Foolishly, the perceived trade off of more economic growth equals more pollution still wins the argument in the halls of power of the Chinese government and in the actions of China's millions of manufacturers and farmers.

A Plague Upon the Land

As daunting as China's water pollution problems are, its defilement of the land is no less of a threat to the survival of tens of millions of people in the not-so-distant future. China has a particular and enduring challenge of feeding its people that other nations do not. With over 20 percent of the world's people but only 7 percent of its arable land, management of food production resources is a strategic and humanitarian necessity. To make matters worse, half of China's land is arid or semi-arid, making it "vulnerable to drying out in the early stages of climate change." But it doesn't end there. Eighty percent of the air and water pollutants end up in the earth anyway via toxic irrigation water, acid rains, and polluted water tables. Add to that the systematic polluting of it, building on it, flooding over it, and expanding desertification, and there exists the definite likelihood of another catastrophic famine in China sooner than later. Furthermore, when construction and population growth have reduced per capita cultivatable land in China by 60 percent in the past

50 years, it doesn't take a genius to figure out that China is devouring the very earth that sustains it at a suicidal rate, and that in the not so distant future, the country will no longer be able to feed itself.

How dire is the arable land situation in China?

By some estimates, 28 percent of China's land has been stripped of its topsoil from deforestation and soil erosion. Desertification has also increased due to drier conditions, over development, deforestation, and over-grazing, while much arable land has been ruined by acid rains as a result of heavily polluting industrial regions. About 10 million of China's 120 million hectares of arable land are polluted today, with another 133,000 hectares of cultivated land poisoned or degraded by solid waste. Half the soil in the industrialized south of China is toxic with cadmium, arsenic, mercury and other poisons. Farmers are aware of how bad the soil is and will not eat from their own crops.[72] Grasslands are increasingly overused, resulting in 130 million hectares having already degraded, losing vegetative cover, and another 2 million hectares added to that number every year.[73]

As a result, the long term trend is for China to have increasing difficulty in feeding its people.[74] Given that development is the main driver of the Chinese economy, the loss of arable lands may be expected to accelerate. Expecting a fundamental change in behavior from developers, local authorities, and party elite is irrational, because a change in course would cause economic hardship at all levels in the near term. If past is prologue, the probability of any meaningful change in direction or enforcement of environment laws while the CCP is in power is practically zero.

China's Dead Zones

As China's twin evils of overdevelopment and pollution eat up its arable land, the prospects for the future grow more desperate as the land deteriorates. As *The Guardian* reported on June 12, 2012:

> Nowhere is the global push to restore degraded land likely to be more important, complex and expensive than in China, where vast swaths of the soil are contaminated by arsenic and heavy

metals from mines and factories. Scientists told the Guardian that this is likely to prove a bigger long-term problem than air and water pollution, with potentially dire consequences for food production and human health.

Zhou Jianmin, director of the China Soil Association, estimated that one-tenth of China's farmland was affected. "The country, the government and the public should realise how serious the soil pollution is," he said. "More areas are being affected, the degree of contamination is intensifying and the range of toxins is increasing."

Other estimates of soil pollution range as high as 40 percent, but an official risk assessment is unlikely to be made public for several years. Scientists: China's soil pollution could be a bigger long-term problem than air or water.[75]

And, as in the case of both air and water pollution statistics, the CCP is loath to tell the truth to the very people who are suffering from the pollution. A six-year government soil survey was conducted, but the CCP authorities prevented the release of the findings.[76]

The Land of Arsenic

As a result of China's extensive mining industry, arsenic has become one of the main soil pollutants, bringing with it horrendous consequences for soil toxicity. By some estimates, China has about 70 percent of the world's arsenic in its soil, and its drive for precious and rare earth metals is causing it to come to the surface.[77]

But the emergence of toxins from below seeping into China's farmlands is not just limited to arsenic; this also includes lead and heavy metals from mining and from industrial discharges and heavy use of pesticides and chemical fertilizers. The costs are high: upwards of 20 billion yuan ($3.21 billion) every year.[78]

How much of China's soil is polluted either with arsenic or cadmium? Estimates vary and the true numbers are probably not known. If they are known, they most likely have not been released to the public. Still, by some estimates, at least 10 percent is contaminated with both arsenic and cadmium from industrial waste and China's 280,000 mines.

A scientific survey revealed that fully 10 percent of China's rice is tainted with unsafe levels of cadmium.[79] But the Chinese Academy of Agricultural Sciences estimates that about 16 percent of China's 120 million hectares of farmland are tainted. However, given the extreme levels of pollution in the air and water coupled with the CCP's resistance to releasing data, 16 percent of farmland pollution seems like a very low number. Government plans to remediate 27 million hectares by 2015 would seem to suggest that over 25 percent of the land is contaminated and that the situation will get worse rather than better.[80]

Like its polluted air and water, China's land degradation is a clear and present threat to China's ability to feed itself. However, compared to air and water pollution, soil decontamination is a much more difficult proposition, and can take hundreds of years if not treated correctly, and in some cases, is irreversible.[81] It is difficult to imagine that a government— one that has supposedly been fighting pollution for years and yet has only seen pollution levels continue to rise to devastating levels as recently as in 2013—is serious in its efforts.

Why Is Such Pollution Tolerated?

Although there is official lip service given to the need for changing the way the land is treated by the farmers and industry, there has been little change in their policies and practices. One main reason is that the CCP regards industrialization as key to their power and to the rise of China as a great power in the world. China's clout in the world is dependent upon China being the world's factory. Remember: It was China's low costs that attracted the world's manufacturers to China in the first place (and its billion-plus population as a potential market). Today, however, there is greater pressure since labor costs are much higher than even 10 years ago and manufacturers are beginning to move their factories elsewhere. Cutting costs wherever they can is what attracts the foreign investment into China. Adding pollution-controlling costs into the equation is mostly a non-starter with Chinese manufacturers.

Another reason related to the prior one is that the CCP fears the economic costs of pollution reduction efforts, which would include inspecting and closing hundreds of thousands of factories, mines, mills, and other industrial sites. The amount of people put out of work would be intolerable and, the CCP fears, cause greater unrest than is caused by the high pollution levels. Also, consider the perspective of the hundreds of millions of Chinese citizens who have risen from poverty to a middle-class lifestyle. While the pollution is bad, these Chinese are living lives their parents would likely have never dared to dream about living. Therefore, to them, the pollution, though not desirable, is a cost worth bearing for the middle-class rewards.

Of course, there are other reasons, as well, such as the political structure of the CCP and its inability to withstand reform and openness. Graft and corruption also play their parts. In lower party levels, local government authorities are paid—or bribed—by industry and farmers to look the other way, as well as rewarded by party officials for delivering economic growth. Thus, there is no incentive to change the *status quo*; local officials have often been known to even provide official cover for polluters.

Given all of the above, it is easy to see why there is the resistance and inertia against pollution reform from official quarters in China. At the same time, polling indicates that pollution is regarded as one of the top threats that China faces. So far, the CCP has not come to grips with the urgency of their problem, and when they have, the CCP has shown itself unable to effectively address the problem. In many instances, they just don't seem to care.

CCP Land Policies Promote Abuse

In his book, *China on the Edge: The Crisis of Ecology and Development* (China Books and Periodicals, Inc., 1991, translation), He Bochuan argues at the time of its writing that in many ways, China's environmental problems had already reached catastrophic levels. First published in 1988, *China on the Edge* sold 430,000 copies before authorities banned it as part of the post-Tiananmen crackdown. In his book, He Bochuan does not content himself with merely listing China's ecological problems: He goes one step further and connects these environmental horrors to government mismanagement and policy failure in virtually every sector of Chinese affairs, and he details how years of overpopulation and the demands of a growing economy have combined to put China on the brink of a major environmental disaster.

As Bochuan keenly observed, a key reason behind the rampant land pollution is the structure of land ownership imposed by the CCP. To a great extent, the state—that is, the CCP—owns the land used by farmers and industry. In order to work the land, farmers have to obtain temporary land use rights by entering into multi-year contracts with local authorities.

One of the problems with this arrangement is that when those contracts expire, the land often changes hands. Therefore, the land is used by one party for a while, and then left behind for someone else. Since there is no ownership interest in the property, and no consequences for polluting it, there is little incentive not to use and abuse the land without caring for its ultimate condition. It's another aspect of the tragedy of the commons with tragic results, brought about by the CCP.

But there are other shortsighted CCP policies that have backfired, as well.

For example, according to China's Land Administrative Law, for every piece of arable land that is turned over for housing or industrial projects, it must be replaced by an equivalent amount of land. One recurring problem is that the replacement land is not nearly as arable as the farmland taken for industrial or construction purposes. "China should improve its policy to ensure reclaimed land matches the used arable land not just in area, but also in production capacity," said Zeng Xibai, a researcher with the Chinese Academy of Agricultural Sciences.[82]

Another unintended consequence of this CCP land policy, according to Qiu Baoxing, vice minister of housing and urban-rural development, is the clever trick of local authorities destroying forestland to replace taken arable lands, which serves only to further damage the environment for decades and perhaps hundreds of years to come, by adding to desertification rather than enhancing it or merely restoring it.

Losing the Breadbasket

China's loss of land through the various means noted here comprise an aggregate threat of China's future inability to grow enough grain to feed itself. As far back as 1997, satellite photos showed that China was losing cultivated land to development 2.5 times faster than was previously thought. As a result, China is now dangerously close to not being able to feed its population, and is doing little to stop the processes that are devouring its farmland.[83]

According to China's Ministry of Land and Resources (MLR), China's ability to feed itself is benchmarked to maintaining at least 1.8 billion mu (120 million hectares) for grain production. In 2010, the country was approaching that level, with just 1.826 billion mu available as of the end of the prior year. In fact, from 1997 to 2009, during its development rush, China's arable land decreased by 123 million mu.[84]

Another fact in the precarious position of China's food chain is simply climate change—that is, anthropogenic global warming or rising temperatures due to the natural, recurrent cycle of warming and cooling periods, whichever may be the case. There is acceptance among some Chinese scientists that a warming trend in China is a definite threat to food production. However, the cause of warming temperatures in China is immaterial for this discussion, since it is not likely to be effectively addressed by the CCP. Zheng Guoguang, who runs the State Meteorological Administration, thinks that global warming may reduce China's grain yields by 5 to 10 percent, or 30 to 50 million tons by 2030. This projected fall in grain production poses a huge problem because China's population is projected to reach 1.5 billion in 2030, as well. With an additional 200 million people to feed, China would need to increase grain yields by another *100 million tons* of food per year.[85]

To reach the necessary food production levels, Zheng estimated that China would require another 10 million hectares of arable land, which is what China is in the process of destroying at an astonishing rate. Without importing massive amounts of grain from other parts of the world, this equation of growing population and shrinking food production is, in itself, nothing short of a recipe for another great famine in China.

A specific symptom of China's vanishing arable lands is the rapid depletion of *black soil*, the fertile part of the topsoil in northeastern China. That region, including Heilongjiang, Jilin, and Liaoning Provinces, is the country's breadbasket, accounting for 20 percent of all of China's grain production. It is thought that 50 percent of the black soil has gone away in the past 50 years. This is another tough problem to overcome, since one centimeter of black soil layer takes hundreds of years to be formed. Today, it is vanishing at a rate of one centimeter per year.

According to Director Hu Ruixuan of the Soil and Fertilizer Administration in Heilongjiang Province, "Black soil layer was as deep as one meter in Heilongjiang Province during the early years after the founding of the PRC (People's Republic of China) in 1949. Nowadays, it's hard to find black soil of half-meter deep. Some areas are even left with only a thin layer due to severe soil erosion."[86]

He Bochuan puts the loss of arable land in even starker but more realistic terms when he says that on a *per capita basis*, "Construction and population growth have reduced per capita cultivatable land in China by 60 percent in the past 50 years."[87] There is no longer any question of China losing its ability to feed itself through its own abuse and mismanagement of its land and resources; the only question that remains is, "How long does China have until that day comes?"

The answer to that question is not a happy one, as the arable land in China diminishes and becomes more exhausted year after year. This presents another set of specific problems. As the land loses more and more of its fertility, it becomes more depleted and requires greater amounts of fertilizer to get the same yields. But, as noted above, over-fertilization is also a major factor in both water and land pollution in China. It's a vicious cycle of dying farmland and overmedicating it to the point of toxicity with diminishing returns.

Lao Zhang, a farmer in Heignagzi village in Jilin Province observed, "Ten years ago, only 30 kg of fertilizer was used for one mu (0.07 hectare) of rice production. This has now doubled to 60 kg; otherwise, the yield would be reduced by 50 percent."[88] The trade-off between growth and pollution that China faces with its water and air pollution carries over into its land and farming output as well, but is only temporary. As is already apparent, as soil pollution increases, output decreases, with devastating implications for future food production in China.

The prospect for China to be able to grow enough food to feed itself in the coming years is increasingly a dubious one. Not only is China's land the most polluted on the face of the earth, but the country is destroying, at a fast clip what remains of its arable land for the sake of development and short term profit. In 2011, The Ministry of Environmental Protection began monitoring pollutants in the soil. Out of 364 rural villages' soil samples, studies found that 21.5 percent of them failed to meet national soil quality standards.[89]

Again, given the manner in which true statistics are often withheld in order to avoid public reaction, who knows how bad things *really* are? It is a fair bet that things are actually worse than reported. Furthermore, there is no reason to believe, regardless of what official policies are adopted, that things will improve over the next decade. For years, China has been the most polluted land on the planet; that is not about to change. Rather, China's ability to feed itself will most likely continue to decline over the next 30 years and will reach a crisis point by 2030.[90]

The truth of that statement applies not only to China's farmlands, but as we shall see in the next section, it applies to *all* of China's lands.

The Deforestation and Desertification of China

Besides polluting its farmland and turning it over for development, China is also in the process of denuding its hinterlands of their forests and grasslands, causing a rising level of desertification throughout the country. Like China's pollution levels in its waterways, coasts, and disappearing arable lands, these dual threats have reached crisis proportions and pose yet another threat to China's future existence. And yet again, the policies of the CCP drive these destructive trends.

Deforestation

Today, forestlands cover about 14 percent of China's landmass. Most of China's remaining forests are located in the northern, southern, and mountainous central parts of the country. Also, tropical rain forests are found in Yunnan Province in the south and in other provinces on the southern coast. Both sources of wood are being decimated as China's insatiable hunger for wood grows year after year.

For example, producing something as basic as disposable chopsticks uses 1.3 million cubic meters of timber annually. With China's furniture industry growing from 4 to 19 percent of the larger global market in only 10 years, the country's consumption of wood not only is stripping China of its forests in record time (50 percent of China's northern and central

forests have disappeared in only 20 years from both legal and illegal logging), but also is causing deforestation from Indonesia to the Congo and
Cameroon in Central Africa to the rainforests of the Amazon.

China's demand for wood is so great that it threatens forests on three
continents and is the cause of floods, soil erosion, mudslides, destruction
of rivers, desertification, loss of Giant Panda habitat, a 4 percent decline
in rainfall, and overall, has cost the country billions of dollars in damage.

The good news is that even with all of the damage that has been
done, in some areas of China, reforestation efforts are now being made;
in fact, China has undertaken the largest afforestation effort in the world.
Unfortunately, despite such efforts, it's a long-term proposition to replace
what has been lost—about 300 years' worth of tree growth.[91]

There are, however, some obstacles to this effort. One is that some
of the afforestation policies are ignored by local authorities. Another
is that the afforestation efforts are more difficult in higher elevations
and are more sensitive to temperature changes. Also, as drought persists
and temperatures rise, repelling desertification becomes more difficult.
Climate simulation models project a 17 percent increase in desert areas
with each degree rise in temperature. Also, reforestation efforts may not
be as successful as they need to be, since they often involve replacing the
natural level of diversity and varieties of trees lost with fewer, cheaper
varieties. The net result is a flawed and insufficient reforestation effort
and, therefore, a permanently diminished environment.

Desertification

Desertification is often a result of deforestation. It is a process and an
effect that also occurs when grasslands are overgrazed, due to farmers
trying to produce more food in response to the greater demand. Just as
the population has increased, and hundreds of millions of Chinese have
been lifted from poverty, so too has demand risen in response to these
phenomena. Enormous flocks of sheep and goats are a huge factor in
grassland depletion in Inner Mongolia, as the livestock population has
exploded from 2 million in 1977 to 18 million in 2000. A direct result
has been the desertification of one-third of the total grassland area. Some
estimates indicate that the entire Xilingol Prefecture of Inner Mongolia may be uninhabitable as early as 2020, as the two deserts in Inner

Mongolia and Gansu Province are in the process of merging into one larger desert.[92]

But desertification is not just a problem for Inner Mongolia; the Gobi Desert is expanding at a rate of *two miles every year* and is within 240 kilometers of Beijing itself. And in western China, the huge Taklimakan and Kumtag deserts are expanding at such a high rate, they are expected to merge in the not too distant future, creating one enormous desert.[93]

Then there's the Chengdu plain, one of China's primary grain-growing areas. It is threatened by sands from the Ruoergai grasslands. They were fertile and plenteous grazing areas until just a few decades ago, when great numbers of cows and goats began to overgraze the land. There is a danger for a dust bowl, similar to what occurred in the United States in the 1930s. There is already massive rural migration away from the depleted regions into the urban areas as wells have dried up and grain supplies diminish to where emergency measures have had to be taken to prevent starvation.

There's also the Tengger desert, which is encroaching from the southeast, and the Badain Jaran desert, from the northwest. The oasis between the two has shrunk by 111 square miles since 1950, while the number of super dust storms has grown by more than 400 percent. And, in places like Liangzhou district, for example, 240 of the 291 springs have dried up. Global warming is thought to be a part of the problem, since evaporation rates go along with rises in temperature, but the main cause of desertification is by far human activity such as over plowing, water mismanagement, increase migration and the transition to a market economy.[94]

The desertification process is most advanced in the northwest, where desert sands are devouring farmland, homes, and towns. Mingqin, a shrinking oasis area in Gansu Province, is an ecological disaster that may be just the beginning for other regions. The Yellow River has been diverted there by more than 100 kilometers just to replenish dried-up reservoirs and aquifers in Minqin, where the population has exploded from 860,000 to 2.3 million over the past 60 years, even as water supplies have steadily diminished.

Some reports say that as much as one-quarter of China's lands remain degraded, deforested, desertified, or despoiled from all the factors and causes noted herein. Those causes include over-pollution, under-regulation, corruption, water pollution from industry and human disregard, illegal logging, clear cutting, and overgrazing, as well as natural factors such as droughts and rising temperatures. The current set of objectives and political process of the CCP have made the prospect of reversal a difficult one. The process they have set in motion is a self-perpetuating one, but ultimately, like the Beijing Model, is self-terminating, too. As an area becomes degraded through deforestation, for example, the population moves to another area, does the same there, inflicting damages in a few years that takes decades or centuries from which to recover, if it ever can. Dr. Sing Yuqin of Beijing University told the *New York Times*, "Once the process gets started it tends to expand exponentially. And the people are pushed into a poverty trap from which it's hard to escape."[95]

What Is the *Real* Cause of Desertification?

Ultimately, desertification is caused by human activity. Humans change what has—or had—existed in the land for millennia relatively quickly, and nature does the rest. It is the arrogance and stupidity of the CCP—and of Chairman Mao, in particular—that bears the greatest responsibility for turning the largest country in the world into the largest desert in the world. Mao's policy, beginning in the 1950s, of turning grasslands into crop fields succeeded in only turning the topsoil into dust, which the wind carried away. The grain plan was another tremendous failure of the CCP. What were once grazing lands have now become deserts that threatened the very lives of hundreds of millions of people.

And even when signs are clearly posted against grazing, herders continue to do so anyway, because the land is so infertile, it's the only way they can eke out a living. But even that is a losing proposition. As the deserts grow, the food produced diminishes, forcing tens of millions into the cities to avoid starving today, and over a hundred million to do the same thing in the near future. That in itself is a demographic and logistical nightmare, and portends of a human services disaster on an enormous scale.[96]

As noted above, China has taken some steps to restore stripped forestlands and reclaim the encroaching desert sands, but the record of success is mixed at best. The survival rate for trees planted varies anywhere from less than 10 percent to maybe one-third, and even those surviving trees often hasten desertification rather than stop it.[97] Additionally, China faces huge problems with soil erosion and soil salination—another source of soil pollution—that depletes China's ability to grow the grain it needs to sustain its growing population. The ecological disaster that China has created for itself is seemingly not fully acknowledged by the CCP leadership—or perhaps it is, and they are playing a game of manipulating perception for the sake of their political and personal interests—but in any case, the damage done to the lands, the seas, the air, and the inland waterways is impossible to overstate. In the case of deforestation and desertification, China is literally many, many decades—if not hundreds of years—away from restoring the land to what it once was, if they are capable of doing so at all.

Ghosts of Famines Past

The same political and governing forces that have resulted in the mismanagement of China's economy and development paths are in charge of restoring China's environment. How likely is it that they will be successful? With corruption levels what they are, not very likely.

And most of the Chinese people understand this reality. In a study by the Lowy Institute for International Policy and the MacArthur Foundation, 75 percent of Chinese view environmental problems and climate change as a major threat to China's security. That is a staggering statistic, especially when one realizes that the CCP puts out almost daily propaganda citing the United States as the biggest threat to China. But according to the study, the United States is not even in the top on the list of perceived threats.[98]

The second biggest perceived threat among the Chinese (67 percent) is water and food shortages. This is very important because the Chinese know better than anyone else what is happening in their villages, towns, and cities.[99] However, it is also important because it serves as a persistent reminder for the Chinese people to recall the famines of the past brought about by the CCP. The worry over the ability of the CCP to continue to provide the very basic sustenance of life is a damning indictment of the CCP, regardless of what the latest GDP statistics might show.

The third biggest perceived threat to China, according to the afore-mentioned study, is internal strife. That is, 58 percent of Chinese view *internal separatists* as a threat to the country.[100] This widespread percep-tion is, again, a perception that is not born in a vacuum, but rather, comes from a reality in China today that cannot be ignored or glossed over. Indeed, the dangers of potential separatism within China are not lost on the CCP, which may explain the constant anti-American drum-beat in the Chinese news releases as an effort to redirect the animus of the Chinese people against an easily identifiable *foreign aggressor*, rather than against the CCP.

Such efforts are not new in China. In fact, keeping the memory of Western domination alive—even though it has not been the case in over 100 years—has been a policy of the CCP for decades. For example, at the Tiananmen Square Memorial in Beijing—if it can be called that—it does not mention the demonstration for democracy, nor of its bloody ending at the hands of the CCP. Rather, the memorial is a testament against the dangers and the threat of division of China by the Western Powers.

This constant focus on foreign aggressors—real or imagined—is an old ploy used by despots the world over throughout history as a way to keep the people's grievances pointed outward, rather than at the real source—in this instance, at the CCP. Unfortunately, when such propaganda stops working, usually when continued deterioration occurs, the next step is to *confront* the foreign aggressors as a way to unify the country behind the leadership. This, of course, means foreign adventurism to settle old scores—or, for that matter, some new or imagined ones.

What is crucial to understand from this study is that of the three main perceived security threats alluded to earlier—environmental prob-lems, food and water shortages, and internal strife—the latter two derive from the first. That is, China's horrendous environmental degradation, which is another way of saying environmental *problems*, is in large meas-ure what is causing the food and water shortages and internal strife. Granted, internal strife is also being generated by growing economic disparity, the abuse of privilege, corruption, and other factors we have talked about, but the wholesale polluting of the country by the CCP's policies is what is worsening food and water shortages and underscoring the lowly position of the vast majority of Chinese. With regard to the relationship between the CCP, pollution, and shortages, most Chinese, as the study confirms, are able to see what little remains of the forest for the trees.

That brings us to the viewpoint of the United States as a threat to China. Even with the nearly constant braying of official anti-U.S. pronouncements by the CCP, only half of the Chinese view the United States as a security threat. This, as noted above, is to be expected not only due to the reasons given, but also because as both economies begin to suffer more in the global slowdown, as the United States continues to borrow from China and export inflation via stimulus spending, and as China seeks to expand its reach to disputed islands that are also oil-rich areas of the Pacific, China has valid reasons to view the United States as an adversary. There is also, of course, the United States' continued military support of Taiwan. Interestingly, almost as many Chinese—about 45 percent—still view Japan as a major threat to China.[101] Old memories live long lives indeed in China.

The pollution levels we've talked about represent political, social, and economic threats to China; but they also represent an *existential* threat. Three-quarters of a million people die every year from pollution, and the shortage of food and water as well as internal instability pose grave dangers to China, as we know it today. This makes China's environmental degradation a qualitatively different crisis than all the others that it faces. The severe depletion of the environment at large as well as their own urban and rural habitats makes the environmental disasters that China has created for itself multi-dimensional and extremely complex to solve.

The necessary time, political will, economic costs to be borne, and massive national effort that will be necessary to even somewhat slow down the spread of the *environmental disease* would be monumental, if it was to ever come about. And even then, those efforts, both in time and expense, to restore the damage that has been done so far would be well out of the abilities of China's current economic arrangements. The CCP has proven beyond any doubt that it is simply not willing or able to absorb the costs of curbing its pollution levels and restoring the environment to where it needs to be, much less *allowing* the political changes that would be necessary to do so to unfold.

It is reasonable to conclude that the current economic structure in China will have to be radically altered in order to affect the changes that would be necessary to even begin to heal China. The scope of those efforts needed to change the economy and reverse the trend of environmental degeneration will only grow greater as time passes and the damage continues to worsen.

But will such necessary changes ever come about? Extreme environmental degradation is a problem that will not be resolved by treaties, fiscal policies, or relaxation of social policies. The system that caused the problem also perpetuates it, and provides neither the knowledge nor desire, nor even the incentive or tools to do otherwise.

Although there are different estimates as to how long China will be able to feed itself, it is clear that China's rate of development grows more unsustainable as more of the country becomes unable to support life. But rather than do what is necessary to correct the major pollution problems, the CCP is finding it much easier to buy the resources it has depleted and destroyed in China, elsewhere. For the past several years, China has been on a food and natural resources shopping spree, scooping up forestland in Canada and the United States and acquiring farms in sub-Saharan Africa and in South America.[102]

As the CCP continues its current scorched earth development and policies, the end result will be similar in scope to the two other great crises that were brought upon China by the CCP many decades ago. China will, sooner or later, be faced yet again with a crisis of famine and death on a truly industrial scale that will be unrivaled anywhere else, or in any other time, on Earth. As observed earlier in this book, the consequences of committing great and terrible errors in policy are themselves great and terrible as well.

Notes

1. "7 of World's 10 Most Polluted Cities Are in China: Report," *Want China Times*, January 16, 2013, www.wantchinatimes.com/news-subclass-cnt.aspx?id=20130116000083&cid=1105.

2. Michael Zhou, "A Stunning Visualization of China's Air Pollution," *The Atlantic*, July 5, 2012.

3. Richard MacGregor, "750,000 a Year Killed by Chinese Pollution," FT.com, July 2, 2007, www.ft.com/intl/cms/s/0/8f40e248-28c7-11dc-af78-000b5df 10621.html#axzz2JZnnah1s; Fred Pearce, "As China's Pollution Toll Grows, Protesters and Media Push Back," *Yale Environment 360*, March 18, 2010, http://e360.yale.edu/feature/as_chinas_pollution_toll_grows_protesters_ and_ meda_push_back/2254/.

4. Calum McLeod, "China's Rapid Industrialization Fuels More Public Dissent," *USA Today*, July 29, 2012.

5. Nicholas Eberstadt, "The Great Leap Backward," review of *Hungry Ghosts: Mao's Secret Famine*, by Jasper Becker, *New York Times Book Review*, February 6, 1997.

6. Sean Foley, "Three Gorges Dam," Toxipedia, updated July 6, 2009, www .toxipedia.org/display/toxipedia/Three+Gorges+Dam.

7. Thomas J. DiLorenzo, "Why Socialism Causes Pollution," *The Freeman* 42, no. 3 (March 1992).

8. Edward Wong, "On Scale of 0 to 500, Beijing's Air Quality Tops 'Crazy Bad' at 755," *New York Times*, January 12, 2013, www.nytimes.com/2013/01/13/ science/earth/beijing-air-pollution-off-the-charts.html.

9. Carl Delfied, "The Inconvenient Truth about China," Forbes.com, October 12, 2007, www.forbes.com/2007/10/12/china-environment-green-pf-etf-in_ cd_1012etfbriefing_inl.html.

10. Richard Brubaker, "China and Sustainability: Connecting the Dots between Economy and Ecology," *Guardian Sustainable Business Blog*, September 10, 2012, www.guardian.co.uk/sustainable-business/blog/china-sustainability- economy-environment-ecology.

11. Joe Jackson, "Political Pollution: How Bad Air Is Slowly Changing China," *Time/Science & Space*, January 22, 2012.

12. Jonathan Ansfield and Keith Bradsher, "China Report Shows More Pollution in Waterways," *New York Times*, February 9, 2010.

13. Thomas J. DiLorenzo, "Why Socialism Causes Pollution," *The Freeman* 42, no. 3 (March 1992).

14. Ibid.

15. Eudel Eduardo Cepero, "Environmental Concerns for a Cuba in Transition," Cuba Transition Project (CTP), Institute for Cuban and Cuban-American Studies, University of Miami, 2004.

16. DiLorenzo, "Why Socialism Causes Pollution."

17. Andreas Lorenz, Spiegel Interview with China's Deputy Minister of the Environment, "The Chinese Miracle Will End Soon," Spiegel Online International, March 7, 2005.

18. Eric Neumayer, "Do Democracies Exhibit Stronger Environmental Commitment? A Cross-Country Analysis," *Journal of Peace Research* 39, no. 2, 2002, Department of Geography and Environment, London School of Economics and Political Science, www2.lse.ac.uk/geographyAndEnvironment/whosWho/profiles/neumayer/pdf/Article%20in%20Journal%20of%20Peace%20Research%20(Environmental%20Commitment.pdf.

19. Austin Ramzy, "China's Industrial Accidents Quietly on the Rise," *Time Magazine*, July 29, 2010, www.time.com/time/world/article/0,8599,2007319,00.html.

20. Guy Sorman, "Destroyed by Communism," *City Journal*, June 16, 2009, The Manhattan Institute, www.city-journal.org/2009/eon0616gs.html.

21. Lorenz, Spiegel Interview with China's Deputy Minister of the Environment.

22. Christina Larson, "The Great Paradox of China: Green Energy and Black Skies," Yale Environment 360, August 17, 2009.

23. Peter Galuzka, "China & India Are Building 4 New Coal Power Plants—Every Week," *New York Times*, November 14, 2012, www.thegwpf.org/china-india-building-4-coal-power-plants-week/.

24. Stephan Lovgren, "China's Boom Is Bust for Global Environment, Study Warns," *National Geographic News*, May 16, 2005, http://news.nationalgeographic.com/news/2005/05/0516_050516_chinaeco.html.

25. Larson, "The Great Paradox of China."

26. Elizabeth C. Economy, *The River Runs Black: The Environmental Challenge to China's Future*, Council on Foreign Relations Books, 2010, cited in Stephan Lovgren, "China's Boom Is Bust for Global Environment, Study Warns," *National Geographic News*, May 16, 2005, http://news.nationalgeographic.com/news/2005/05/0516_050516_chinaeco.html.

27. Fang Jia, "Car Society Replacing Bike Kingdom," *China Daily*, updated October 6, 2004, www.chinadaily.com.cn/english/doc/2004-10/06/content_379974.htm.

28. R.A., "The largest migration in history," *The Economist*, February 24, 2012, www.economist.com/blogs/freeexchange/2012/02/china.

29. Michael Wines, "Majority of Chinese Now Live in Cities," *The New York Times*, January 17, 2012, www.nytimes.com/2012/01/18/world/asia/majority-of-chinese-now-live-in-cities.html.

30. Justin Gillis, "Carbon Emissions Show Biggest Jump Ever Recorded," *The New York Times*, December 4, 2011, www.nytimes.com/2011/12/05/science/earth/record-jump-in-emissions-in-2010-study-finds.html?_r=0; John Vidal and David Adam, China overtakes US as world's biggest CO2 emitter," *The Guardian*, June 19, 2007, www.guardian.co.uk/environment/2007/jun/19/china.usnews.

31. Marc Lallanilla, "China's Top 6 Environmental Concerns," *Live Science*, March 15, 2013, www.livescience.com/27862-china-environmental-problems.html.

32. Steven Jiang and Faith Karmini, "Beijing adopts emergency measures for harsh pollution," CNN, January 16, 2013, www.cnn.com/2013/01/14/world/asia/china-smog-blanket.

33. "Mongolia: Air Pollution in Ulaanbaatar—Initial Assessment of Current Situations and Effects of Abatement Measures," The World Bank. 2010.

34. Te-Ping Chen, "Air Pollution Fuels Hospital Visits in Hong Kong," China Real Time Report, *Wall Street Journal*, May 21, 2012.

35. Bryan Wash, "The World's Most Polluted Places," *Time Magazine*, September 12, 2007.

36. Alexis Madrigal, "China's 2030 CO2 Emissions Could Equal the Entire World's Today," *Wired*, February 8, 2008; and "Climate Change—the Chinese Challenge," *Science Journal* (2008).

37. Thomas Glaswin and Jonathan Porrit, "China Facts and Trends," 2007 Edition, www.globalchange.umich.edu/globalchange2/current/2007/Labs/China%20Facts%20and%20Trends%20(2007%20edition).htm.

38. "Air Pollution in Notoriously Polluted Beijing, China at Dangerous Levels," Fuel-Efficient-Vehicles.org, January 12, 2013.

39. Lovgren, "China's Boom Is Bust for Global Environment, Study Warns;" and Carl Delfied, "The Inconvenient Truth about China," Forbes.com, October 12, 2007, www.forbes.com/2007/10/12/china-environment-green-pf-etf-in_cd_1012etfbriefing_inl.html.

40. David Feinberg, "Chinese coal-mining city is world's most polluted," CNN, June 3, 2010, www.cnn.com/2010/WORLD/asiapcf/06/02/toxic.linfen.vbs/index.html.

41. Edward Wong, "On a scale of 0-500, Beijing's air quality tops 'Crazy Bad' at 755," *New York Times*, January 12, 2013, www.nytimes.com/2013/01/13/science/earth/beijing-air-pollution-off-the-charts.html.

42. "Beijing Admits Fish in Yangtze River Are Dying," AsiaNews.it, April 16, 2007, www.asianews.it/news-en/Beijing-admits-fish-in-Yangtze-River-are-dying-9011.html; "Fish Dying in Yellow River," AsiaNews.it, January 18, 2007, www.asianews.it/index.php?l=en&art=8264.

43. Jonathan Ansfield and Keith Bradsher, "China Report Shows More Pollution in Waterways," *New York Times*, February 9, 2010; and Shai Oster, "China Report Finds Extensive Pollution," *Wall Street Journal*, February 10, 2010.

44. Ibid.

45. Tai Lake, "Raising a Stink," *The Economist*, August 5, 2010.

46. Brian Handwerk, "A Third of Fish Species in China River Extinct, Officials Say," *National Geographic News*, January 19, 2007, http://news.national geographic.com/news/2007/01/070119-fish-china.html.

47. Chao Shengyu, "Underground Water in 90 Percent of Chinese Cities Polluted," Jinhua News Network, December 28, 2005, www.jhnews.com.cn/ gb/content/2005-12/28/content_552266.html.

48. Lester R. Brown, "Could Food Shortages Bring Down Civilization?" *Scientific American*, April 22, 2009.

49. Avraham Ebenstein, "Water Pollution and Digestive Cancers in China," Working paper, http://paa2009.princeton.edu/papers/91541.

50. Chris Buckley, "China Says Water Supplies Exploited by 2030," Reuters, December 14, 2007, uk.reuters.com/article/2007/12/14/environment-china-drought-dc-idUKPEK13275320071214.

51. Jonathan Kaiman, "Chinese Environment Official Challenged to Swim in Polluted River," *The Guardian*, February 21, 2013.

52. AP, "China punishes 7 officials for water contamination," *U.S. Water News Online*, March 5, 2009, www.uswaternews.com/archives/arcglobal/9chinpuni3 .html.

53. Joe Romm, "Chart of the Week: China's Pollution Crisis Is Worse Than Living In A Smoking Lounge," *Climate Progress*, January 31, 2013, http:// thinkprogress.org/climate/2013/01/31/1523611/chart-of-the-week-chinas-pollution-crisis-is-worse-than-living-in-a-smoking-lounge.

54. Lee Liu, "Made in China: Cancer Villages," *Environment*, March/April 2010, www.environmentmagazine.org/Archives/Back%20Issues/March-April%20 2010/made-in-china-full.html.

55. United Nations, "Natural Resource Aspects of Sustainable Development in China," Sustainable Development (UN), Agenda 21, April 1998, www .un.org/esa/agenda21/natlinfo/countr/china/natur.htm.

56. Lee Liu, "Made In China: Cancer Villages."

57. Ibid.

58. Will Clem, "Villagers tormented by stench of toxins and smell of fear," *South China Morning Post*, March 31, 2013, www.scmp.com/article/733795/ villagers-tormented-stench-toxins-and-smell-fear.

59. Dennis Walsh, "Dirty Laundry," *Sustainable Industries Magazine*, December 20, 2011, http://sustainableindustries.com/articles/2011/12/dirty-laundry.

60. Edward Wong, "Cost of Environmental Damage in China Growing Rapidly Amid Industrialization," *New York Times*, March 29, 2013, www.nytimes .com/2013/03/30/world/asia/cost-of-environmental-degradation-in-china-is-growing.html.

61. Wang Qian, "Most northern plain groundwater unsafe to drink," *China-Wire*, November 5, 2010, http://china-wire.org/?p=6858.

62. Susan Moran, "Nitrogen pollution disrupts Pacific Ocean," *Nature International Journal of Science*, 22 September 2011, www.nature.com/news/2011/110922/full/news.2011.552.html.

63. World Watch Institute, "China's Rivers: Frontlines for Chemical Waste," April 1, 2013, www.worldwatch.org/chinas-rivers-frontlines-chemical-wastes; Mathew Garland, "China's deadly water problem," *South China Morning Post*, March 27, 2013, www.scmp.com/comment/insight-opinion/article/1199574/chinas-deadly-water-problem.

64. Kyodo, "Greenpeace identifies 5 polluting factories in southern China," *The Free Library*, 2009, www.thefreelibrary.com/Greenpeace+identifies+5+polluting+facilities+in+southern+China-a0211000206; Xinshua, "Nine tonnes of chemical contaminate N China River," *Want China Times*, January 7, 2013, www.wantchinatimes.com/news-subclass-cnt.aspx?id=20130107000008&cid=1105.

65. Zhou Wei, "Textile industry poisoning China's Qiantang River," *Chinadialogue*, May 12, 2012, www.chinadialogue.net/blog/5435-Textile-industry-poisoning-China-s-Qiantang-River/en.

66. "Water Pollution in China," Scipeeps.com, May 18, 2009, http://scipeeps.com/water-pollution-in-china.

67. Lily Victoria, "China's Seven River Systems Are All Polluted," Peakwater.org, June 6, 2011, http://peakwater.org/tag/huai-river.

68. Huang Yan and Ben Blanchard, "Garbage islands threaten China's Three Gorges Dam," Reuters, August 2, 2010, www.reuters.com/article/2010/08/02/us-china-threegorges-idUSTRE6710SH20100802.

69. Lester R. Brown, "Expanding Deserts, Falling Water Tables, and Toxic Pollutants Driving People from Their Homes," Earth Policy Institute, August 23, 2011, www.earth-policy.org/book_bytes/2011/wotech6_ss2.

70. Mitch Moxley, "Pollution Rising Fast in China's Seas," Inter Press Service, June 20, 2011, www.ipsnews.net/2011/06/pollution-rising-fast-in-chinar squos-seas.

71. Ibid.

72. Nadya Ivanova, "Toxic Water: Across Much of China, Huge Harvests Irrigated with Industrial and Agricultural Runoff," *Circle of Blue*, January 18, 2013, www.circleofblue.org/waternews/2013/world/toxic-water-across-much-of-china-huge-harvests-irrigated-with-industrial-and-agricultural-runoff.

73. "Deserts Swallowing Up China's Grasslands and Cities," World Watch Institute, April 2, 2013, www.worldwatch.org/deserts-swallowing-chinas-grasslands-and-cities.

74. Ed Flanagan, "China can feed itself today, but what about tomorrow?" NBCNews.com. November 16, 2010, http://behindthewall.nbcnews.com/_news/2010/11/16/5470494-china-can-feed-itself-today-but-what-about-tomorrow?lite.

75. Jonathan Watts, "The Clean-Up Begins on China's Dirty Secret—Soil Pollution," *The Guardian*, June 12, 2012, www.guardian.co.uk/environment/2012/jun/12/china-soil-pollution-bonn-challenge.

76. Ibid.

77. Ibid.

78. Huang Rongfang, "Heavy Metal Pollution of Grain Costs China 20 Billion Yuan Annually," *Guangzhou Daily*, October 11, 2011.

79. Gong Jing, "Heavy Metals Tainting China's Rice Bowls," Market Watch/*Wall Street Journal*, Caixin Online, February 14, 2011, http://articles.marketwatch.com/2011-02-14/industries/30715843_1_cadmium-poisoning-rice-bowls-metals.

80. Xinhua, "Pollutants, Pesticides Threaten Farmland," ChinaDaily.com.cn, June 12, 2012, www.chinadaily.com.cn/business/2012-06/12/content_15496585.htm.

81. Ibid.

82. Xinhua, "Shrinking Arable Land Threatens Grain Security," *China Daily*, October 18, 2010, www.chinadaily.com.cn/china/2010-10/18/content_11423618.htm.

83. "China's Farmland Loss Rings Alarm—Satellite Photographs Reveal a Serious Problem," a report from U.S. Embassy Beijing, June 1997, www.fas.org/spp/guide/china/earth/landloss.htm.

84. Xinhua, "Shrinking Arable Land Threatens Grain Security."

85. "More Arable Land 'Needed' by 2030," China.org.cn, *China Daily*, August 23, 2007, www.china.org.cn/english/China/221782.htm.

86. Guo Jiali, "Gloomy Outlook for China's Black Soil," China.org.cn, June 12, 2012, www.china.org.cn/environment/2012-06/12/content_25629451.htm.

87. He Bochuan, "China on the Edge: The Crisis of Ecology and Development," China Books and Periodicals, Inc., translation, 1991.

88. Jiali, "Gloomy Outlook for China's Black Soil."

89. Professor Pan Genxing of Nanjing Agricultural University, report, *Economic Observer*, June 11, 2012.

90. Catarina Bouca, "Soil Pollution a Growing Problem in China," *Toonari Post*, March 27, 2011.

91. Jonathan Watts, "China Makes Gain in Battle against Desertification but Has Long Fight Ahead," *The Guardian*, January 4, 2011, www.guardian.co.uk/world/2011/jan/04/china-desertification.

92. Lester R. Brown, "Plan B: 2.0: Rescuing a Planet Under Stress and a Civilization in Trouble" Earth Policy Institute, 2006, www.earth-policy.org/books/pb2/pb2ch5_ss5.

93. Ibid.

94. "Desertification in Mongolia," Swiss Agency for Development and Cooperation, September 30, 2009, www.greenmongolia.mn/en/about-codep/facts-about-desertification.html.

95. Eric Eckholm, "Chinese Farmers See a New Desert Erode Their Way of Life," *New York Times*, July 30, 2010, www.nytimes.com/2000/07/30/world/chinese-farmers-see-a-new-desert-erode-their-way-of-life.html.

96. Jonathan Watts, "'We Have Taken Every Measure We Can Think of to Stop the Desert Moving Closer and Submerging Our Crops and Villages,'" *The Guardian*, May 18, 2009, www.guardian.co.uk/world/2009/may/18/china-ecorefugees-farming.

97. Jon R. Luoma, "China's Reforestation Programs: Big Success or Just an Illusion?" *Environment 360*, January 12, 2012, http://e360.yale.edu/feature/chinas_reforestation_programs_big_success_or_just_an_illusion/2484.

98. Katie Baker, "China's Biggest Threat," *Newsweek*, December 12, 2009, www.thedailybeast.com/newsweek/2009/12/11/china-s-biggest-threat.html.

99. Ibid.

100. Ibid.

101. Ibid.

102. Malcolm Farr, "Chinese Government Buying Up Our Farms, says Senator Bill Heffernan," *The Daily Telegraph*, June 28, 2010, www.dailytelegraph.com.au/archive/national-old/chinese-government-buying-up-our-farms/story-e6freuzr-1225881085302; Alexei Barrionuevo, "China's Interest in Farmland Makes Brazil Uneasy," *New York Times*, May 26, 2011, www.nytimes.com/2011/05/27/world/americas/27brazil.html?pagewanted=all&_r=0; and Richard Spencer, "China Looks Abroad to Grow Its Own Food," *The Telegraph*, May 9, 2008, www.telegraph.co.uk/news/worldnews/asia/china/1942254/China-looks-abroad-to-grow-its-own-food.html.

Chapter 7

Political Transition and the Breaking Point

The transition of power from the old guard to the new generation of Chinese Communist Party (CCP) leaders has resulted in change at the top, but not in the challenges they face. We have shown how command economies fail in the long term by inefficiencies, widespread corruption, and a lack of an accurate market mechanism for everything from raw materials to finished goods. We have also identified the negative attributes and effects of China's command economy, in terms of the *tragedy of the commons* effect that has led to such damaging results as extreme levels of pollution, social decay, and obscene levels of economic inequality.

With that reality, and with the understanding that the new leadership of China is aware of the state of their economy, society, and environment, will they be willing or able to make the policy changes necessary to at least decrease the severity of the oncoming crises? The context of this question involves the fading—and failing—political trade-off of prosperity for the middle class in exchange for political compliance that was agreed to in the wake of the Tiananmen Square massacre in 1989. That contract is fast becoming untenable. The economy is now failing the middle class as the Party grows ever richer and the income gap widens and the Beijing Model continues to devour the wealth and resources of the country.

The CCP is acutely aware of the rising instability, but also realizes that its political exclusivity and the policies that help it maintain that power are a major source of alienation and civil unrest in China.[1] In this light, Xi Jinping's recent call for the CCP to be more open to criticism and receptive to non-party member oversight is an interesting development. In his Lunar New Year speech on January 31, 2013, Xi said, "The CCP should be able to put up with sharp criticism, correct mistakes if it has committed them and avoid them if it has not," and "Non-CCP personages should meanwhile have the courage to tell the truth, speak words jarring to the ear, and truthfully reflect public aspirations."[2]

Xi went on to praise the efforts of other political parties in China (there are eight other parties, none of which have any real power) and asked "party committees of all levels to readily accept and welcome supervision from other political parties and personages so as to improve their work style and quality." Additionally, Xi said that he appreciated "the hard work of the country's other political parties and personages in the past five years."[3]

What should we make of these pronouncements? The CCP is quite used to having its unfettered way with the people, the country's resources, and all sources of national wealth with an unsurpassed brutality that belies the moral vacuity and the inhuman, monstrous beasts behind the calm, well-fed public faces that populate the echelons of the Party. The dilemma the new leadership faces seems to be how to quell, reduce, or at least control the tsunami of protests sweeping China whilst holding onto power as long as it can. It is also reasonable to assume that the new leadership is not in the business of intentionally undermining the CCP's grip on power.

This conundrum was similarly spelled out in Hu Jintao's last speech to the Politburo Standing Committee in November 2012:

We must continue to make both active and prudent efforts to carry out the reform of the political structure, and make people's democracy more extensive, fuller in scope and sounder in practice. . . . However, we will never copy a Western political system . . . (but rather) adhere to the principle of party exercising leadership over personnel management and promote party building in an innovative way . . . (and) widely consult with democratic societies and grassroots systems.[4]

How should these two ideas of continued Communist Party domination in all spheres of the economy and the refusal to adopt any "Western political system," juxtaposed with the call for open criticism, reform, and oversight, be regarded? After all, political exclusivity and secrecy are part of the very nature of the CCP, and along with political and economic violence, are what have kept the Party in power. Yet, Xi has specifically asked for a critique of the CCP by non-Party members, which has quite possibly painted him into a political corner. It is, outwardly, a grand admission that things are not going nearly as well as China's GDP statistics would have most of the world believe. But it is also not clear what the political ramifications of Xi's statements will be.

For instance, how much criticism will Xi allow? In what forum will such criticism of the CCP be allowed? How about large public protests? Will those expressions of political criticism be tolerated? Will the criticisms be published in China's government daily or broadcast on state television for the entire country to see and respond to? How will the CCP react to the criticisms? What happens if the criticism gets so bad, so out of hand, that it sparks more and larger civil protests in the streets of Beijing or throughout China (which is a very plausible outcome)?

Are mass protests deriving from public criticism of the CCP leadership what Xi, whose father was a supporter of Hu Yaobang's liberalization policies back in the 1980s, has in mind? (Interestingly, Xi has never disavowed his father's support of Hu.) Are his political adversaries in the Party agreeable to such openness? If so, does it mean that Xi Jinping might consider sharing power with other political parties in China? Or is Xi attempting to defuse public discontent and alienation by co-opting the sources of discontent, making public gestures toward addressing the problems while working to maintain the *status quo*?

If his objectives aren't any of the above, what else could they be? Does Xi Jinping think that openness and reform will save the CCP? That would be a dangerous political game to play, as Mikhail Gorbachev discovered when his similar attempts led to the disintegration of the Soviet Union. It is, however, rational to think that Xi's immediate objective in terms of public policy is to stabilize the levels of dissent by clearly letting the people know that he has heard them and is initiating policies to address their concerns, even if he has no intention of following through with any of them.

Sharing power is quite likely far from Xi's current intentions, if his stated objective of avoiding Western forms of political systems is true, which it probably is. If this is indeed the case, then his calls for constructive criticism would have to considered as, at best, only conciliatory remarks meant for public consumption, as hollow as the empty ghost cities that China counts as real GDP.

It is also important to understand that Xi has many audiences—domestic and foreign—to speak to at once. His pronouncements are subject to the political interpretations of both his allies and adversaries in the Politburo Standing Committee, in the Party as a whole, as well as in the powerful People's Liberation Army (PLA, whose support is crucial), the wealthy merchant class, regional authorities, disaffected regions and peoples within China, and of course, the general Han population. Abroad, Xi knows that regional adversaries such as Taiwan and Japan will be paying close attention, as will their ally Russia and their ersatz strategic military adversary and trading partner, the United States.

There is little question that in calling for reforms and open criticism, as well as expressing his intent for the CCP to adhere to "socialism with Chinese characteristics," Xi was sending signals to the masses—ones that require assurance from the CCP that they intend to improve Chinese society for the benefit of its people. His message also spoke to those in the Party who want assurances that Xi's liberal past is behind him. Will this apparent *middle path* be the way in which to minimize or pacify the unrest in China without resorting to greater levels of oppression?

Or, is Xi simply attempting to buy time for the regime? Does he think he needs to maintain the status quo until the hour arrives when

China is ready to engage in foreign adventures as a way to not only acquire much needed resources, but also to settle historic grievances with Japan (with whom tensions are already high) and Taiwan, push the United States out of the Asian–Pacific region, and vent high domestic social tensions in the process?

Such foreign engagements would certainly be a qualitative shift in China's global status, elevating it to the great power status militarily that it currently enjoys in the economic realm. That line of thinking carries considerable weight when one considers all of the social problems that beset China today, which we have discussed herein and will only grow worse over time. It wouldn't be the first time that a powerful, dictatorial nation looked to war to accomplish all of the above objectives and direct attention away from its own grand failures.

In the face of such broad domestic failures, what more can the Party offer?

Will Xi Jinping Unify the CCP?

It's no secret that Xi Jinping was carefully groomed for leadership of China by the outgoing regime. With power over both the CCP and the military, he will be the driving force that shapes China for the next decade. That is not to say that he will enjoy unanimity within the Party, because he certainly will not.

There are fierce struggles for power and competing visions of where China ought to be headed in terms of regional foreign policy, its dealings with the United States, and various domestic issues such as how to deal with rising civil tensions and China's pollution crisis. The Party's political divisions fall along predictable lines among areas and interests within China and are typically not resolved without bitter debates, political maneuvering, and byzantine deal-making among the most powerful Party members. This ponderous, deliberate process is by design.

As noted, rule by committee in today's CCP doesn't allow for the radical policy changes that rule by personality allowed both Mao and Deng to pursue. In the past, the domination of the CCP by one supreme personality is what made massive policy shifts possible. Bear in mind that it was Deng's vision and personal decision to open China to the capitalist

West that set the country's current state of affairs in motion. Since Deng's departure from the scene, however, ruling China has shifted from the job of one supreme leader to the joint effort of a committee with shared and often competing powers at the highest levels of the Party.

Given that the CCP is a divided body with fierce power struggles behind the scenes and distinctly different political visions, it is unlikely that Xi Jinping will be able to rule from a position of absolute strength and therefore, he will have to compromise with and be wary of his party adversaries along the way. This reality is important regarding the prospect for reform in the new government in the context of the two competing factions within the CCP. Recall that the two major party divisions are the *taizidang*, or *princelings*, and the *populists*, which are led by the *tuanpai*. The princelings are those members brought up in power, privilege, and wealth, who hold a very elitist view. They regard China as worthy of world leadership, favor the urban industrial regions and interests over the rural agrarian ones, and have a more forward-leaning posture with regard to asserting China's power regionally and around the world.

The tuanpai are those Party members who have come up through the ranks, and typically see the difficulties of the rural areas as a priority; they also tend to favor more liberalization and a less bellicose approach in China's regional policies and in its attitude toward the West and the United States in particular. The focus of these two major factions will remain in the struggle for power within the CCP to a much larger degree than would occur in other parties simply because there is no other political alternative by which to gain and exert influence. Xi Jinping is considered allied with the reformist wing of the Party, but the memory of what happened to Hu Yaobang in 1987 must surely serve as a warning to him as well.[5]

But regardless of which group dominates the Party, the days of one-man rule in China, with a carefully crafted cult of personality within the cadre and the public supporting him, appear to be over. This reality was amply demonstrated when Bo Xilai, the favored Party member to take over the leadership of the CCP, was very publicly ousted by the Party in the spring of 2012. Bo's fatal political sin was appealing directly to the masses on a personal level, bypassing the Party in the mold of Mao Zedong. He had hoped to secure his rise to supreme power over China and the CCP based upon his widespread, highly cultivated popularity with the public.

Party leaders, wary of one-man rule and the havoc that it can bring to the country—as well as to one's well-being—summarily crushed Bo's ambitions, exiled him from the Party, stripped him of most of his status, and handed down a suspended sentence for his and his wife's role in the murder of British businessman Nick Heywood. It is instructive to note that the offense of murder was not the problem with Bo—done correctly, murder is entirely acceptable in the Party—but seeking to usurp all political power for himself was just plain unforgivable in the eyes of the political elite.[6]

In spite of stated long-term economic plans, the struggle within the Party is for power, influence, and benefits in the near term, which will always outweigh the need for reform and restructuring that are necessary for long-term sustainability. Regarding the CCP as a very powerful guild or union is a useful analogy, where its primary mission is to perpetuate and enrich itself at the expense of all other competitors or objectives, with no-holds-barred infighting for control and survival.

With the Party divided by two competing factions with conflicting visions for the country, and wherein the entire CCP relies upon graft, force, and corruption in its rule, the result of *rule by committee* has been a relatively stable yet inefficient ruling process, with changes introduced and executed only gradually. Inwardly, the Party is thuggish and mafia-like, where interests of cliques must be fought for and protected. No big changes are likely to occur quickly; rather, the momentum of current policies is likely to remain the course of the CCP.

But what is an advantage in Chinese politics when things are going well is also a disadvantage when things go south. With the Bo Xilai example fresh in everyone's minds, the overriding political objective among Party members will be political survival—to protect one's turf by balancing carefully orchestrated political alliances. Thus, even though the transition of power may be officially over with, there is no reason to believe that behind the scenes deals are not continually being made both in support of the new leadership, and just as importantly, against it. But either way, the majority of their focus will be on forming advantageous political alliances in the new regime and staying on the familiar path rather than facing or resolving the crises at hand.

What does this mean for the possibility of reform and addressing the crises?

Despite Xi Jinping's call for criticism of the Party, publicly pointing out the failures of Party members—whether it is the low air quality in Beijing, the toxic water table throughout China, or the rising level of desertification—may not be a wise political strategy for survival in the CCP or outside of it. Giving the issues lip service is one thing; challenging the policies that create them is quite another. Therefore, political survival within the Party will be the word of the day going forward.

Thus, even though laws against pollution, corruption (Xi has announced a new anti-corruption campaign), and murder are passed—some with great publicity—these actions are, for the most part, for public consumption. It will be nearly politically impossible to follow through with reforms of any meaning or substance because that would not only highlight all the wrong-headed policies and graft that are going on, but it also would be an admission of guilt by the Party and its leaders. And as we discussed earlier, large-scale reformation would create greater short-term hardship for the Chinese people in higher costs and lost jobs. None of these outcomes is acceptable to the CCP or to the people of China. It is hard to imagine that there will emerge another Party member who is willing to launch a personal crusade in a public manner as a way to crystalize support for cleaner water, a more open market, or better working conditions. The lessons and legacies of Bo Xilai and Hu Yaobang seem to have made such political maneuvers out of the question in the current political environment.

The upshot of all of this is that rule by committee, with closed-door negotiations between the two main factions, will continue to be the manner of rule in China. The top-down stability imposed by CCP oppression and political domination, sweetened by economic growth and materialism, has yielded to rising political and economic instability, which have proven to be difficult to manage by the consensus-based rule of committee of the CCP. But it remains the only political game in town. Individual political visions and ambitions will likely remain couched in the continued division of the economic and financial spoils that Party rule and leadership affords the political elite in China, rather than in grand expressions of reform and openness.

This brings another possible reason for Xi's speech to mind. Could it be that he is looking to the past for solutions to domestic unrest? Do Xi's calls for reform, collaboration with opposition parties, and invitations for open criticism that is jarring to the ear have a more sinister motivation? Could it be that such announcements are a *false spring* tactic designed to attract the main opposition leaders—the troublemakers—out into the open, where they can then be dealt with swiftly and surely?

This is an old tactic used by Mao Zedong during the "100 Flowers Campaign" in the late 1950s, when he invited open criticism of the CCP leadership under the pretext of improving the country. The critics were then persecuted in anti-rightist campaigns and sent to re-education camps.[7] This may well be a strategy under consideration of the new leadership; the CCP are certainly budgeting for more internal security, aren't they? On the other hand, the status of the CCP in Chinese society is greatly diminished from where it was in 1957, is riven with dissent, and is ruled by committee rather than a Maoist figure. Such a crackdown would signal a return to the ultra-violence of those horrible times and cause further deterioration in the economy, leading to more instability.

Some may view Xi Jinping's recent consideration of adopting Singapore's "flexible authoritarianism"[8] in China to address the crises facing China as a genuine effort to find a path forward for the CCP. Again, such posturing is likely nothing more than a self-deluding fiction; the Chinese Communist Party is rigid to the point of being brittle and is falling in upon itself as I write this. With an economy based on corruption and theft, China can neither function well without the authority of the CCP, nor, as has been shown of late, can it function well with it.

Therefore, Xi's pronouncements notwithstanding, the political exclusivity of the CCP will remain—and remain as a major obstacle to reform. Likewise, Xi's opportunities for achieving real party unity is highly unlikely in areas other than those that bolster CCP domination. The strongest force to accomplish that objective is China's embrace of a strident nationalism,[9] which, given the continued economic slide, is really the only direction left for the CCP. It is not only useful as a unifying force, but it is also one which feeds the national pride the Chinese feel for their nation's meteoric economic rise in only one generation, and also justifies their concurrent disdain for the sinking Western powers—especially the United States.

Liberalization versus Stability

Calls for liberalization are present in China, but the same reasons and forces that prevent shared political power and economic reforms while the CCP is in power apply to political liberalization in China. Any meaningful reform would mean opening up the black box of the CCP and letting the people see just how corrupt and distorted the CCP really is. The people of China know that things are bad, that the Party leaders are corrupt, serving their own interests in state-owned enterprises, and that the environment and inequality are both growing worse in their country. They just don't have *full* knowledge as to the degree the degradation has reached, or how much it is truly harming them and the country. The openness of reform would certainly provide clearer and unmistakably damning evidence against the CCP's leadership and would not survive such disclosures. Undoubtedly, Xi Jinping is aware of this.

The events in the final years of the Soviet Union under *glasnost* and *perestroika*, as well as the events in Tiananmen Square, are not lost on the new leadership. They understand exactly what reform is and what it means to them and to the Party. That is why the so-called Arab Spring of 2011, which saw the overthrow of various despotic regimes in the Middle East, as well as the riots in Greece, have prompted the CCP to engage in the most intensive crackdown on dissent since Tiananmen Square in 1989.[10] The calculus is simple: Liberalization spells the end of the CCP. The CCP is, in all its propaganda and self-identity, the *savior* of China. The last thing a thin-skinned and ultimately false savior like the CCP can tolerate is open and persistent criticism by the people.

Thus, a liberalization effort from the top would only hasten the end of the CCP and quite likely mean the end of the lives of many Party members. The challenge for the leadership of the CCP, therefore, is to keep enough people happy enough of the time to justify their continued leadership. And, of course, when that no longer works, even higher levels of oppression are always on the table.

Passing the Torch: China's New Nationalism

There is another aspect to the power transition that presents a very real danger to China's future, as well as to that of the entire region and the rest of the world. With power shifting from the old generation to the new, there is always the temptation—or even the probability—for the new leadership to make rash and unwise decisions, especially in the beginning of their rule. Some of those decisions may be advantageous in their outcomes, but others may well not be.

The biggest temptation for Xi Jinping and the fifth generation of leadership is the adoption of an active and outward-facing nationalism. As alluded to earlier in this chapter, there are a number of reasons for this. For one, because all people are products of their experiences, the new generation knows only relatively good times in China, with memories mainly made of their country's rising wealth and power in the world. Unlike the old guard, they have grown up under the protective wing of the Party and its privileges. With an average age of 63, the leaders of China were born around 1950, the time of the revolution.[11] Even so, any memories of the starvation, terror, and deprivation of the Cultural Revolution era, or before that, of the Great Leap Forward have been more than likely eclipsed by the enormous rise in wealth and power China has experienced the past three decades under the leadership of the CCP. Those earlier days of struggle, though perhaps not forgotten, do not so heavily influence the thinking of the prior generation sheltered under the protective wing of the CCP, but they do provide a historical lens through which to view past difficulties and injustices.

The new generation of leadership remembers the end of the Mao era and the Open Door Policy, but for the past 30 years, they have seen a rising China become a major player on the world stage in the twenty-first century, which is also juxtaposed against the Western powers of the twentieth century falling rapidly into decline. As noted in earlier chapters of this book, they view the rise of China as a validation of the Beijing Model, as well as of the Party, and give very little credit to the West for helping them along the way. Ultimately, the Party leadership tends to regard their rise as a sign of their country's destiny to rule the world.

This has tremendous implications for Sino-U.S. relations, especially with regard to the American influence in the region. The new leadership regards China as the rightful hegemon in the Asian-Pacific region, and deeply resents the ongoing defense arrangements between Taiwan and the United States and the fact that they are funding the U.S. defense budget with their support of the U.S. bond market. Furthermore, the new leadership also sees a China that was a weak country historically, bullied by Japan in World War II, and is now in a position to return the favor.

As a result of this generational shift in power, coupled with its relative and absolute gain in power in the region and around the world, China has adopted a more forward and outward-looking foreign policy posture, and there is little reason to think that this will change in the near future. The more likely scenario is that China's behavior will grow worse as conditions on the ground deteriorate. The push for China's new nationalism is coming from within the party. The hard landing of its economy and growing internal dissent will continue to compel the CCP to bring hardline tactics to bear on the population and seek means of relieving internal pressures. Foreign aggression fulfills this need.

The pull toward an aggressive nationalism will be the need to capture oil and other resources upon which China depends, as well as the need to be able to defend sea lanes for oil shipments, which are currently dominated by the United States, and the desire to supplant the United States for regional domination. This new, overly confident attitude toward America and neighboring Asian countries extends to bellicosity and beyond. In recent dealings with its smaller, weaker neighbors, China has not hesitated to saber-rattle whenever it has served its interests.[12]

The undersea oil field disputes near Vietnam and the Philippines are a prime example. Recall that the *Global Times* in Beijing, an official newspaper of the Chinese Government, openly called for war against those nations who seek to deprive China of oil that is rightfully theirs.[13] There is also the impending necessity for a more extroverted foreign presence from China that is driven by basic needs in other areas. For example, with its seas nearly bereft of life, Chinese fishermen have been fishing in their neighbors' territorial waters for their catch. This imperative of scarcity applies across the entire spectrum of China's needs, from oil to food to water.

Politically, the new leadership undoubtedly needs to consolidate its position and power within the CCP, and in doing so, they may make decisions intended to accomplish their immediate political needs— to the further detriment of the country. The impact of this dynamic nationalism will thus be seen in domestic policy. Again, the trade-off in China that has been continually made between economic development and environmental degradation for its entire existence under the CCP will continue. This is because in the leadership's desire and need to project power, confidence and competence, a weaker economy, higher unemployment, or any other domestic downturns, like the one affecting China today, would seriously threaten their positions and the legitimacy of the Party.

With so much at stake, is there any real doubt that the new leadership will not adopt a more formidable nationalistic posture? In fact, it is doing so already. Other provocative actions and policies include the stoking of anti-Japanese sentiment while also laying claims to traditionally Japanese islands.[14] However, China's assertiveness goes further afield than that. China engages in continuous cyber attacks against the U.S. defense establishment for theft of defense secrets, technology, disruption, and disablement of U.S. military assets as well as command and control centers.[15] Though a softer offense than, say, attacking a U.S. warship, cyber warfare is still warfare, and puts the lie to the quaint and quite dangerous notion of China's *peaceful rise*.

Also, as described in Chapter 5, China's currency policies are correctly characterized as disruptive to—if not intentionally destructive of—the current international financial system. China's massive gold purchases could easily and quite correctly be perceived as a maneuver to affect the rise of a gold-backed yuan becoming a new reserve currency, replacing the fiat dollar. Expanding *dollar exclusion zones* for trading and bilateral currency agreements are other examples of attacks on the U.S.-led global trading system and the far more dangerous threat to very existence of the dollar itself. However, given China's rise to a level of a great power after centuries of humiliation by Western powers, does the country adopting a new nationalistic posture really come as a surprise?

Another possible indicator of the new regime's intent to assert itself might be the map of China watermarked on new Chinese passports. It shows a version of China that includes disputed territory claimed by India, a vast stretch of the South China Sea, including islands claimed by several other countries, and the entirety of Taiwan.[16] Though China is not the only nation to indulge in such passport fantasies, their printed claims ought not to be ignored. After all, China's greatest weakness is its lack of resources, primarily oil.

This particular energy weakness has had a significant impact on the thinking of the Chinese defense establishment. Like much of the world,

China must rely on a steady flow of foreign oil sources for its economy to keep moving forward. This strategic weakness is amplified by the fact that it is the United States' naval power that controls the sea lanes through which China's oil supplies travel. Thus, as it stands today, when push comes to shove, the United States has the power to decide whether China is to receive oil or not. As of yet, China is in no position to challenge U.S. naval power on the high seas; but that is exactly what China has in mind. More time is needed, however. Perhaps that is closer to the true context of Xi's statements.

It is illustrative, if for just a moment, to postulate China's policies were it to suddenly become a democracy. A democratic China would certainly be less likely to be an aggressive China, given that a plurality is necessary to rule, and the vast majority of the people's interests lie in bettering their own lives rather than conquering foreign lands. In contrast, an authoritarian, nationalist China's allocation of its resources to both domestic security and military expansion leave little doubt that Xi intends to maintain CCP power exclusivity and pursue greater regional ambitions.

Strategically, an assertive, if not outright aggressive, foreign policy based upon the projection of power is a crucial part of the CCP's vision for China's future and will be the next phase of Chinese foreign policy doctrine. Ideologically, it is a fitting and dangerous bookend to its already assertively violent domestic policy. It has recently begun Pacific training for its first, albeit refurbished, Soviet-era aircraft carrier and has pledged to produce a fleet of aircraft carriers and increase its submarine force from 62 to 100 by 2020, as well as to deploy strategic "carrier killer" missiles to counter U.S. naval superiority.[17] Given these developments and postures, political plurality in China is not likely to be allowed to come about willingly under the new CCP leadership.

Unless a sudden enlightenment descends upon the minds of China's new leaders, CCP policies will become even more bellicose at home and abroad going forward. They will do so even though such a course enhances the odds for conflict among nations, and the present political and economic systems in China offer neither sustainability nor renewability. It is both of these concerns—a lack of sustainability and renewability—that will also play a part in China's deteriorating domestic crises as well as in its shifting foreign policy posture.

Domestic Crises for the New Leadership

As we discussed in Chapter 4, concerning the Beijing Model, the big problem today is that when it comes to the biggest social benefit of China's development—a rising middle class—the problem today is sustainability, or rather, the lack thereof. As we are already seeing, China's Beijing Model is simply not sustainable. The direct result of that fact is that the shrinking middle class means the economic miracle is fading.

It is important to remember that China's shrinking middle class—that is, the growing number of Chinese whose middle-class expectations are no longer being met or who are growing increasingly impoverished—is not only due to the effects of the global financial crises, but more importantly, is also due to the deleterious effects of the Beijing Model, as well as the endemic theft of the nation's sources of wealth perpetrated by the CCP. These destructive processes have brought China to a crossroads in its development, both politically and economically. China's new leaders have tremendous problems facing them, with few if any workable solutions that include them remaining in their current positions of power.

One of those problems is China's aging workforce. As noted earlier, China must become rich before it becomes old. China must develop its own domestic economy in order to establish a sustainable, wealth-creating economy of its own, rather than relying on foreign investment and phantom real estate development projects to create domestic demand and keep workers employed, and that is a political problem for the CCP as much as it is an economic and social emergency. As China is discovering, with rising wages and a slowing global economy, foreign investment is certainly not reliable over the long-term and is limited in creating domestic demand. And, in the absence of true domestic demand driven by consumption, China is finding that a real estate industry funded by stimulus is not real GDP if the properties do not sell, are not used, and do not help create long-term demand in the economy.

Similarly, it has been noted that China must proceed up the development food chain from manufacturer to a knowledge economy of high tech research and development, along with a strong and rising domestic market. This is also a necessity, so the thinking goes, for China to be able to afford the medical care and other social benefits that its aging workforce will need in the very near future. The assumption underlying that statement is that China will—or wants to become a modern welfare state, with all the social safety nets and old age pensions that have become the hallmark of them. That has yet to be determined, but the evidence points elsewhere.

In the wake of the harsh economic struggles that the European welfare states are now facing, including deep cuts in their cherished welfare and pension programs, such assumptions are not as well-founded as they might have seemed only a few years ago. Another problem with that assumption is the fact that China cannot afford such welfare plans. Additionally, the assumption that the CCP even cares for the aging workforce as a whole is, sadly, untrue. Since the Party has shown so little regard for its working population, it doesn't make much sense to imagine that it will care more for its retired—and thus unproductive—workforce in the same way that European states do. There is no such need for the CCP to be politically accommodating to its retirees, since, like the rest of the country, they have no political voice.

The reality is that for much of China's aging population, no such benefits are expected from, nor will be offered by the state. This seems much more likely the case when you consider that China's GDP per capita, as well as its human development level (which is a United Nations ranking of standard of living) are 120 and 101 in the world, respectively.[18]

What does this mean from a domestic policy perspective?

It means that China doesn't have the resources on a per capita basis to treat its elderly as they are treated in developed nations. There are about 590 million people living in China's rural areas, with over 150 million of those living on less than $2 per day. That's about 42 percent of the rapidly aging Chinese population barely scratching out a living.[19] Thus, what actually exists of China's old age pension system will most likely be targeted at those workers with an importance attached to those at the top, whether it is Party affiliation, working in critical technological areas, or living in those regions where political accommodation is most needed. The rest of China's aging workers will be on their own. This will add fuel to the fires of civil unrest as old workers are callously tossed aside by the CCP.

One other major problem that is related to the throwaway workforce mentality is the idea of a privileged class emerging, which manifests itself in everyday occurrences. Disdain for those lower on the economic food chain is tearing the fabric of Chinese society not from above, politically, but from within and below. This rising development will vex the new leadership for it is caused by the growing socioeconomic gap between the people and the privileged elite.

The rampant sense of privilege among the wealthy and Party classes has its expression in not only how the common man lives, but also how he is treated at the hands of the privileged classes. For instance, the son of a police official killed a student with his car, and when stopped, the boy simply said, "My father is Li Gang!" This incident became a national symbol of CCP abuse and privilege, reflecting a deep-seated social division in China between the elite few and the poor masses that is toxic to social cohesion.[20]

This division by privilege has spawned a relatively new sense of anger and dissent within China. It wasn't much of an issue when everyone was sporting Mao jackets in the bicycle kingdom 30 years ago. When everyone is poor, that's one thing; but when the privileged class lords it over the lower classes in such blatant and callous ways, the gap becomes a big problem.

Another, though by no means the least or last, internal or sociopolitical problem that the new leadership faces is the decline in traditional values among the privileged class. The traditional, paternalistic culture of the past has been replaced with a freer, more materialistic mindset that pervades the younger generation. Reverence for one's elders, traditional authority, and social norms have given way to resentment of authority, an adoration of Western goods, and a general disdain for the old ways. To the younger generation steeped in social media and exposed to Western ideas and the existence of a democratic Taiwan, the CCP is definitely *old school*. The false idea put over by the CCP that democracy is chaos and the CCP is necessary for stability is no longer valid. In a tense time of economic decline and political oppression, old school can easily translate to illegitimacy.[21]

The new leadership will have to deal with these social shifts and it won't be easy to do. That's because it is with the manufacturing and merchant class that the CCP made the deal of allowing those people to become rich in exchange for their political obedience. This subculture is found mainly in the eastern coastal regions where industrial and financial development are heavily concentrated and culturally attuned to the Hong Kong and Shanghai societies.

However, as noted earlier, with the declining wealth among the middle class, that bargain is becoming harder to honor, and the new generation of wealthy Chinese are not inclined to go backward into material deprivation and meekly obeying their elders. With the declining economic climate that China is now in, it will become a politically volatile issue for the new political leadership to finesse—if they can—or to simply suppress, which they have proven over and over again that they are more than willing to do.

How Will the New Chinese Leadership Navigate the Rough Waters Ahead?

The crises that are even now beginning to erupt within China are important in their financial and environmental impacts and are potentially devastating to the economic and physical well-being of the great majority of Chinese, not to mention their impact on the rest of the world. For example, in the previous chapter, we noted that the extensive environmental damage that China has sustained over the past several decades, and continues to endure today, has concrete consequences not only on the lives of the hundreds of millions of people scattered across the great distances that the nation covers, but on nations near and far as well.

Likewise, the great development imbalance of the southern and eastern coastal regions, and the relative backwardness of others has great and dangerous impacts upon the livelihoods of hundreds of millions in China, as well as shaping their perceptions of the CCP vis-à-vis their personal lives and their region or province. Alienation from the government is a rising trend throughout China, but especially with those most negatively affected by the current economic policies. Alienation or even revulsion are not a small thing; what it really means is illegitimacy in the eyes of the masses and finger pointing at the highest levels of the Party. That is a condition that brings about rifts and fractures in a society, and political infighting at the highest levels of the CCP.

We noted also the cultural decline in China today, resulting in the callousing of society and an ingrained disdain for ethics and moral behavior, an indifference to their fellow human beings, and an embracing of getting ahead no matter what the costs. The moral crisis in China is perhaps the deepest malaise and the most dangerous; a society stripped of its morals has little regard for anything else other than the most immediate and self-centered of interests.[22]

Given that the preceding discussion paints a powerful and, for the most part, utterly negative portrait of the true, long-term impact of China's economic miracle, the bigger miracle might just be that the regime has lasted as long as it has. In prior chapters, we've shown how the challenges facing China are deadly serious and growing in their potential magnitude the longer the CCP drags its feet in effectively addressing them.

We've also conveyed the rising level of civil unrest throughout China that foreshadows higher levels of internal conflict going forward. Using the new media as effectively as any other country on earth, even in the face of the CCP's monumental attempts at censorship, the Chinese people are continually protesting against economic injustice, political privilege, and environmental degradation at the hands of the ruling elites in the CCP. One of the most noteworthy protests was the social-media–coordinated, pro-democracy Jasmine Revolution of 2011, where public security forces illegally detained at least 600 citizens and tortured 354 to prevent the spread of the pro-democracy movement throughout China.[23]

Such has been the CCP's standard response over the past several decades. China's political leaders have shown a marked preference to address the problems they themselves have created by applying state violence upon those whom they view as *troublemakers*. The troublemakers have been and continue to be those people who protest the long train of injustices suffered at the hands of China's pervasive state, such as forced abortions, the forced relocation of millions of workers into slave-like conditions, the confiscation of farmland, and the polluting of the environment, as well as the illnesses and deaths that come with it.

China's state violence has been shown in a variety of forms, including the firing upon of unarmed citizens, the burying of people alive, mass beatings by state thugs, poisonings, tortures, rapes, the sentencing of tens of millions to hundreds of gulag-style torture camps,[24] and the always theatrical crushing of human beings by running them over with large construction equipment.[25]

The short answer is that there are some very fundamental changes afoot in China that are happening faster than most Western observers either understand or are able to admit to themselves as being possible. The portentous realities in these statements and admissions by both the outgoing leadership and the new leadership regarding the state of the CCP and the future path of the CCP in its rule over China are nothing less than earthshaking in their consequences. Reform and openness are incompatible with the CCP's rule.

Up until today, the CCP's survival has depended upon secrecy, political exclusivity, brutality, and corruption. Those aspects, however, are proving to be no longer sufficient. That is why aggressive nationalism will be the next phase in China's metamorphosis, which began in 1979. But ultimately, whether the CCP liberalizes or pursues resources through aggression with its neighbors, in the end, will matter little. Its cannibalistic tendencies will eventually prove to be fatal to the *ancient regime* of the CCP.

The truth is that the CCP can no more adapt to the changes and challenges before it today than the Soviet Union could in the late 1980s and early 1990s. Recall that the Soviet navy was formidable and many lands were under the rule of the Soviet Army, yet neither of these facts changed its fate. China's communist regime, like the Beijing Model it has adopted, is also, ultimately, a self-terminating process. Recall the fear that the Soviets felt in the latter years, in the face of courageous dissidents. China may well be feeling that fear, as well.

Take for example, Chen Guangcheng, the so-called "barefoot lawyer," whose protest against the brutality of the One Child policy gained him global notoriety and house imprisonment. Over 5 million people visited the blind activist who had been at various times beaten, put in detention, and held under surveillance at his home in Shandong province in support of his cause before he was arrested.[26] And yet, this blind man was able to outsmart the Chinese authorities in Beijing and secure visas for himself and his family to the United States. Does that seem plausible? Maybe it does.

But it seems just as plausible, if not more so, that the Chinese leadership understood that letting Chen out of the country unharmed was wiser than having him in the country as a martyr—or a catalyst—who would incite widespread protests and perhaps even a revolt in the mold of Tiananmen Square. At some level, the CCP might be coming to the realization that there are costs, even for them, in how they treat their people, especially when the world is watching.

Recall in Chapter 6 how pollution statistics were withheld from the public or modified for fear of the people's reaction. Recall also Deng Xiaoping's fear of revolt in 1978, thus begetting the Open Door Policy to introduce capitalism into China. And finally, recall the old Soviet Union's reaction to political dissenters who were too effective and well known. They came to similar conclusions with regard to their political dissidents, like Andrei Sakharov, Alexander Solzhenitsyn, and Natan Sharansky—who threatened and foreshadowed the decay and the ultimate end of their society in the 1970s and 1980s. It is quite possible that the CCP may have reached the same point regarding the dissident Chen.

If so, it portends a more severe yet very human catalyst to the coming collapse in China, which, I believe, is the more likely scenario. It may well be that we will see catastrophe unfold in perhaps a very unexpected, and at first, innocuous way—such as when the next Chen event occurs and the authorities apply one too many beatings and thereby trigger a mass response. It may originate from any one of several sources: growing food shortages, revolts against the privilege and theft of the Party, where one too many plots of land have been stolen or one too many infrastructure failures from shoddy work have led to the deaths of hundreds or even thousands.

Whatever the intentions of the leadership, whatever the CCP thinks it will gain under the cloaks of nationalism, crackdowns, or any other false refuge, the meaning of Xi Jinping's statements is clear: *The CCP truly fears for its continued existence.* As Minxin Pei observed in a recent article, the CCP has long since lost its moral authority; it is rapidly losing its political authority as well. The politics of oppression are reaping diminishing returns.[27]

The existence and toleration of unofficial urban militias and security forces is another strong indication of both the CCP fearing blame for the continued oppression of the Chinese people, as well as its inability to handle the hundreds of daily protests around the country. As it is, over 500 protests take place every day, a 400 percent increase from just a decade earlier. In many places, the government is now backing down in the face of such public protests.[28] This is yet another indication of a regime in rapid decline in power over its people, political legitimacy, and perhaps most importantly, a lack of belief in itself at the highest levels.

Hell and High Water

The Shakespearean quote from *Henry IV*, "Uneasy lies the head that wears a crown," seems appropriately meet for the new leadership of China. The new generation that wears the crown of leadership in China today faces many obstacles that stand in the way of a successful future for the country. Every way they turn, there is degeneration in the very engines of growth that have led them this far, and deterioration in the assumptions upon which the political system is based.

As I have attempted to illustrate in this chapter, one of the main obstacles to a brighter future is China's current political and economic systems. The nature of the political structure of the CCP, its recent and past history of ruling arrangements, and its current committee structure all mitigate against China being able to effectively meet its challenges and thus continue its rise. The argument that compels the CCP onward down the current path—accruing wealth and holding onto power no matter what the cost or damage to the country—is based upon false premises and supported by levels of fraud that are the seeds of its own destruction. These same arguments will consign their leadership into a growing series of crises, which they will very likely badly mismanage.

As I noted earlier in this book, the CCP, in all its rigidity, paranoia, and oppression, is a nineteenth-century political artifact proven to be a disaster in the twentieth century, attempting to remain relevant and effective in the twenty-first century. Like its leaders of the past, the consistent inability of the CCP to reconcile social needs with political and economic policies has created a nation on the edge of disaster. And, like the Great Leap Forward and the Cultural Revolution before it, the next catastrophe in China will have been brought upon the people of China by a leadership and political system that is, in the long run, virtually incapable of doing anything else.

Notes

1. Steve McCann, "Civil Unrest in China," *American Thinker*, June 18, 2011, www.americanthinker.com/blog/2011/06/civil_unrest_in_china.html.
2. Xinhjua and Staff Reporter, "Xi Jinping Urges Party to Be More Open to Criticism," *Want China Times*, February 10, 2013, www.wantchinatimes.com/news-subclass-cnt.aspx?id=20130210000008&cid=1101.

3. Ibid.

4. Mamta Badkar, "Hu Jintao: Corruption Could Be 'Fatal' for the Communist Party but China Will Never Copy Western Political Systems," *Business Insider*, November 7, 2012.

5. Jeremy Page, Bob Davis, and Tom Orlik, "China's New Boss," *Wall Street Journal*, November 21, 2012.

6. Lin Feng, "Exclusive: Why Bo Xilai Fell and Xi Jinping Disappeared, Part 1," *The Epoch Times*, October 31, 2012, www.theepochtimes.com/n2/china-news/exclusive-why-bo-xilai-fell-and-xi-jinping-disappeared-part-1-302461.html.

7. Oliver Chou, *The South China Post*, December 4, 2012, from factsanddetails .com, http://factsanddetails.com/china.php?itemid=1153&catid=2.

8. Edward Wong and Jonathan Ansfield, "Many Urge Next Leader of China to Liberalize," *New York Times*, October 21, 2012, www.nytimes.com/2012/10/22/world/asia/many-urge-chinas-next-leader-to-enact-reform .html?pagewanted=1&_r=1&ref=world.

9. Baogang He and Kingsley Edney, "Chinese Nationalism and Where It Might Lead," East Asia Forum, September 21, 2011, www.eastasiaforum .org/2011/09/21/nationalism-and-where-it-might-lead.

10. "China's Crackdown," *The Economist*, April 14, 2011, www.economist.com/node/18560351.

11. Susan Shirk, "Age of China's New Leaders May Have Been Key to Their Selection," *ChinaFile*, November 15, 2012, www.chinafile.com/age-chinas-new-leaders-may-have-been-key-their-selection.

12. J. Michael Cole, "Chinese Analyst Calls for War in South China Sea," *Taipei Times*, September 30, 2011, www.taipeitimes.com/News/front/archives/2011/09/30/2003514541.

13. Ibid.

14. Chris Buckley, "China Accuses Japan of Escalating Tensions over Disputed Islands," *New York Times*, February 28, 2013, www.nytimes.com/2013/03/01/world/asia/china-accuses-japan-of-provoking-tensions.html.

15. "China Cyber Attacks on U.S. Targets," *The Associated Press*, February 19, 2013, www.wjla.com/articles/2013/02/china-cyber-attacks-on-u-s-targets-85396.html.

16. Max Fisher, "Here's the Chinese Passport Map That's Infuriating Much of Asia," *The Washington Post*, November 26, 2012, www .washingtonpost.com/blogs/worldviews/wp/2012/11/26/heres-the-chinese-passport-map-thats-infuriating-much-of-asia/.

17. Bernhard Zand, "Power in the Pacific: Stronger Chinese Navy Worries Neighbors and US," *Der Spiegel*, September 14, 2012, www.spiegel.de/international/world/strengthening-of-chinese-navy-sparks-worries-in-region-and-beyond-a-855622.html; Mackenzie Eaglen and Jon Rodeback, "Submarine Arms Race in the Pacific: The Chinese Challenge to Undersea

Supremacy," The Heritage Foundation, February 2, 2010, www.heritage.org/research/reports/2010/02/submarine-arms-race-in-the-pacific-the-chinese-challenge-to-us-undersea-supremacy; and Julian E. Barnes, Nathan Hodge, and Jeremy Page, "China Takes Aim at U.S. Naval Might," *Wall Street Journal*, January 4, 2012, http://online.wsj.com/article/SB10001424052970204397704577074631582060996.html.

18. Jeffrey Hays, "Income Gap and Poor People in China," factsanddetails.com, updated August 2012, http://factsanddetails.com/china.php?itemid=155.

19. Ibid.

20. David Bandurski, "China's 'Symphony' of Privilege," China Media Project, September 9, 2011, http://cmp.hku.hk/2011/09/09/15376.

21. Martin Jacques, "How the Chinese Communist Party Convinced the World to Accept It," *The Epoch Times*, October 5, 2012, www.martinjacques.com/when-china-rules-the-world/how-the-chinese-communist-party-convinced-the-world-to-accept-it/.

22. Stanley Lubman, "Fraud, Culture and the Law: Can China Change?" *ChinaRealTimeReport* (blog), August 24, 2012, http://blogs.wsj.com/chinarealtime/2012/08/24/fraud-culture-and-the-law-can-china-change.

23. "Chinese CIA Spy Unveils Power Struggle between Security Ministries," *Want China Times*, February 15, 2013, www.wantchinatimes.com/news-subclass-cnt.aspx?cid=1101&MainCatID=11&id=20130225000030.

24. A.M. Rosenthal, "On My Mind: China's Black Book," *New York Times*, July 7, 1992, www.nytimes.com/1992/07/07/opinion/on-my-mind-china-s-black-book.html.

25. Sarah C. Nelson, "He Zhi Hua, Protester Crushed to Death by Steam-roller in Chinese Government Relocation Drive," *The Huffington Post*, September 27, 2012, www.huffingtonpost.co.uk/2012/09/27/he-zhi-hua-protestor-crushed-to-death-by-steamroller-in-chinese-government-relocation-drive-_n_1918494.html.

26. Asia One News (AFP), "Chen Gungcheng: China's Blind 'Barefoot' Law-yer," May 3, 2012, www.asiaone.com/News/AsiaOne%2BNews/Asia/Story/A1Story20120503-343679.html.

27. Minxin Pei, "China's Troubled Bourbons," Project Syndicate, October 31, 2012, www.project-syndicate.org/commentary/rising-political-uncertainty-in-china-by-minxin-pei.

28. Deng Jingyin, "Beijing Police Crack Down on Black Jails," *China-Wire*, December 2, 2011, http://china-wire.org/?p=17603; and Daniel Wagoner and John Margeson, "The Rise of the Chinese Urban Militia," *The Huffington Post*, October 8, 2012, www.huffingtonpost.com/daniel-wagner/the-chinese-urban-militia_b_1946099.html.

Chapter 8

Empire Decline
and Complexity Theory

I n this chapter, I want to introduce two additional ways of looking at China's multiple crises that it now faces from a macro perspective. Empire decline and complexity theories provide different contexts and analysis for evaluating the prospects of China's ability to renew itself. Both also offer different yet compelling reasons for China's collapse in the near future. By viewing China as both an empire and as a complex system, we gain a deeper understanding of the steep challenges that threaten the CCP and the *status quo*.

In the preceding chapters, we identified major issues in China that are clearly visible and undeniable, and yet remain unresolved. For instance, we established that China's command economy, like all command economies, suffers from the *tragedy of the commons*; this leads to chronic and pervasive despoliation of the environment and gross inefficiencies in the allocation of labor and capital. We also discussed the mortal threat that China's insatiable drive for economic development (with little regard for the quality or highest use of that development) and market share represents to its own environment as well as to the world's resources. And we underscored the dangerous phenomenon of rising civil unrest in response to the cannibalistic tendencies of the Beijing Model and the inability of China's one-party political system to adequately address its distorted economy and its growing internal conflicts.

To further understand the context of China's challenges, we can compare it to similar circumstances elsewhere, both past and present, and draw reasonable conclusions from such comparisons. Specifically, it is helpful to recall that I have drawn several parallels and conclusions from China's shared political ideology with the old Soviet Union and single (communist) party rule. There is, of course, a danger in drawing too many comparisons between one country and another, since no two countries are alike in terms of culture, history, geography, demographics, technological advancements, regional influences, and other factors. However, drawing comparisons between the former Soviet Union and China remains valid and useful because they share many macro characteristics of the tragedy of the commons: fraudulent economics, political oppression, widespread corruption, and extreme environmental degradation. They also share a similar geopolitical burden as communist empires spanning thousands of miles of territory, relatively large and diverse populations, and multiple languages and cultures.

Aside from those reasons, the Chinese themselves provide one other excellent point for doing so: They were drawing comparisons between themselves and the Soviets for decades, and rightly changed course when they saw the undeniable destination of the path they were on. The irony of that decision is that the path China is following today, though a departure from the Soviet experience, still circles around to the same dismal destination.

China as an Empire

Why would China face a similar fate to the Soviet Union's even after fully integrating itself into the global economy? Why would it still face a Soviet style collapse—or worse—when it has opened itself to the West and allowed certain aspects of capitalism to catapult it into great power status with the second largest economy on Earth? How can such a fate still be not only possible, but probable?

The answer is that not only does China suffer from many of the same ill-advised policies and limitations under the rule of the CCP that the Soviet bloc nations suffered beneath the yoke of the Kremlin, but there is also one other crucial area in which China mirrors the old Soviet Union—or, for that matter, the defunct Yugoslavia—and that is in its composition. The old Soviet Union included many different nations within its borders, and multiple languages, religions, and regions that had historical ties elsewhere and were adversarial to both communist rule and the cultural and political supremacy of the dominant Soviet power structure. The old Soviet Union was an empire—an evil one at that—and the very same can be said of China today.

When we think of China, we may often think of it as a nation in the way we might think of Japan, for example. But China is much more complex. As a nation, Japan is, generally speaking, much more culturally and linguistically homogenous, and has a pluralistic political system that discourages rebellion by encouraging political and economic participation as well as providing social benefits. But applying that same general idea of nationhood to China is not an accurate representation at all. China is indeed a nation; but in its current political and geographical arrangements, it is more accurate to categorize China as an empire, ruling over many peoples, cultures, languages, and religions. It is also worth keeping in mind that China's composition and borders have ebbed and flowed through the centuries and millennia and even in the past 63 years. This fact is part of the cause of the problems that they face today.

Why Is the Distinction of China as an Empire Rather Than a Nation Important?

Distinguishing China as an empire is important because it brings into focus another challenge that the Chinese leadership faces, which is the dilemma that all empires face: *How to maintain the empire against the contrary forces of language, culture, ethnicity, and religion that are constantly at work in pulling it apart.*

Like all empires, the simple fact is that several parts or regions of China's empire have no wish to be a part of it. Perhaps the main difference in China's case is that there are few, if any, direct benefits, economic or otherwise, for those peoples who would prefer not to be a part of China. Violence, political oppression, forced relocation, pollution of the environment, and outright military occupation are among the negative outcomes that suppressed regions endure as vassals of the Chinese Empire.

Of course, there are also the costs of empire that China must pay. The economic and political price of maintaining power over disaffected provinces, rebellious ethnic groups, and their separatist agendas is considerable, ongoing, and has proven to be only marginally and temporarily successful, at best. The end result of China's efforts to pacify or otherwise contain separatist passions, subversive political ideas, and outright attacks against Chinese rule is only an increase in both expenditures and in the CCP's illegitimacy in the eyes of those it continues to oppress. Again, as observed before in this discussion, as economic conditions continue to deteriorate in China, the costs and levels of resistance will likely increase. What is more, the malaise of empire that plagues both the Chinese leadership and its captive regions also applies to the vast majority of the Chinese people themselves.

There are many studies devoted to the rise and fall of empires—what it is that keeps them together, as well as those factors that cause them to fall apart—but if China is to take over the role of the United States, it must attract the support and cooperation of a considerable portion of the world. Granted, China's empire already encompasses about one-fifth of the world's population within its own borders, but as the theme of this book explains, that will not be sufficient to allow China's empire to expand, much less to maintain itself. To do both of those things, China must successfully sell the China "brand" abroad.

This involves much more than simple foreign relations and foreign aid (which China is already mishandling badly[1]), but much more broadly, involves the receptivity abroad of the Chinese model. It is, by its secretive, authoritarian nature, a power that other nations are intrinsically wary of and viscerally uncomfortable at the idea of a living in world led by China.

> (A)utocracy has hobbled China's bid to put a friendly face on its rise. Institutions associated with authoritarian rule such as pervasive state secrecy and official censorship mask China's ambitions, leading outsiders to focus on what they can easily observe: diplomatic behavior and military capabilities. Beijing's more assertive rhetoric in territorial disputes coupled with the

rapid modernization of the People's Liberation Army has generated unease across Asia, the US and even Europe. Exacerbating
these concerns is the lack of opportunities for shaping China's
future course. With basic information about China's decision-
making process obscured under an authoritarian regime, and
domestic actors either co-opted or controlled by the state, outsiders have little capacity to influence Beijing's foreign policy
from within.

China's lack of domestic political reform is now becoming
a strategic liability. No matter how many times a rising China
reiterates its commitment to "peaceful development," no matter how many confidence-building dialogues a rising China
participates in or free trade agreements it signs, the anxieties
generated by its authoritarian system will remain. Rightly or
wrongly, China will be mistrusted and even feared. Wary of
China's growing power, the US, India, Japan, South Korea,
Australia, Indonesia and others will behave in ways that harm
China's interests. Although China will not face a unified alli-
ance like the Soviet Union did during the Cold War, it will
confront an international landscape that is increasingly unwel-
coming. This forecast is already coming to pass; even Burma,
China's erstwhile ally, is now looking to reduce its reliance on
Beijing by opening up to the United States.[2]

China's prospects for successfully assuming the global hegemon
mantle from the United States are also problematic from a historical perspective. Note that in the early twentieth century, Great Britain's decline
from its position of global hegemon had two continental powers—the
United States and Germany—ready to take the leadership baton from
the British Empire. Although the obvious cultural legacy of the United
States was a factor, Great Britain found America's open democratic society the key reason for cooperating in the transition to the U.S. global
hegemony. In contrast, Britain found Germany's secretive, authoritarian
regime nearly impenetrable, its leadership unreasonable and bellicose, its
foreign policy intentions veiled, and its way of governing its own people
contrary to Britain's understanding and view of how the world ought
to be. China is the twenty-first century Germany, hoping to replace a

global hegemon but severely lacking in the necessary cultural and political attributes to successfully pull it off.[3]

That said, in our digital age of an expanding global culture, it is most useful to explore and leverage those necessary political and cultural attributes that are particularly applicable and necessary to our time. Thus, we will discuss in broad terms three concepts or factors that would seem best to apply to the idea and needs of a modern, sustainable, hegemonic power, or empire, that China vainly hopes and wishes to be. These concepts are simple yet profound in their impact.

The first concept we'll consider is the Chinese culture. Does China have an exportable culture? That is, do other people in the world want to be Chinese? The second concept is soft power. Are there more subtle attributes of Chinese power that are easily leveraged and yet markedly beneficial to other nations? And third, is China feeling the strain of imperial overstretch? That is, has China overextended itself in terms of being able to maintain itself, its economy and its military commitments? It may seem premature to ask such a question regarding China, especially as China seems to be still rising in power, but when one frames the question in economic and geopolitical terms, the answers are there for all to see. It is these three concepts that are key in understanding, from a macro perspective as it relates to the rest of the world, why China's empire is facing decline.

Although there are 1.3 billion Chinese within China, the Chinese culture in terms of language, alphabet, and outlook, is a non-starter to most of the world. Learning to speak Chinese is very difficult, learning to write the thousands of characters is daunting, and the ideas and images that emanate from China are a hard sell to the rest of the world. And frankly, the pollution levels, the political violence, and the captivity of China are less than attractive to most other cultures.

Culturally, the Chinese are not an open, friendly, or inclusive people. To the Chinese, there are Chinese and there are outsiders, who are typically viewed as inferior. This characteristic may well be a product of decades of deprivation and oppression, resulting in a very short-term, "get what you can" mentality, but whatever the cause, it is not a cultural trait that translates well. The simple fact is that most of the world does not want to live like most of the Chinese do.

The Chinese mindset is typically self-centered, inward-looking, suspicious, and opportunistic.[4] China pushes people out of itself; it sends its people emigrating throughout the world, engendering rancor from their hosts. Unlike America, Britain, or Europe, or Africa, Australia, and Canada, China does not attract masses of people to its shores; it largely repels them. To put it in rather stark yet generally accurate terms, the world does not like China and China does not like the world.[5] Regardless of its efforts in cinema and its excellent cuisine enjoyed the world over, or even the vast amounts of money China invests in other countries, Chinese culture as a whole, unlike that of America and Europe, is simply not easily exportable to the majority of the world.

Soft power, those areas of a nation or empire's resources that can be successfully leveraged for influence around the world consist of diplomacy, economic relations, and cultural exchanges.[6] As a one-party state dictatorship, China's experience in managing power relationships is limited in its development and in its outlook. It is well equipped to apply the stick in its policies to get its way, but is clumsy, arrogant, and inept in offering carrots in its diplomatic efforts that don't come across as condescending or as ultimatums. China's choice to wield its economic resources as a coercive tool rather than as a reward is the growing trend as China's relative power grows:

> (I)t's strange that as China's economic clout rises—and its leaders have grown more enamoured of using commerce as a tool of diplomacy—Beijing has become, strategically at least, less prudent. Instead of showing restraint on issues ranging from climate change, territorial disputes, trade and human rights, China has opted for assertiveness and confrontation. As a result, fear of China has driven Chinese neighbours—notably India, Japan, South Korea, Vietnam and Indonesia—into the ready arms of the United States. Economically, China and these countries have never been closer. Strategically, they've never been farther apart.[7]

Given the opportunities to build mutually respectful diplomatic relationships with its trading partner, China continues to build resentments within its trading partners. It is as if the larger its economic clout grows, the more it forgets the meaning of diplomacy and the value of cultivating good will with its neighbors and other nations.[8]

In the space of only a few years, China's diplomatic *"savoir faire"* has successfully alienated its Asian neighbors from communist Vietnam, Japan, and Singapore to the Philippines. Even neighboring Myanmar (Burma), which was heavily reliant upon Chinese foreign aid, has decided that hitching its wagon to China was not worth being dominated and abused, as if it were just another Chinese province to exploit. In fact, Myanmar is moving away from the authoritarian political model altogether, and has now distanced itself from China and turned to the much friendlier Japan for infrastructure investment.[9] For most countries, even those with close economic ties, the China story is a scary one that no one wants to commit to over the long term, as there seem to be no happy endings associated with it.

Finally, China is already suffering from its own version of imperial overstretch, which has arrived surprisingly early in its incarnation as a modern empire. The typical causes of imperial overstretch are a core nation of great economic and military power having overextended itself in far-flung places around the globe, exhausting its economy in managing its empire and keeping its vassal states in line and under control. That, however, is not the source of China's economic exhaustion.

In China's case, as outlined in Chapter 4, it is its own Beijing Model that is exhausting its economy at breakneck speed. There is no need to repeat all the aspects of China's cannibal capitalism here, but the bottom line is that unlike typical empires that exploit other nations' resources and lands for its own gain, China is doing the same to its own nation, with little regard for the costs, the waste, or defilement. Its own economy faces the near-term prospect of reaching the point of no return—if it hasn't already— regarding sustainability or renewability.

In the international sphere, rather than enlarging the economic pie through mutual gains of trade and investment, China's economic and trade policies have been largely adversarial. Consequently, China has repeatedly created a trading zero-sum game where there need not be, by displacing other producers on the one hand through low prices and technology theft, and not buying other producers' products on the other. This practice ultimately leaves the seller (China) unable to sell to buyers who are diminished in their buying power or even no longer in existence because their economic base has moved to China.[10] Even its own population cannot buy because it suppresses wages and pushes the lion's share of taxes upon the bent shoulders of the middle and lower classes.

China's trade policies are thus parasitical on the international system, selling the world many times more goods than it buys. But it is now boomeranging back on China as the economies upon which it depends to buy its products simply buy less and less as their economies cave in. The encroaching imperial overstretch that is hitting China is one of its own making. Having treated the rest of the world just as it treats its own people, it is learning—or perhaps not yet—that zero-sum games ultimately end with everybody losing.

Within China itself, China is finding that maintaining control over its own people is consuming the level of resources that would ordinarily obtain with controlling a rebellious and hostile nation outside of one's borders, not within it and throughout the nation, as is the case. The task gets even more expensive and less successful in the more distant regions. More to the point, China faces the challenge that all empires have faced, which is maintaining sufficient force and political influence in those provinces and regions that do not identify themselves as being a part of or belonging to China. This should not be surprising, given that China has five distinct language groups and 129 different languages, not counting dialects or sub-dialects, a continental land mass over 3,000 miles across, and of course, contains one-fifth of the world's people.

Like the Soviet Union before it, China has undertaken draconian emigration and population redistribution policies. In Tibet, just one example among many, China has relocated 80 percent of the indigenous population under the guise of creating a "socialist countryside."[11] China's efforts to counter uncooperative indigenous ethnicities also include relocating millions of ethnic Han—the dominant Chinese ethnicity—to trouble areas as a way to strengthen CCP control and diminish separatist passions. The results are a mixed bag at best; some areas have seen a reduction in tension, while in others, such as Xinjiang province, it has engendered greater tensions.[12]

Is regarding China as an empire in the preceding contexts a useful perspective? It certainly allows us to see China from a different macro point of view, doesn't it? The Soviet empire context fits China particularly well when it comes to the similar challenges and symptoms China has concerning managing its restless and alienated internal populations. This is especially evident in light of China's problems with some of its more troublesome provinces that underscore major differences with the CCP leadership, Chinese culture, territoriality, and religion. Although there are divisions along economic development, regional, and ethnic lines throughout the Chinese empire, the biggest problems can be identified in three particular provinces—China, Hong Kong, Xinjiang, Tibet—and one "renegade province," as the CCP likes to refer to Taiwan.

Hong Kong

We have already discussed how Hong Kong (which is referred to as a Special Administration Region in China, but is equivalent to a province) reverted back to the PRC by treaty from British control in 1997 and is proving to be a political headache for the dictatorial powers in Beijing. Hong Kong's annual observation of the Tiananmen Square massacre, for example, is a thorn in the side of Beijing and a notice that the people of Hong Kong are not about to give up their freedom of expression or forget about the brutality that marks the CCP's rule over China.

But there is more than just Hong Kong's observance of the Tiananmen Square anniversary that troubles the CCP about Hong Kong. Hong Kong's long history with Great Britain and the West also poses a steep cultural and financial challenge to the CCP. Hong Kong's cultural identity is deeply attached to personal expression, financial freedom, mobility, and historical attachment to a free press. Every one of these cultural and political attributes is an inherent challenge to Beijing's repressive government, just as is the fact that Hong Kong grew rich by trade and finance decades in advance of mainland China's turn to Western capitalism in a desperate attempt to rescue itself from itself.[13]

Furthermore, as China's main financial center, the *idea* of Hong Kong as a free and prosperous part of China remains a constant threat to the CCP's vision of a united and prosperous country united under the boot heel of oppressive communist leadership. Not surprisingly, Hong Kong resents the inundation of Mandarin-speaking Mainlanders swarming over real estate, exacerbating housing shortages, and driving inflation upward. Additionally, the Cantonese-speaking residents of Hong Kong are growing ever more distrustful of the CCP, its leadership, and its motives.

> "Hong Kong is a free society. We treasure different views," says Robert Chung, director of the University of Hong Kong's Public Opinion Program. "And when we see dissidents in China being oppressed and being jailed, of course people are skeptical about it. That has been very clear to us and Chinese officials know that too."[14]

Thus, China is finding it difficult to gain traction there for its preferred level of censorship, and culturally, Hong Kong residents have almost no affinity with the Mainland Chinese, regarding them as coarse invaders from a lesser society.[15] The notion that in 36 years, Hong Kong will be "reabsorbed" into Mainland China, and the "One China, Two Systems" arrangement will cease to be is difficult to imagine coming about peacefully. It is at least as difficult to imagine the CCP lasting that much longer as it is to imagine that Hong Kong would so easily give up its entire identity in exchange for what the CCP has to offer. It is easier to imagine the Mainland seeking to adopt Hong Kong's ways in the liberating wake of the CCP's rapid and final demise.

Taiwan

We also discussed the impact and importance of China's renegade province, Taiwan. Even more so than Hong Kong, Taiwan is not only a living, breathing, politically liberal alternative to what the CCP keeps selling its people through official media outlets day after day, but it is also a much more advanced nation economically, with per capita income over five times greater than China's and one of the most ecologically minded populations in the world. Meanwhile, China as we know, is without question the worst polluter on the planet.

Furthermore, Taiwan is a living, breathing reminder of Mainland China's impotence to impose its will upon its renegade province for over 60 years. With its military partnership and defense treaty with the United States, Taiwan is heavily armed with advanced weaponry and intelligence from the United States. Perhaps even more dangerous to the CCP than Taiwan's defense capabilities is its mere existence as a free and thriving democracy just offshore of the world's largest prison nation. It is, to the CCP, a constant and growing ideological threat.

Is tiny Taiwan really such a threat to the colossal People's Republic of China? China boasts the world's second largest economy, nuclear weapons, an enormous standing army, and 1.3 billion people. What could it possibly fear from Taiwan?

The deep fear lies in the CCP's inability to close the gap with Taiwan and bring it under their control; it is a constant black eye for the Chinese leadership. Its inability to control its own "renegade province" without the interference of the United States speaks volumes about China's political failure and gives hope to its millions of dissidents. It's also a constant reminder of China's inability to compete with American military power. Other than China's own angry population, Taiwan, a mere 140 miles off the coast of China, is the CCP's greatest political threat. The greater the oppression that China exerts upon its own population, the bigger Taiwan grows in the eyes of millions of China's younger generation, who see Taiwan as a stable, prosperous democracy and wonder to themselves why they can't have the same.[16]

The two other regions that are a continuous challenge to the leadership of China and its claim on them are the Western provinces of Xinjiang and Tibet. Both of these are not only constant sources of political resistance, but are also noted for their strong and historical religious affiliations, which seem to grow stronger the more China attempts to suppress them.

China's Uighur Problem in Xinjiang

Some of China's more distant provinces have ties to other nations and cultures that border China and feel more a part of the cross-border culture than they do a part of China. Xinjiang province is a prime example of this. Xinjiang is a Western province that makes up one-sixth of China's landmass with a population of 20 million. It has a wealth of minerals and oil and is home to the Uighur nation of people, the largest ethnic minority group in the province, with over 8 million people.

Not only are there ethnic and cultural tensions between the Uighurs and the Chinese leadership, there are also deep religious ones as well. The Uighur population is mainly Muslim. As in many other parts of the world, a resurgent Islamic cultural and religious identity is a force that China's officially atheistic government is finding increasingly difficult to deal with.

Xinjiang is a "designated autonomous region" in China and is tellingly also known as East Turkistan, with historical and religious ties to several Central Asian nations. In fact, it shares borders with Mongolia, Russia, Kazakhstan, Kyrgyzstan, Tajikistan, Afghanistan, Pakistan, and India, as well as with Tibet. Uighur populations are found in some of these countries, and in recent years have been providing greater levels of support to the Uighurs' separatist movement in Xinjiang.[17]

The Uighurs view China's presence in Xinjiang as imperialism and identify themselves as belonging to the Central Asian Islamic republics more than they do with China. An independence movement has been in existence since the early 1990s, when Uighur separatists staged numerous attacks against Chinese rule over the region. In response to those attacks, China has maintained a demographic policy in Xinjiang of migrating ethnic Han Chinese (which is 80 percent of the Chinese population) as a means of displacing Uighurs and minimizing their disruptive influence. The "Uighur problem" is viewed by China as highly inflammatory, since the province borders five Muslim countries with a history of supporting Islamic militants.

China's problems with the Uighurs have involved numerous outbreaks of rioting and protracted violence with death tolls in the hundreds. China has accused Pakistan of allowing Muslim terrorists to traffic and train unhindered within Pakistan, causing fractures in their relationship. Tensions and instability remain high due to recent killings by armed Muslims of ethnic Han Chinese in the province, and a meeting of 200 Uighurs—hosted by Japan—to publicize their demand for independence, which was met with condemnation by China.[18]

The Uighurs' religious intransigence is a challenge that China's leaders have so far been unable to address successfully, even though it has resorted to drastic measures to quell the rise of Islamism. From teachers force-feeding Muslim children candy during Ramadan to bans on religious expression throughout Xinjiang, such measures have not produced the desired outcomes, but rather, have only succeeded in provoking more violence in the province and increased separatist sentiment.[19] The situation has also worsened China's relations with Pakistan, who it suspects is supporting Islamic radicalism in the province. An oppressive communist empire having a difficult time with its Muslim population sounds familiar, does it not?

China has tried to bring Xinjiang's orbit closer to Beijing, to quell the unrest of its Islamic population by force, migration, and accommodation, but has yet to realize success. In fact, it has achieved just the opposite. There is little reason to doubt that as economic conditions continue to deteriorate and Beijing's oppression of the province escalates, that Xinjiang will seek further involvement and deeper ties with its Muslim neighbors and grow more distant from the CCP's authority. That eventuality is a great worry to the Chinese communist leadership, and well it should be.

The Sandals and Saffron Threat of Tibet

The threat that Tibet poses to China's empire is of a particularly moral—as well as political—nature, with its roots based in the Buddhist religion. The Dalai Lama, as the exiled Buddhist leader of Tibet, is widely respected, even revered worldwide. He is regularly welcomed in the world's capitals and international gatherings, and exerts tremendous moral authority and political influence in Tibet and throughout the world, including in China. But the CCP's regard for the Dalai Lama and his powerful influence in Tibet is not one of admiration, but of outright fear. A March 20, 2008, *Christian Science Monitor* article explains the viewpoint of China's powerful Party leaders regarding the threat that Tibet, and its exiled religious leader, the Dalai Lama, pose to China's empire:

> The saffron-clad monk, widely admired in the West as an icon of nonviolent struggle against the occupation of his homeland, was described Wednesday by a top Chinese official as "a wolf wrapped in monk's robes, a devil with a human face and a beast's heart."[20]

As communist party leaders view it, the Tibetan-born Dalai Lama, cloaked in saffron robes, sandals on his feet and thick eyeglasses on his shaved head, is a threat to the entire unity of China. But how can this be? He commands no military divisions, has no missiles or tanks at his disposal, no air force or navy to dispatch, nor does he possess financial resources to bring to bear, and yet his very existence threatens the stability of the CCP's rule. "Chinese officials have offered just one explanation for the unrest in Lhasa: a plot by the Dalai Lama and his government in exile to further their alleged goal of breaking up China by winning Tibet's independence."[21]

The viewpoint—and fear—of one religious leader in exile tells a lot about the brittle nature of the Chinese leadership and how they view their own legitimacy in their positions of power. Is China's Communist Party so weak and unstable as to fear one Buddhist monk? The answer, apparently, is yes. China's military occupation of Tibet since 1949 does not make Tibet a true part of China, nor has it made China any more powerful or stable. Like the Chinese finger trap made of thin, woven strips of bamboo, the more China struggles with Tibet, the more of a difficult time it has in managing it.

The larger threat isn't just Tibet's independence from China *per se*, but also how Tibet's resistance to Beijing, expressed through the Dalai Lama's speeches and religious followers, may well bring about similar responses in other provinces. This could lead to what the CCP fears most: the breakup of China. Given this possibility, it becomes clearer how China is much more an empire made up of disparate and antagonistic groups, regions, peoples, and ethnicities than it is a nation in the traditional sense of the word.

Are the pressures and strains of maintaining its empire already starting to show in China? The answer seems rather obvious. Beset by multiple concurrent and crippling crises, China is losing its ability to control its own captive population, much the way the old Soviet Union failed to do at the end of its existence. The key point to keep in mind is the overarching theory of this book: that the greatest threat to China is China itself. Perhaps the most powerful evidence of this point comes from the actions of the Chinese leadership itself. Recall that on the one hand, the leaders of the CCP are moving hundreds of billions of dollars *out of China*, while at the same time, they are committing the greatest single portion of the national budget to internal security. Like everybody else, one can determine a government's aspirations, and its fears, by where it puts its money.

Is there any other financial activity or budgetary item that could be more illustrative of the ironic twist of China's economic miracle? In 1978, Deng Xiaoping worried about the revolt of the people in light of China's economic backwardness and poverty. To remedy the problem, he opened China to the West and China became rich. Thirty-five years later, the same fears are in the minds of China's leaders today, even as China is reaching the apex of its economic development and power.

Fear and Greed in the New Leadership

Like the two basic drives of most human behavior, fear and greed are the base forces driving the CCP today. Fear that their greed is becoming a source of instability and the cause of a well-earned revolt is an enormous concern of the new leadership. And their greed in reaping the wealth from China's economy knows no limits. As mentioned in previous chapters, China's new leadership, headed up by Xi Jinping, is made up of so-called *princelings* or Marxist royalty, an oxymoron if there ever was one.

The new wealthy political class has become viewed as untouchable royalty with enormous privilege in the *new China*. The scam of this new royalty in China is to portray themselves on the one hand as the rightful rulers of China—a cluster of collective dynastic families, as it were—and yet on the other hand, as the ones who are best suited to look out for the Chinese people's interests; best accomplished, of course, through the wise guidance of the CCP. But the fact is that the Marxist Party, full of communist doctrine of equality and united workers, is no more in China.

Today, as it has from the very beginning, the Party exists for a certain minority of China to get rich and hold onto power.[22] As Deng Xiaoping so famously said, "To get rich is glorious." He could have added, "It's good to be the king."

But getting rich is hardly the creed of the Communist Party, is it? Nor is it a legitimate reason for the Party's continued existence in China, especially in the face of rising inequality and privilege that Party membership provides. Today, the CCP leadership and its wealth-usurping cadres' lives much more resemble the reign of Louis XIV in France, or the Mandarins of a bygone era, than those of egalitarian communists, which is what the Party ostensibly once represented.

However, as is politically correct to do in these times in China, when dissent continues to rise throughout the country, the new leadership has made the proper pronouncements of reform and anticorruption as important policies going forward. But realistically, the Marxist royalty are hardly interested in ceding political or economic power or diminishing their positions in any way since their families and friends literally own the major industrial interests in China. Reform and anticorruption would be a direct threat to the way things are run in China and would threaten the entire existing wealth and power structure; it simply can't happen without undermining those at the very top.

This becomes abundantly clear when one realizes that the entire top level of new leadership is comprised of multibillionaires.[23] This also explains why the internal security budget has become greater than the defense budget. For China to maintain its empire, it can brook no defections from any of its troubled provinces. The loss of one would almost certainly embolden the secession of others. The only real question is, which province will be the first to turn its back on Beijing?

Complexity Theory

From both a philosophical perspective and a theoretical one, *complexity theory* offers an insightful way of looking at systems and why they fail. With regard to China—or any other complex political, financial, or economic system—complexity theory's scope and analytical focus helpfully takes us a step or two back from the human and political passions of analysis. Rather, complexity theory provides both a philosophical and an analytical framework that are descriptively elegant and—contrary to its name—also rather simple to understand and apply. Among other factors, complexity theory considers the exponential energy usage—in all its forms—that is necessary to maintain an increasingly complex system. The theory illustrates how a complex system is ultimately prone to sudden collapse due to its inability to provide sufficient amounts of energy to maintain itself.

To begin to understand the concept of energy use in a complex system—Chinese society—and its consequences, think about the meaning of China's internal security budget becoming larger than its entire defense budget for a moment. The takeaway from that dreary statistic is simple but alarming: The Chinese government fears its own people more than it fears U.S. military power or any and all other foreign powers in the rest of the world combined. Or, put another way, more energy and resources in China's vast state apparatus and in the economy as a whole are expended in *suppressing the energies of its own people* than in allowing the release and expression of those energies in productive ways, or even in defending against foreign aggressors, real or imagined.

The idea of energy exertion and suppression as they relate to China's political and economic systems is a fascinating perspective by which to assess its prospects for the future. We can apply *complexity theory* as a way of viewing and assessing China's current condition and potential longevity. Complexity theory has been used in various scientific paradigms, but as James Rickards has so clearly expressed in his book, *Currency Wars* (Penguin Portfolio, 2011), it can be successfully applied to the global financial and currency systems. However, the principles of complexity theory are also quite applicable to the situation in China (or many other nations, as well). For the purposes of simplicity and accuracy, Rickards' definitions and explanations of complexity theory are used throughout this part of our discussion.

Complexity theory is based upon several premises, the first being that complex systems originate from the bottom up, not from the top down. Does this apply to China and the CCP? Was Mao's Marxist revolution a grassroots campaign? Let us agree that it was, even though today, China's command economy is in most ways very much a top-down process. But clearly, even today, the *reaction* to CCP policies remains very much an evolutionary process from below (i.e. China's shadow banking system, its tens of millions of *netizens* on the internet, its hundreds of daily protests, etc.).

The second premise or principle is that a complex system will behave in ways that cannot be determined simply by looking at the parts of the system. Put another way, the individual parts interact with one another and with the system itself to produce unpredictable outcomes and unintended consequences. Such unpredictable yet highly impactful events might also be understood as *Black Swan events*, as referenced in Nassim Nicholas Taleb's influential book, *The Black Swan: The Impact of the Improbable*, (Penguin, 2007). The main difference between it and complexity theory may be simply that complexity theory predicts unpredictability as an outcome or result of the rise of complex systems, whereas Black Swan events are just simply unpredictable. Regardless of which form of reference one may prefer, unpredictable reactions and interactions within China should be a given in such a highly complex and utterly distorted society of 1.3 billion people, should they not? That said, complexity theory gives us a framework for understanding and of seeing some levels of causality, even though there may be little one can do to alter the eventual outcomes.

The third premise of complexity theory concerns the necessary energy to run a system as it increases in size. That is, complex systems require exponentially greater amounts of energy as they grow in scale. Therefore, when a system increases in scale by, say, a factor of 10, its energy requirements increase by a factor of 1,000. This is an interesting and quite powerful concept with regard to stimulus spending, if one regards money, as Rickards does, as *a store of energy*. That is, money is a way to transfer energy—labor or intellectual capital or the fruits thereof—through society. Now, think about the hundreds of billions of dollars' worth of stimulus spending that China has released and will continue to release in one form or another, in order to keep China running.

Of course, the same argument could be applied to the United States, as well. The current "eternal stimulus" policy of the Federal Reserve creates trillions of dollars—erstwhile units of energy—from nothing and injects them into the economy, putting enormous downward pressure on the dollar's value, and upward pressure on price levels. (It also transfers ownership of the real assets of the United States to the Federal Reserve as the stimulus buys millions of residential and commercial mortgages in the stimulus process.) How long this policy can last without catastrophic reactions in the system—or its total collapse—is a worthwhile and urgent question, but one that is beyond the scope of this book.

The fourth foundational idea of complex systems is that catastrophic collapse is actually a *likely* outcome (emphasis is mine), since the energy necessary to sustain the system once it reaches a certain scale becomes

unattainable as available energy sources are exhausted. Even though, the-
oretically, there may be no limit to how much energy can be created or
transferred via economic activity or even stimulus spending, there *is* a
limit on human capacities and energies. Thus, complex systems develop
autonomously in response to stimuli, act in unpredictable ways, eventually exhaust resources necessary for their continued existence, and then
collapse. It should be evident by now that China, like other developed
nations, with all its aspects and features of political, ethnic, economic,
environmental, and other activities, is a complex system or even a series
of interrelated complex systems.

In addition to the four premises above, two additional and very
important characteristics of complex systems apply. They are *emergent
properties* and *phase transitions*. Emergent properties, as Rickards notes,
are the whole being greater than the sum of its parts. In highly complex
systems, emergent properties are far more powerful and unexpected.
Or, put another way, catastrophes occur, whether they are hurricanes of
unrecorded magnitude and impact, or the *sudden* collapse of a political
system or nation. That is a phase transition. Either of these is predictable
in that at some point in time, both will eventually occur; but the exact
timing is impossible to predict. However, as emergent properties develop
within a complex system, they create the right environment, or what is
called a *critical state*, for a phase transition to occur.

Phase transitions are, as Rickards says, "a way to describe what happens when a complex system changes its state." The analogy of a snowflake falling on a steep mountainside triggering a massively destructive
avalanche is used to show how one small event, a snowflake falling, can
trigger a huge, violent, and permanent change to the landscape. It is
important to understand that the fault for the phase transition lies not in
the snowflake falling, but in the unstable nature of the mountain in the
unstable situation of too much snow on too steep of a slope.

Let's look at China in all of its current conditions in the context of
emergent properties, phase transitions, critical states, and add in snowflakes, mountainsides, and avalanches. The point of this analogy is to
show how the policies of China's leadership—policies are choices, by
the way—have created today, as they have at least twice before, conditions or "emergent properties" within China that are trending toward
a critical state. That is, China's leadership has created the environment

and processes of its own collapse, and today, conditions in China have reached a critical state.

China's critical state means that its systemic elements are now arranged in such a way as to require only a small event to trigger an enormous and system-destroying collapse. Think of that in terms of how much energy is being destroyed by state-owned companies taking over profitable ones and destroying them? Think how many billions of yuan-units of energy are wasted in unnecessary projects and in stimulus money to support over-valued real estate, zombie companies, and the debts they carry. Consider the value and energy being destroyed by the ravaging of their life-giving rivers, lands, oceans, and atmosphere. Most importantly, imagine the levels of energy that are exerted and spent by the government to suppress the natural energies of the people 24 hours a day, day after day, month after month, year after year. Think, finally, of the units of energy that are destroyed by the negative returns on a national savings rate in China that is equivalent to 50 percent of its total (reported) GDP.

How much longer can China's system produce the necessary energy to replace that energy which is being destroyed? Not to mention the additional levels of energy needed as more demands are put upon the entire Chinese socioeconomic system. When China's energy-destructive patterns are viewed from this perspective, the systemic collapse seems not only inevitable, but also imminent.

To complete the metaphor, the CCP has created a mountain of economic inequality and privilege, raised the mountain higher with decades of state theft of land and intellectual property, steepened the slope by means of extreme environmental degradation, and added multiple layers of instability through its economic and financial distortions, corruption, and political and financial repression. There are too many snowflakes on the mountainside, and the mountain itself is unstable. Viewed from the perspective of complexity theory, China seems quite well positioned for a catastrophic avalanche.

But it gets worse in complexity theory, as applied to China, when two more aspects are added to the analysis.

Degree distribution refers to the frequency of extreme events versus mild events in complex systems, and the *concept of scale* applies to the level or scale of the impact of catastrophic events. Rather than apply the law of averages to extreme events, where extreme events are rare, which is typical of a bell curve, complexity theory applies the *power law curve*. The power law curve confers a direct relationship between complexity levels and extreme events. That is, as a system grows more complex, there are more underlying unpredictable activities occurring within it with more frequent and more impactful, yet unintended, consequences. Essentially, a rise in complexity means a correlated rise in extreme events.

Does China's Exponential Complexity Mean Catastrophe in China?

In the context of complexity theory, the scale of the impact of the extreme events is limited to the scale of the system itself. This is important for two reasons. Recall that China's two prior catastrophic collapses in the Great Leap Forward and the Cultural Revolution occurred when China was a largely agrarian society, with a much simpler economy, as well as existing in the isolated state of autarky. That is, China was cut off from the rest of the world. Its systemic collapses, as bad as they were, were limited in their scale (a difficult truth to face) due to the following two factors:

1. A lower level of social and economic complexity.
2. The catastrophes did not affect the rest of the world in any major way.

Put simply, China did not operate on the level of integration and interdependence with the global trade and financial systems that exist today. In a global context, one could rightly argue that the world itself has become a highly complex system of complex systems, one within another within another, all affecting each other. James Rickards makes just such a point with the global financial system, which has become several times larger and more complex than when it collapsed in 2007. It was only *rescued* by the injection of massive amounts of capital—that is, money or "units of energy" created out of nothing—as a stopgap measure to prevent the total collapse of the global financial system *at that time*.

Applied in a historical context, who would argue that the world itself hasn't grown exponentially more complex in the past 100 years? And, as the complexity theory predicts, large-scale catastrophes have occurred with greater frequency in the same time frame. In the twentieth century, World War I saw the collapse of the Ottoman Empire and the decline of the British Empire. The Great Depression followed two decades later, followed by World War II, which gave rise to the U.S. and Soviet empires. Other events also occurred, like the nuclear age, the space age, and the information age. Although these were not catastrophes in the complexity theory sense, they did lead to the development of even more complex systems. In his landmark book *The Structure of Scientific Revolutions* (University of Chicago Press, 1962), Thomas Kuhn called such developments, going all the way back to the printing press, catalysts that allowed sudden leaps in scientific knowledge. Those leaps also resulted in leaps in social and political complexity.

From a sociopolitical perspective, however, collapses in current structures and thought patterns of complex systems are also *paradigm shifts* and serve to fundamentally alter the prior reality and allow for new ideas and systems to emerge or re-emerge as the case may be. When we look at China, and in one way or another anticipate its collapse, whether from the perspective of it as a failing empire or as a complex system falling in upon itself, or even as the simple idea of single-party dictatorships driving their nations into the ground through corruption and degradation of all kinds, the unknown variable is, of course, timing.

It is the contention of this book that the timing of China's collapse is now on the event horizon, and not below it. That thinking may also be applied, as by Rickards, to the international financial system. After all, risk is present or latent in every manmade system, as well as every natural system, such as earthquakes, tsunamis, hurricanes, and yes, snow avalanches. Government intervention cannot eliminate the systemic risk; it can only postpone it. But in doing so, a government allows the risk to grow exponentially larger and the system more complex and fragile as it awaits the next destabilizing event.

What will be the catalytic snowflake on the mountainside in China's ultimate collapse? Will it be skyrocketing food prices? Will it be riots against China's extreme pollution deaths? Perhaps it will be one too many Tibetan monks acting out with self-immolation or the killing of a dissident?

It is not known what the catalyst for change will be, but it is predictable that any one of many relatively minor events can become the event that forever alters the country. It is useful to consider that China's third collapse was very likely postponed by grafting Western economic and financial energies onto its vast impoverished labor force, saving the nation's leaders from death by ideology. Today, however, that happy ending is no longer an option.

Is predicting another catastrophic collapse in China a wise proposition or is it a foolish one? Would it be a desirable outcome for China, or a disastrous one? And what about the rest of the world? How would a China crisis impact the global economy? The implications of this prospect are explored in the following and final chapter of this book.

Notes

1. "Zambia Takes over Chinese-Owned Mine because of Safety Problems," *Africa-News and Analysis*, February 20, 2013, http://africajournalismtheworld. com/tag/zambian-anger-at-chinese-mine-owners; Janet Otieno, Jonstone Ole Turana, and Saudah Mayania, "Afro-Chinese Labor Relations Turn Sour," *Africa Review*, October 18, 2010, www.africareview.com/Special-Reports/ Icy-Afro-Chinese-relations/-/979182/1035242/-/vde64k/-/index.html; Jian Junbo, "China Losing Asian Popularity Contest," *Asia Times Online*, August 17, 2011, www.atimes.com/atimes/China/MH17Ad01.html; and Sonia Gallego, "Chinese-Run Sweatshops Anger Italy Workers," *Al Jazeera*, March 6, 2012, www.aljazeera.com/video/europe/2012/03/201236194151497656.html.

2. Daniel M. Kliman, "Advantage India: Why China Will Lose the Contest for Global Influence," Global Asia, June 2012, www.globalasia.org/V7N2 Summer_2012/Daniel_M_Kliman.html.

3. Michael J. Green and Daniel M. Kliman, "China's Risky Bet against History," *The Diplomat*, December 23, 2010, http://thediplomat.com/2010/12/23/ chinas-risky-bet-against-history/2.

4. Mark Kitto, "You'll Never Be Chinese," *Prospect*, August 8, 2012, www.prospect magazine.co.uk/politics/mark-kitto-youll-never-be-chinese-leaving-china.

5. Andrew Jacobs, "In Singapore, Vitriol against Chinese Newcomers," *New York Times*, July 26, 2012, www.nytimes.com/2012/07/27/world/asia/in-singapore-vitriol-against-newcomers-from-mainland-china.html.

6. John Feffer, "When Soft Power Fails," *The Huffington Post*, January 21, 2013, www.huffingtonpost.com/john-feffer/china-soft-power_b_2519954.html.

7. Minxin Pei, "China's Money Diplomacy Hits Limit," *The Diplomat*, January 4, 2011, http://thediplomat.com/2011/01/04/china%E2%80%99s-money-diplomacy-hits-limit.

8. Bonnie S. Glaser, "China's Coercive Economic Diplomacy," *The Diplomat*, July 25, 2012, http://thediplomat.com/2012/07/25/chinas-coercive-economic-diplomacy.

9. Thomas Fuller, "Long Reliant on China, Myanmar Now Turns to Japan," *New York Times*, October 10, 2012, www.nytimes.com/2012/10/11/world/asia/long-reliant-on-china-myanmar-now-turns-to-japan-for-help.html.

10. "Difficult Tradeoffs," The Drucker Institute, January 25, 2012, http://thedx.druckerinstitute.com/2012/01/difficult-tradeoffs.

11. "World Report 2012: China," Human Rights Watch, www.hrw.org/world-report-2012/world-report-2012-china.

12. Preeti Bhattacharji, "Uighurs and China's Xinjiang Region," Council on Foreign Relations, May 29, 2012, www.cfr.org/china/uighurs-chinas-xinjiang-region/p16870.

13. Kevin Drew, "In Hong Kong, Frustration 15 Years after Return to Chinese Rule," *New York Times*, June 29, 2012, www.nytimes.com/2012/06/30/world/asia/in-hong-kong-frustration-after-return-to-chinese-rule.html.

14. Mary Kay Magistad, "Growing Rift between Hong Kong and Mainland China," PRI's *The World*, February 21, 2012, www.theworld.org/2012/02/hong-kong-mainland-china-rift.

15. Ibid.

16. Martin Jacques, "How the Chinese Communist Party Convinced the World to Accept It," *The Epoch Times*, 10/05/12, www.martinjacques.com/when-china-rules-the-world/how-the-chinese-communist-party-convinced-the-world-to-accept-it/.

17. Michael Wines and Declan Welsh, "China Says Wanted Militants Use Nearby Countries to Stage Attacks," *New York Times*, April 6, 2012, www.nytimes.com/2012/04/07/world/asia/china-says-wanted-militants-use-nearby-countries-to-stage-attacks.html.

18. "Hundreds of Uighurs Lobby China for Independence," *The Telegraph*, May 14, 2012, www.telegraph.co.uk/news/worldnews/asia/china/9263756/Hundreds-of-Uighurs-lobby-China-for-independence.html.

19. "China Seeks Global Help in Fighting Uighur Separatists," *Voice of America*, May 4, 2011, www.voanews.com/content/china-seeks-global-help-in-fighting-uighur-separatists-121313539/138977.html.

20. Peter Ford, "For Beijing, Tibet Threat Is 'Life and Death'," *Christian Science Monitor*, March 20, 2008.

21. Ibid.

22. Mike Forsythe, "China's Billionaire People's Congress Makes Capitol Hill Look like Paupers," *Bloomberg News*, www.bloomberg.com/news/2012-02-26/china-s-billionaire-lawmakers-make-u-s-peers-look-like-paupers.html.

23. Ibid.

Chapter 9

The Fall of the Red Dragon

A t the outset of this book, we observed that the Chinese Communist Party (CCP) operates by exercising repression of all kinds on its subjects, promotes corruption throughout society, and that China's command economy is inherently inefficient and destructive. We also determined that the policies of the CCP have led not only to great economic distortions, but also to serial catastrophes that have cost, and will continue to cost, the lives of tens of millions of people. Finally, it was also established that the CCP lives in a constant state of fear. The main source of that fear is the continued legitimacy of the CCP, or the lack thereof, in the eyes of the 1.3 billion people over whom it rules.

Aptly enough, China's leaders have publicly lamented the country's moral bankruptcy and the coarsening effect it has had on Chinese society. Culturally, China is not the same as it was before the Cultural Revolution. The Cultural Revolution detached Chinese culture from its mooring to Confucianism, repudiating its central ideas in favor of revolutionary ones.[1] Those revolutionary values, in turn, have since been replaced with an unbridled materialism that has no overarching philosophical idea to temper the baser aspects of human nature and ultimately has effectively dehumanized much of Chinese society.

The CCP has been successful in leveraging the people's—and its own—insatiable appetite for acquisition into a political acquiesence of the subjects in return for fulfilling their materialistic urges. Ironically, or perhaps not so much so, the CCP has recently attempted to cloak itself in Confucian rhetoric in some instances, as a means of culling legitimacy from the traditional Chinese philosophy that revered order, obedience, and traditional hierarchical structures. After over 60 years of tyranny and 30 years of a debased materialistic culture, Confucianism as well as Protestant Christianity are both experiencing resurgent popularity in China. This is no coincidence, given that the people have no faith in a Marxist ideology, nor faith or allegiance to the thugs who run the government that oppresses them, nor in the vile and cruel culture that is the legacy of the CCP.[2]

We also noted that the errors China had made in causing the prior catastrophes were large and pervasive, and stemmed from many causes, but mainly were performed under the broad idea of a greater China developed and guided by the dictatorship of the CCP. We recalled that the two great cataclysms of China during its time of isolation from the rest of the world were the Great Leap Forward and the Cultural Revolution. These two national disasters were not only systemic in their impact and effect, but were also products of ideological (and self-serving) policies of the CCP.

We also underscored the point that China, with its command economy, has fallen under and suffers from the *tragedy of the commons*, which causes tremendous economic and human losses in addition to extreme environmental degradation. Finally, we concluded that the same apparatus that led China to ruin twice before, the CCP, has positioned itself for a third cataclysm by way of the numerous policy errors, culminating in the Beijing Model, which will have vast political, social, and economic consequences for China, and ultimately lead to a systemic collapse that, in spite of China's seemingly uninterrupted rise to power, is already on the event horizon.

China's War with China

What will China's collapse look like and how will it impact China's internal situation and its relations with its neighbors? Any prediction as to what will happen in the future, even the collapse of China, is, at least to some degree, speculative in nature. But that does not diminish its relevance or importance. Military planners develop many versions of contingency plans for future events that may or may not occur as a way to at least be somewhat prepared for what may develop, even if the events they correctly anticipate do not play out exactly as they thought they would. With that in mind, we can look at several possible, and even probable, events and actions that could occur or be undertaken as China's leadership finds itself able to control neither events within the country nor the actions of the people as the existing order deteriorates from within.

As our discussion on *complexity theory* illustrates, once a complex system reaches a critical state, the catalytic event that causes cascading failure and collapse can be almost anything. It is worth remembering here that the financial system in China—and in the rest of the world—is larger and more complex than in 2007, when it began its collapse. But as the problems in China grow, they are becoming exponentially bigger than the government's ability to control them or react correctly toward them. China has reached—or is approaching—a *critical state*, wherein a small event will have an exponentially large impact and lead to its collapse.

Given the precarious state of China's environmental resources and disappearing arable lands, along with a demographic shift to Western dietary patterns, climate change, rising global demand for food, and metastatic corruption throughout the country, the most likely event leading to China's collapse will be food riots. These will be due to the aforementioned factors contributing to rapidly rising national food prices and shortages that are endemic to command economies.

Another likely catalytic event is the revolt of people whose lands have been seized by the state. This phenomenon is increasing as the output of the Chinese economy continues its decline and is cited as a main cause for the hundreds of protests that now take place in China on a daily basis. For that reason alone, there is no real expectation that state land seizures will abate in the near future.

A third transformative event may well be Xinjiang province, with its deep and historical Muslim ties to neighboring states, declaring its allegiance to a neighboring Islamic state, or at least its independence from China. Xinjiang province's proximity to several Muslim nations, including Pakistan, makes it a likely suspect for the importation of firearms into China and into the hands of the Muslim people in that province, at the least. In fact, China suspects that this has already been happening.[3] Nonetheless, as global Islamism continues its rise, China will remain a target to the many Muslim states that lie on its Western border. The tensions will become particularly more acute as China ramps up its oppression of the Uighurs in the province. But regardless of whether food riots or any of these other catalytic events are the trigger for China's collapse, several things will likely transpire within a short period of time of a catalytic event occurring.

The first response will be reactive. The CCP will crack down heavily on the riots; as we know, this is already transpiring. As pointed out in the previous chapters, China's internal security budget surpassed its defense budget in 2010 and continues to supersede it each year. This is a major development in the mindset of the CCP toward their people and the rising anti-CCP sentiment or illegitimacy. In a very real sense, China is already at war with its people. However, as the crackdowns become greater, and the response from the people becomes greater and more widespread, not only will the People's Liberation Army (PLA) be brought in to restore order, just as it was in Tiananmen Square in 1989, but urban militias will also be relied upon to control civil unrest.

One of the difficulties for the PLA, urban militias, and the CCP leadership will be the sheer number of places where disorder and civil violence erupt. This will require a greater commitment of PLA resources and personnel, and the civilian battles in the streets against the PLA will be the beginnings of a civil war in China. The CCP will not be able to control the responses of the urban militias, which will likely overreact and bring about more chaos, not less.

At about the same time, sensing an opportunity, Xinjiang province, as well as others, may well attempt to secede from China.

Tibet, for example, may also seize upon the opportunity. The Dalai Lama, if he were to be still around at that time, would likely be the moral voice speaking against the elevated level of Chinese violence, while the Muslim nations bordering Xinjiang would likely be tempted to funnel larger amounts of arms and explosives, if not fighters, into the rebel province.

In response to Xinjiang and Tibet, the CCP may well increase their military forces in those provinces, with resistance and escalating violence as a result. Religious minorities would be heavily persecuted as foreign agents, enemies of Chinese culture, and saboteurs against the state. China's immediate focus will be inward, to control renegade provinces as they try to secede from Beijing's control.

Meanwhile, Hong Kong and Shanghai will be watching it all with the eyes of an interested observer backed into a corner with few good choices, which would certainly be the case. There would likely be a massive outflow of financial assets that would funnel through Hong Kong and Shanghai, for however long as permitted by Beijing. As noted in earlier chapters, CCP leadership has been fully involved in moving billions of dollars out of the country for the past several years, if not longer.

In the process of food shortages and civil violence, China would probably continue and escalate its standing policy and publicly blame the United States for its woes, as well as those nations in the region aligned with the United States. That would specifically include Taiwan. Whether or not China would invade Taiwan is, of course, unknowable. In the face of famine and civil war, however, China's leaders may calculate that the United States will be unable or unwilling to come to Taiwan's defense. China may also see that an invasion of the island would serve several purposes, including providing access to food and other vital materials. Such a decision is plausible, if for no other reason, because China has wanted the United States out its sphere of influence since 1949. Besides, China may in fact have rendered the United States financially unable to come to the aid of Taiwan with a gold-backed yuan either before the crisis or in the midst of it.

Why would this happen?

In the midst of China's growing civil conflict, foreign investment flows would slow down even more, if not stop altogether. Additionally, output at factories would also slow down in the civil crisis, as would foreign demand. It also seems likely that China would cease its purchases of U.S. Treasuries as a way of crippling its regional hegemony adversary, the United States. This would be a strategic move, planned for well in advance.

China's policy planners know that withdrawing support of the dollar would send the U.S. bond market into a free fall. This would result in the United States falling into its own financial crisis—if it had not already done so—which would cause a ripple effect throughout Europe and the rest of the world. In that scenario, the United States would face an immediate existential threat to its financial system, which would consume the sitting administration for the weeks and months ahead. An invasion of Taiwan by China—or even just the threat of invasion if they didn't cooperate—would seem more likely than not to be on the table, and probably successful.

As China's internal stability declines, the yuan may not be an acceptable currency for trade. Or, it might. A crash in the U.S. bond market followed by a collapsing dollar is what may prompt the CCP to introduce a new, gold-backed yuan. As a way to attract foreign investment—or at least foreign trade for food, fuel, and other essentials—a gold-backed yuan would certainly be alluring, and necessary, in light of the greater danger in investing in China. Furthermore, China has the gold reserves necessary to do so on some level. But even though China may indeed put the final nail in the dollar's coffin, it is not so likely that the yuan will be able to replace the dollar as a reserve currency if China has descended into a state of civil war and its economy is in the throes of collapse.

With regard to the Asian-Pacific region, China would likely intensify its aggressive policy of resource conquest, specifically with regard to oil, as indicated by its current policy toward Vietnam, Japan, and the Philippines, and the undersea oil fields in various disputed waters. It is reasonable to assume that China will desperately need resources and food, and will do whatever it has to in order to acquire them. Local wars with the above-mentioned nations would not be out of the realm of possibility or reason given the existential crisis that communist China would be facing.

The Breakup

Eventually, as China loses its tight grip on Xinjiang and Tibet and the internal situation deteriorates, the CCP will lose all ability to control China as a whole. It would likely retain some control over the urban regions for a time, but even that will not last in the face of famine, an inflow of arms to rebel provinces, and economic collapse. The CCP will have lost its legitimacy and its power base in the country, as well-heeled Party members and business owners will flee the sinking ship. When high-ranking members of the Communist Party leadership begin to take early morning flights out of China with their families, fortunes, and bankers in tow, the world will know that the game is over for the CCP. There will be a great reckoning for those members of the CCP who did not leave China, and there will be a great need to gain control of the PLA in order to obtain a cease-fire within the country, which may prove quite difficult to bring about with any expediency. China, finished with the yoke of centralized tyranny around its neck, will then probably break apart into several autonomous regions.

At some point, before or after the breakup occurs, a new leader or leaders will emerge as an alternative to the CCP. Perhaps the leader will come from Taiwan, which would not be out of the question and would be a politically legitimate source for an anti-CCP leader other than a Mainland Chinese individual with proven liberal ideas who might rise to the occasion. Or, it may be a group of leaders from various regions and provinces, who collectively wish to not be held under the boot of a central government in Beijing. They may agree to a loose federation of Chinese states. This outcome might look like and be fashioned similarly to the breakup of the old Soviet Union.

China's newly autonomous regions would also be aligned with their historical and ethnic ties rather than be subordinated to the domination of the "one China" vision of the CCP. Although this may seem to be presumptuous, it is not at all historically inaccurate. China has been unified and divided many times throughout history, and the post-Soviet Russian Federation is as reasonable—and ideal—an outcome as one could hope for from China's collapse. But in the context of a major civil war in China, such a process could take many tragic years of crisis, heartbreak, and suffering throughout the Middle Kingdom.

What Impact Will China's Collapse Have on the World?

The effect of China's financial and political collapse will be multidimensional in its unfolding, and its impact will be felt throughout the world. Remember, the China that closed itself off from the world for nearly 30 years to develop—or not—in autarky, no longer exists. In that period, China's crises were limited in their scope and effect because China was limited in its scope—it was separate from the rest of the world. This is no longer the case.

Today, China is fully engaged with the world, a crucial part in an interdependent and highly sensitive global financial system. Nowhere else is this more true than with regard to the United States. China is the largest foreign buyer of U.S. debt, holding over $1.2 trillion of U.S. Treasury bonds. Their large bond holdings provide the liquidity needed for the United States to turn around and use that money to buy Chinese goods as well as to fund the world's greatest military, which supports U.S. foreign policy around the world. Chinese loans also allow for the funding of the United States' ever-expanding social programs, and China's deep involvement in U.S. Treasury markets, banking, and trade means that any interruption in China's participation in the U.S. Treasury bond market would have an immediate impact on the United States' ability to continue to exist in its current state and status.

If there is a collapse in China, as this book argues is inevitable, there are many possible scenarios and outcomes, some seemingly more likely than others, but all of them seem to lead to a withdrawal from the purchase of U.S. debt by foreign nations. This will have an enormous impact on the United States and the global economy as a whole.

As mentioned above, when China finally decides to withdraw its participation in U.S. Treasury bond auctions and proceeds to dump large amounts on the open market, the U.S. bond market will collapse overnight, as will the dollar. The dollar will probably not survive such an attack, at least not as a reserve currency. The crashing of the bond market will cause nations to dump the dollar literally overnight. Either or both of these events will tip the balance of an already feeble world economy into a Great Depression, marked by naked competition for resources and, as much as anything else, for food.

The immediate effect of a bond market crash and the collapse of the dollar will likely be a significant level of civil unrest in the United States. From a financial standpoint, interest rates will rise, as will inflation. Hyperinflation may even come about as dollars lose virtually all of their value in a matter of days. However, all dollar-denominated assets will also lose their value. This means stocks, real estate, and whatever else might be priced and valued in dollars.

This also applies to all Chinese assets valued in yuan, as well. As we talked about earlier, the fraud and deception of Chinese companies on the U.S. stock exchanges will result in hundreds of billions—if not trillions—of dollars of losses to Americans, and anyone else who had money in those companies. That would be virtually anyone who holds a portfolio of mutual funds.[4]

Both U.S. banks and international banks would also find their asset base decimated by China's collapse and the dollar's collapse shortly thereafter. International trade and credit agreements would likely have to be voided as well. And, since the U.S. economy is the engine of growth for the world, as the U.S. economy collapsed from the fall of its currency from reserve status and suffering from hyperinflation, the foundations of the global economy would be no more. Taking a double hit from China's economic collapse and the United States' deep depression and worthless currency would leave the international trade and finance systems in a state of anarchy. The Eurozone economy would continue to shrink, as both its largest source of capital and its largest market suddenly went away.

Perhaps the greatest impact on the dollar and the global financial system will be the end of the petrodollar arrangement. Since 1975, OPEC has agreed to price and sell its oil on the global market in dollars. This has created a sustained demand for dollars around the world. One could say that the U.S. dollar has been on the "oil standard" since 1975. However, as the value of the dollar plunges in this scenario, OPEC would likely stop accepting dollars for oil almost immediately. In fact, China has already made several assaults on the dollar by creating dollar exclusion zones for trade with countries like Brazil, Chile, India, and

Iran, and it has set up bilateral trade agreements with Japan and Russia, excluding the dollar as an intermediary currency.[5]

The loss of the petrodollar itself, if nothing else happened, would send the United States into a situation of very high inflation, if not hyperinflation, as the value and demand for the dollar disappeared. The U.S. economy—the world's economic engine—would cease to function anywhere near its previous level and would send the rest of the world into a Great Depression.

As predicted herein, China's collapse would trigger a collapse of world trade and finance. Nations like Russia and Iran would be less affected perhaps, but as trade and finance receded in the world, other means of obtaining necessities would come to the fore. The temptation to engage in war for necessary resources would become the new reality as the military treaties and defense capabilities that the United States has enjoyed since the end of World War II fell apart. A broke United States bereft of a viable currency would no longer be able to afford to enforce or honor its treaties around the world. The global system as we know it today, although already in the process of disintegration, would go away altogether in a rapid succession of systemic failures.

Thus, like China's breakup in the aftermath of its collapse, so too will the world break up. The U.S. dollar, the world's reserve currency, will be no more, nor will the world's policeman be on the beat any longer. The deterioration of U.S.-led trade, financial, and defensive systems will lead to a multipolar world marked by shifting alliances and wars for resources and for survival in the new reality.

Regional currencies, such as a gold-backed yuan, a gold-backed ruble, or baskets of currencies backed by commodities such as oil or even nuclear weapons will likely emerge, or in some cases, may already be in place for this contingency. (As noted, China and Russia, as well as other nations, are already in the process of replacing the dollar.) Or, another possibility is that a simple barter system may emerge between some nations and regions, such as oil for food or gold for protection, or the threat of nuclear annihilation to encourage certain transactions.

In broad terms, the consequences of China's collapse will result in the unraveling of the international system, which includes trade and defense treaties, peace treaties, and business agreements. Such devolution will rapidly push the world into a state of treacherous multipolar disorder. All of Europe, North and South America, Japan, and the rest of Asia will struggle to attract investment and revive their economies under great hardship.

Conclusion

In this book, I have sketched a picture of China that is in many ways contrary to how leading China experts view the future of the Middle Kingdom. It is certainly also contrary to the widely held belief that the future belongs to the People's Republic of China, "flexible authoritarianism," and the Beijing Model of economic development.

There are some, of course, who also see China in a similar light as I do and view the serious foundational problems that China faces as the symptoms of decline of a distorted state economy, which they most certainly are. One of those observers is Minxin Pei:

> The latest news from Beijing is indicative of Chinese weakness: a persistent slowdown of economic growth, a glut of unsold goods, rising bad bank loans, a bursting real estate bubble, and a vicious power struggle at the top, coupled with unending political scandals. Many factors that have powered China's rise, such as the demographic dividend, disregard for the environment, supercheap labor, and virtually unlimited access to external markets, are either receding or disappearing.
>
> Yet China's declining fortunes have not registered with U.S. elites, let alone the American public. . . .
>
> One explanation for this disconnect is that elites and ordinary Americans remain poorly informed about China and the nature of its economic challenges in the coming decades. The current economic slowdown in Beijing is neither cyclical nor the result of weak external demand for Chinese goods. China's economic ills are far more deeply rooted: an overbearing state squandering capital and squeezing out the private sector, systemic inefficiency and lack of innovation, a rapacious ruling elite interested solely in self-enrichment and the perpetuation of its privileges, a woefully underdeveloped financial sector, and mounting ecological and demographic pressures.[6]

Like the above quotation, the portrayal herein of a China that most people may not know exists, with all of its failures and falsities, its moral and political bankruptcy, and its headlong rush into environmental catastrophe, is closer to the truth. The temptation to view the rise of China in the twenty-first century as inevitable and permanent is like the observation in the 1970s that saw the rise of communism worldwide as the inevitable model for development: it is reflective of an inability to discern the signs of decay and failure, and perhaps is also a function of bias on the part of the observer. Those who view China as the natural and obvious heir to global leadership and the true economic model for the future, however, are greatly deluded in their expectations.

Notes

1. Yenni Kwok, "You Can't Kill Confucius," *Asia Sentinel*, October 12, 2007, www.asiasentinel.com/index.php?option=com_content&task=view&id=76 2&Itemid=171.

2. Kwok Pui-Lan, "Mao, Meet Confucius: China's Religious Revolution," *Religion Dispatches*, January 18, 2011, www.religiondispatches.org/archive/ culture/4046/mao__meet_confucius__china_s_religious_revolution.

3. "Xinjiang Unrest: China Blames Unrest on Pakistan-Trained Terrorists," *The Express Tribune*, August 2, 2011, http://tribune.com.pk/story/221828/ china-blames-xinjiang-unrest-on-terrorists.

4. Jeff Cox, "China's a 'Roach Motel'; Don't Trust the Numbers: Chanos," CNBC, September 20, 2012, www.cnbc.com/id/49099734/China039s_a_039 Roach_Motel039_Don039t_Trust_the_Numbers_Chanos.

5. Hao Li, "China-Russia Currency Agreement Further Threatens U.S. Dollar," *International Business Times*, November 24, 2010, www.ibtimes.com/china- russia-currency-agreement-further-threatens-us-dollar-248338.

6. Minxin Pei, "Everything You Think You Know about China Is Wrong," *Foreign Policy*, August 29, 2012, www.foreignpolicy.com/articles/2012/08/29/ everything_you_think_you_know_about_china_is_wrong.

About the Author

James R. Gorrie is a freelance writer and editor with a very eclectic background. He began his career in graduate school, becoming a PhD candidate in international relations and comparative politics at the University of California before leaving to work in the private sector. James spent 18 years in the financial services industry, and is a registered investment advisor. Most recently, he was an editorial director and managing editor for an Internet marketing company. He has also ghostwritten for a major reality television personality; wrote, directed, and produced a multi-award winning feature film, *The Indian* (without going to film school); and has written about a dozen screenplays and three novels. James enjoys fiction and nonfiction writing, family activities with his wife and three boys, film, and travel. He lives in Austin, Texas.

Index